T0386382

EUROPEAN DISUNION

STEFAN AUER

European Disunion

Democracy, Sovereignty and the
Politics of Emergency

HURST & COMPANY, LONDON

First published in the United Kingdom in 2022 by
C. Hurst & Co. (Publishers) Ltd.,
New Wing, Somerset House, Strand, London, WC2R 1LA

The poem quoted in the Notes to Chapter 3 is reproduced with the
permission of Penguin Random House:
Ernst Jandl, Werke, hrsg. von Klaus Siblewski
© 2016 Luchterhand Literaturverlag, München, in der Penguin Random
House Verlagsgruppe GmbH

A Cataloguing-in-Publication data record for this book
is available from the British Library.

ISBN: 9781787386846

www.hurstpublishers.com

Printed in Great Britain by Bell and Bain Ltd, Glasgow

For
Thomas, Sebastian, Ben and Dasha

CONTENTS

ACKNOWLEDGEMENTS

This book took much longer than intended. And yet, writing these remarks in the immediate aftermath of Russia's invasion of Ukraine is a sobering reminder of the limitations of this venture. Everything seems so much in flux.[1] I am reminded of Hannah Arendt (Arendt 1958: vii), who reflected on the man-made catastrophes of the first half of the twentieth century, writing 'against a background of both reckless optimism and reckless despair'. What follows, then, inspired by Arendt's approach, are my 'attempts at understanding'. I aim to interpret Europe's present challenges against the background of its conflicting pasts.

I have been researching and thinking about this book for a decade. I have incurred many debts in that time. The ideas that fed into this project are the result of innumerable conversations with friends, colleagues and students in Bilbao, Birmingham, Bologna, Bratislava, Delphi, Dublin, Florence, Košice (my hometown), Lisbon, London, Madrid, Melbourne, Oxford, Paris, Prague, Turin, Vienna and Wrocław—to name just some of the places I visited for short research stays and/or conferences. This time in my life coincided with my move to the University of Hong Kong (HKU), whose School of Modern Languages and Cultures (SMLC) provided me with excellent working conditions, notwithstanding the deteriorating political situation in this remarkable city. I would like to thank Wayne Cristaudo, whose position in European Studies I replaced, for his friendship and intellectual impulses over the

ix

years. Wayne told me that I would love Hong Kong and he was proven right. This was to a large degree thanks to my first Head of School, Kendall Johnson, whose support and friendship made me appreciate my new position so much that my stay, which was meant to last for a couple of years, became semi-permanent. Roland Vogt, my current Head, has been an invaluable interlocutor on German and French politics and a great colleague to teach and work with. At SMLC, I have been very fortunate to receive fantastic administrative support, and I would like to thank especially Zena Cheung and Dorothy Shum for that.

In Hong Kong, I learned a great deal about the history of ideas and Carl Schmitt from Andreas Leutzsch (HKU), Joshua Derman (HKUST) and Ryan Mitchell (CUHK); and about contemporary politics in France, Poland and Europe at large from fellow Europeanists: James Downes at the Chinese University of Hong Kong, and Kenneth Chan Ka-lok, Alistair Cole and Krzysztof Sliwinski at Hong Kong Baptist University (HKBU). I also learned a lot from my brilliant doctoral students, Kenneth Chan Ching-yeung, Thomas Stiegler, Andrew Park and Martin Šebeňa. Andrew and Martin read parts of the book and I wish to thank them for speedy feedback. My teaching and research assistant, Alexandros Tsaloukidis, has been incredibly supportive and kindly helped me with a number of translations from French.

I have always learned through teaching. In this context, I am pleased to acknowledge the EU-funded 2016–20 Jean Monnet Chair project 'Enhancing EU Studies in Hong Kong and China', which enabled me to produce a Massive Open Online Course (MOOC), 'Europe without Borders?'. Particularly rewarding and highly relevant for this book was the opportunity to interview fellow scholars, practitioners and friends, including Timothy Garton Ash, Chris Bickerton, George Papandreou, Helen Thompson, Ben Tonra, Antje Wiener and Jan Zielonka. The Jean Monnet Chair project was greatly supported by HKU's Vice-President for Teaching and Learning, Ian Holliday, and the team at HKU's Technology-Enriched Learning Initiative, particularly Attin Cheng. I would also like to thank one of my most brilliant undergraduate students, Jenny Xiao Wenquan, who helped to develop and deliver the MOOC.

ACKNOWLEDGEMENTS

The decisive impulse for the book in its current form came from Hans Kundnani, with whom I discussed 'The Challenge of Technocracy' in a June 2019 panel discussion kindly hosted by Ivan Vejvoda at the Institute for Human Societies in Vienna.[2] Hans suggested that I write a book about Central Europe that would go beyond worn-out categories of democratic backsliding and populist backlash. Some of those ideas shape the arguments especially in Chapter 5, but the book ended up being broader in scope and perhaps even more polemical. Co-authoring a short paper on the EU's rule of law crisis with Hans and Pepijn Bergsen for Chatham House in October 2021[3] was a useful reminder of the importance of the issues at stake. Hans also recommended my project to Michael Dwyer, Hurst's Publisher and Managing Director. Michael's enthusiastic embrace of this project was instrumental for its realisation. I am heavily indebted to Hurst's excellent and highly professional team: Senior Editor Lara Weisweiller-Wu, Production Director Daisy Leitch, Editorial Assistant Mei Jayne Yew, and my copy-editor Rose Bell—they have been an absolute pleasure to work with. I would also like to thank Emily Matchar, whose attentive copy-editing and feedback helped me to keep going.

A number of friends and colleagues read parts of or the whole manuscript at various stages of writing. I have fond memories of working dinners with Peter Baehr, who read closely a number of chapters and encouraged me to be bold and clear in my argumentation in the early stages of writing. Robert Horvath taught me more than anyone about Putin's Russia, but also how to write neat paragraphs (which is not to assume that I have mastered that craft). The late György Schöpflin read and commented on the first chapter and provided me with numerous sources on both Hungarian and European politics. Marek Cichocki kindly directed to me to relevant sources about Poland's judicial reforms. Tony Carty, Adam Czarnota, Christian Joerges, Martin Krygier and two anonymous reviewers nominated by Hurst kindly read the entire manuscript and provided me with invaluable feedback. I am especially indebted to Martin, whose work I have followed and admired for more than two decades. His friendship and support goes far beyond intellectual exchanges. Adam has provided me with invaluable insights and sources about

Polish politics. It would be remiss of me not to mention colleagues and friends in Melbourne: Philip Bull, John Carroll, the late John Hirst, Robert Manne and Robert Thomson—they have been a source of lasting inspiration.

I do not shy away from controversy and I have learned as much from colleagues whose perspectives and judgements I share as those with whom I often disagree. I thoroughly enjoyed the opportunity to have a frank exchange about the EU–Russia–Ukraine relationship in Beijing in December 2014. While most objections I received in Beijing were based on the kind of realist assumptions that John Mearsheimer popularised,[4] a similar presentation I gave at Florence's European University Institute (EUI), at a conference devoted to '10 Years of the New Europe' in May 2014, met objections from liberal internationalists, including my co-panelist, Andrew Moravcsik.[5] The result of these presentations was an article in *International Relations*,[6] which provides the basis for Chapter 4 of the present book. I would like to thank Tomasz Woźniakowski and Michał Matlak for their invitation to the EUI conference and Jean-Pierre Cabestan of HKBU for the one and only conference I ever attended in Beijing.

This is not the place to list all the conferences at which I was able to engage with fellow scholars, but there are a few that have been particularly rewarding. I am grateful to Doug Webber, one of the first Europeanists to think seriously and systematically about the possibility of European disintegration, for his invitation to chair a panel on that very topic at the July 2015 Council for European Studies conference in Paris[7]—it was one of the most lively and rewarding discussions of Europe's many crises covered in this book. I am grateful to Ruby Gropas and Loukas Tsoukalis for his invitation to a symposium in Delphi in September 2015, which took place at the height of Europe's migration crisis. It was in Delphi that I first met Jonathan White, whose brilliant work on emergency Europe inspired large parts of this book, and Anand Menon, whose insightful approach to the EU as a foreign policy actor and to the EU–UK relationship helped me to think through some of my own arguments.

I would like to thank Agáta Šústová Drelová and Jakub Drábik for their invitation to a conference commemorating thirty years since November 1989, held at Comenius University in Bratislava and organised by the Institute of History of the Slovak Academy of Sciences. My contribution there fed into Chapter 4's historical reflections about the legacy of 1989 in Central Europe. I found particularly rewarding the contributions by, and my conversations with, Hugh L. Agnew, Timothy Garton Ash, Jozef Bátora, Zora Bútorová, Tomáš Gábriš, Michal Kopeček, James Krapfl, Juraj Marušiak, Soňa Szomolányi and Philipp Ther. Further to this, I wish to thank Samo Abrahám, Darina Abrahámová, Vlado Bilčík, Ivan Janda, Ivona Jandová, Peter Konkol, Peter Lipa, James Thomson and the late Pavel Vilikovský for their friendship and support on my numerous visits to Slovakia. Samo's Bratislava International School of Liberal Arts is a true centre of intellectual life in Slovakia; I have been honoured to present some of my work there over the years, and to contribute to teaching. I have fond memories of a short research trip to Bilbao in the summer of 2019, and I would like to thank Felipe Gómez Isa and Laura Teresa Gómez Urquijo for their warm welcome at the University of Deusto.

Of the more recent conferences, I would like to highlight the June 2019 Council for European Studies conference on 'Sovereignties in Contention', for which I organised two panels about 'The European Union between democracy and a Europe of nation-states'. I particularly enjoyed Glyn Morgan's paper advocating 'The Case for a European Superstate', which I found as inspirational as his brilliant book on the same topic (Morgan 2009). Though our positions are fundamentally opposed, I remain in awe of Glyn's depth of analysis, his level of sophistication and his great sense of humour. I would also like to thank András Bozóki, Daniel Hegedüs, Aleksandar Pavkovic and Jiří Přibáň for their contributions. Our discussant, Erik Jones, deserves a special mention. Despite our numerous disagreements over the years, Erik encouraged me to submit my paper on 'Merkel's Germany and the European Union' to the journal *Government and Opposition*. That paper serves as the basis of some of the key arguments in Chapter 2 of the present book.

The Robert Schuman Centre for Advanced Studies at the EUI has offered me a congenial home for a number of short research stays over the last decade. This is thanks to my former colleague and friend, Brigid Laffan, who generously extended me a standing invitation and always found time for engaging conversations. I would like to thank Kalypso Nicolaïdis for her invitation to St Antony's College, Oxford in the summer of 2018, which enabled me to discuss my project with Kira Huju, Joseph Lacey, Petar Marković, David Marsh and David Miller. Kalypso's pioneering work on the EU's 'demoicracy' has influenced my work more than I have managed to acknowledge in the present book. I am grateful to the Aston Centre for Europe at Aston University in Birmingham, which offered a friendly base for my sabbatical leave in 2016. I have fond memories of semi-regular meetings with Willy Paterson, who showed a keen interest in my work, discussions with Nathaniel Copsey and friends from the University of Birmingham, particularly Chris Finlay and Tim Haughton. I would like to thank William Outhwaite for his kind invitation to contribute to an edited volume on Brexit, which served as a point of departure for the second part of Chapter 3 here. Over the last couple of years, in the age of Covid-19 and Zoom conferences, I particularly benefited from the webinar series 'Dissenting voices', organised jointly by Christian Joerges, Michelle Everson, John Erik Fossum, Jiří Přibáň and Agustín José Menéndez.

I would never have written this book, or produced much of my scholarship over the last six years, without my co-author, friend, colleague and the love of my life, Nicole Scicluna. Nicole heard me talking about the book more than anyone ever should, read various drafts and sections, and continued supporting the project despite numerous disagreements over the content. Our sons, Sebastian (4) and Thomas (1) have kept me sane and happy, and I hope that if they ever end up reading this book, they will not find it too boring. I owe special thanks to Jackie Damaso, our amazing nanny. The mistakes are all mine.

Hong Kong, 22 March 2022

PREFACE
COSMOPOLITAN EUROPE OR A EUROPE OF NATION STATES?

Bigger is not always better. Few people would need to be persuaded about the relevance of this commonplace for politics in the city state that is my adopted home: Hong Kong. Though it has its own currency, legal system and some control over its economic and political affairs, Hong Kong's autonomy is limited. It is part of a greater China that is ultimately ruled by the central government in Beijing and the Chinese Communist Party. Twenty-three years after Hong Kong's sovereignty was 'returned' to China, the People's Republic defied both the wishes of the Hong Kong people and its international obligations with a number of controversial policies that betrayed the one country, two systems principle, which was meant to ensure the territory's autonomy, democratic aspirations and strong commitment to the rule of law for fifty years. So far, Hongkongers' fight for democratic self-government, which I witnessed during the 'Umbrella revolution' of 2014, and then again in 2019–20, has resulted in China asserting even more power over the city, diminishing rather than enhancing its autonomy. The implementation of the National Security Legislation in 2020, accompanied by significant changes to the electoral system, appears to have ended Hong Kong's ambition to further democratise its political system.

Europe is different. It invented democracy and remains committed to its basic principles. When the British people decided in a 2016 referendum to exit from the European Union, the EU's political leaders were dismayed, but in no position to prevent the UK from leaving. The question was not so much whether the UK would reclaim sovereignty, but rather how and when that might be achieved. This is not to ignore the formidable opposition to this move both in the UK and in Europe at large. The political establishment in major European capitals considered the step retrograde. Opinion makers were scathing about what they perceived as the victory of populism, not democracy. In fact, most scholars of European integration found any talk about national sovereignty obsolete. They thought of the nation state as a hopelessly outdated container for democracy. The interdependent world of the twenty-first century, they believed, required political entities that were 'de-territorialised' and that would no longer be anchored in a strictly defined place. In such a polity, borders were to be fluid, porous or even non-existent. To be sure, the European Union never fully lived up to this cosmopolitan ideal. Yet, over the last few decades, Europe has steadily moved towards the vision of an 'ever closer union', which paradoxically brought about its exact opposite: a Europe that was internally divided and weakened.

The key argument of this book is that the multiple crises of the European project are caused by one underlying factor: its bold attempt to overcome the age of nation states and the concomitant ideal of territorially bounded political communities. Left unchecked, supranational institutions tend to grow ever more elaborate bureaucratic structures that elude the control of the people they are meant to serve. The logic of technocracy is thus pitted against the democratic impulse, which the European Union is supposed to embody. Democracy in Europe has suffered as a result, vindicating the fear of a great German and European, Hans Magnus Enzensberger, who more than a decade ago warned against 'The Disenfranchisement of Europe' by 'Brussels, the Gentle Monster' (Enzensberger 2011). Since Enzensberger's eponymous book was published, the 'monster' has become less gentle and the resistance against the disenfranchisement all the more determined. The fact that the problem was identified with greater verve and understanding by a poet and novelist than by numerous academics with far more nuanced knowledge of the EU's power structures is itself a part of the problem. Enthused by the idea of Europe's experimental union, many scholars jettisoned impartiality, downplaying the growing disquiet of those who felt disenfranchised. More Europe, they assumed, was better for both European citizens and democracy. If people felt disempowered, so the thinking went, it was because they were misinformed. Not surprisingly then, few mainstream scholars of European integration anticipated the upheavals that the project experienced in its crisis decade. Likened to a bicycle ride, it was assumed that integration had to proceed apace to prevent a fall—an ever wider union was also to become ever closer. My book seeks to challenge this fallacy.

I aim to engage with contemporary European politics via the reassessment of some of the key moments in European integration history and theoretical debates about a number of crucial terms that shaped these developments, such as national sovereignty and sovereign Europe. I will engage a motley crew of thinkers (e.g., Carl Schmitt, Hans Kelsen, Alexandre Kojève and Hannah Arendt) to show the weaknesses of the EU's underlying ideology. I will suggest that, far from being irrational, a number of nationalist rebellions across Europe are based on legitimate grievances that European political elites ignore at their peril. Echoing Yoram Hazony's controversial study, *Virtue of Nationalism* (2018), my book builds on the contradistinction between nationalist and imperialist projects. While very few supporters of European integration would refer to it as imperialist (Morgan 2020), for better or worse the EU came to exemplify the post-1989 tendency 'to remove decision-making from the hands of independent national governments and place it in the hands of international governments and bodies' (Hazony 2018: 4). This in turn exacerbated the growing alienation between national political elites and citizens whose interests they were meant to serve (Czarnota 2020: 40).

Yet, the failure of Europe's cosmopolitan dream should not give rise to nationalist nightmares (Auer 2010). My attempt to defend sovereignty as a meaningful—and practical—normative ideal for democratic government is not an argument in favour of ethnocentric nationalism, which has contributed to numerous violent conflicts in the past. My objective is a frank assessment of Europe's current predicament. The challenges that Europe faces invite a fresh look at age-old questions about the nature of the political, the location of sovereignty and the relationship between law and politics. The protracted crisis of the Eurozone, the refugee crisis, the EU's mishandling of the Ukrainian revolution of 2013–14 and its relationship with Russia, the impact of Brexit and, finally, the numerous challenges presented by Covid-19 have tested the viability of the European project. I argue that the EU's responses so far have been largely inadequate. The main reason for this is a mode of governance that oscillates between the logic of technocracy and the politics of emergency. In fact, the very term 'governance' encapsulates the EU's preference for the depoliticisation of conflicts, which is a method that worked fairly well in the past, but is increasingly becoming a source of new problems rather than solutions.

Writing about 'Europe's Functional Constitution', Turkuler Isiksel observes how both in its official communications and its founding treaties, the EU conceals 'its enormous power behind a dense fog of linguistic obfuscation' (2016: 10). The problem with governance, she writes, is that it implies that 'political power has been sublimated, when in fact it has simply become more opaque' (ibid. 11). In its self-understanding, 'the EU has competences, not powers' (ibid. 10). This process of depoliticisation is mirrored in EU scholarship by approaches that are ever more elaborate, technical and inaccessible to fellow researchers working in cognate disciplines, let alone to the very people who are most affected by the European project—EU citizens. I seek to cut through this fog of obfuscation by bringing politics back into the study of European politics. I will do this by raising some basic questions about power and how it can be made accountable to the people, which in turn is at the heart of perennial debates about the relationship between democracy and sovereignty. As we shall see, in a number of important policy areas the EU has actually weakened democracy at the national level, without being able to compensate for it at the European level.

To address these and similar questions, I believe that it is not enough to reconsider the EU's history; what is needed is 'to change the very terms that frame the discussion of it' (Gillingham 2016:

75), and I seek to do that in Chapter 1. The lofty rhetoric of the EU's founding fathers notwithstanding, the ultimate aim of European integration was never simply to forge ever more unity. Rather, 'an ever-closer union' was meant to create a Europe that was ever more firmly committed to democracy and the rule of law. This was largely the case in the first few decades of European integration, when the idealistic aims of the likes of Walter Hallstein (the first President of the European Commission) were kept in check by pragmatic political leaders such as Charles de Gaulle (the French President) and Konrad Adenauer (the German Chancellor). In the 1990s, Europe took a turn towards a more ideologically based project of a borderless polity that was to be accomplished via the Single European Currency, the euro, and the Schengen Treaty. Both these projects have failed to achieve their intended goals—to promote economic convergence across the European continent and to contribute to the creation of a truly transnational polity. Ironically, instead of strengthening democracy in Europe, they have unwittingly contributed to its decline. This is why the decisive question should no longer be whether more or less Europe is needed, but instead what kind of Europe is best suited to safeguarding democracy, prosperity and political stability.

This contest over the direction of the European project has now gained an interesting spatial and political dimension, pitching some of the core nations of Western Europe (France and Germany) against newer member states (Hungary and Poland). Perhaps surprisingly, national identities matter in this conflict on *both* sides. 'We are good Europeans' is the quasi-nationalist claim of those Europeans who stand for a Europe that is supranational to the extent that national sovereignty is subsumed within the EU's sovereignty. Jürgen Habermas is the exemplar of this stance—his universalist project of Europe based on *Verfassungspatriotismus* (a constitutional patriotism) is, paradoxically, quintessentially German, as I discuss in Chapter 2. In a similar way, President Emmanuel Macron is very French in his push for a 'Sovereign Europe', which builds on France's centralising and statist traditions, embodied, amongst others, by Charles de Gaulle, as shown in Chapter 3. Growing calls for a 'Sovereign Europe' accompanied by the idea of 'European autonomy' have gained resonance in response to a more assertive Russia and the ongoing conflict between the US and China, in which Europeans do not want to be sidelined, which is the focus of Chapter 4. It is striking that the populist anti-EU rebellions in a number of new and old member states are waged in the name of Europe. Like Macron in France, and every German leader from Adenauer to Angela Merkel, sovereignist leaders in Hungary, Poland, Italy *and* France also claim that they are 'good Europeans' as they advocate a Europe of nation states (discussed in Chapter 5). While leaders such as Viktor Orbán in Hungary, Jarosław Kaczyński in Poland, Marine Le Pen in France and Matteo Salvini in Italy aim for levels of national independence that the current level of integration simply does not allow for, they do not advocate that their countries should follow the British example and leave the European Union.

Yet, significant conflicts over Europe exist not merely between EU member states but also *within* them. What is particularly interesting for the purposes of this book is the fact that these different conceptions of Europe are gaining importance owing to a number of significant challenges that have put the EU system of governance under stress. Brexit and the Covid-19 pandemic, for example, have triggered processes that are likely to be transformative not just for the UK, but arguably even more so for Europe. The EU's constitutional settlement is far more fragile than many people are willing to acknowledge, and it will be tested further still—as I discuss in my Conclusion, which focuses on the rise of 'emergency Europe' (White 2015).

In particular, the rule of law crisis, which intensified in late 2021, further destabilised Europe's self-understanding as a community of law and exposed the fragility of its unwritten constitution. To use the more specific German terms, the *Rechtsstaat* crisis coincides with and feeds into the crisis of Europe as a *Rechtsgemeinschaft*. These two concepts are closely related but not identical, and neither of them can be fully captured by the English term 'the rule of law'. Yet the distinction is important because it encapsulates the intractable problem that the EU faces in dealing with this challenge. The EU is not (and arguably can never become) a fully fledged 'rule of law state' (that is, a *Rechtsstaat*), but merely a community of law (that is, a *Rechtsgemeinschaft*). As a post-sovereign polity, it has arguably no sufficient power to enforce the rule of law principles, and it is not obvious how it could acquire such powers without undermining those very principles. As a non-state entity, the EU and its institutions simply do not have enough legitimacy resources to 'discipline and punish' (Kundnani 2018). The more political, assertive and authoritative EU institutions became, the more opportunities they created for nationalist mobilisation. The EU's power has thus been challenged by 'trouble-makers' from within (e.g., Orbán's Hungary and Kaczyński's Poland) and from without (the UK).

Brexit was often seen as having vindicated the superiority of the supranational system of governance. Brexit enabled 'the EU to reveal its essential essence', argued a leading scholar of European integration, highlighting Europe's ability to manage 'deep interdependence' (Laffan 2021). Over the next decade, Brigid Laffan anticipates, the EU 'will provide living proof that pooling sovereignty is a more effective response to the 21st century than the chimera of sovereignty and taking back control' (ibid.). This book takes a different tack. Examining the inability of the EU's supranational structures to effectively address the pressing issues of European citizens, including protecting their lives during the Covid-19 pandemic, I argue that these crises reveal the extent of the EU's dysfunction. Far from being a chimera, the concept of sovereignty has come to play a hugely important role in protecting democracy in Europe (Grimm 2015). In fact, one of the key problems that the EU's post-sovereign polity has created is the erosion of democracy at the national level, without an adequate compensation at the supranational level.

THE RETURN OF SOVEREIGNTY

'The dictator is coming.'

With these words, the then President of the European Commission, Jean-Claude Juncker, turned towards the then Prime Minister of Latvia, Laimdota Straujuma, to announce the arrival of her Hungarian counterpart, Viktor Orbán. Upon his entry, Juncker greeted Orbán as 'dictator'—shaking his hand and playfully slapping him in the face.[1]

It was remarkable that Europe's leading political figures appeared jovial and exceedingly friendly towards Orbán, just at a time when within Europe and beyond there was growing concern about Hungary's turn towards authoritarian rule.[2] The bizarre encounter took place in Riga in May 2015, when the Latvian presidency of the Council of the EU hosted yet another summit chaired by Donald Tusk, then President of the European Council. The leaders gathered according to a well-established ritual of the European Council, a part of which is taking a 'family photo', symbolising Europe's unity. The role of the Council has always been somewhat contradictory—very powerful in practice, as it comprises all the national leaders, though formally its brief is rather circumscribed. In fact, the Council's purpose was only explicitly defined as recently as 2009 in the Treaty of Lisbon, which describes its mission as providing 'the Union with the necessary impetus for its development' and defining 'the general political direction and priorities thereof'. Importantly, the Treaty stipulates that the Council 'shall not exercise legislative functions' (cited in Olsen 2020: 111).[3]

But my focus here is not on the EU's institutional architecture. Instead, this vignette aims to highlight a troubling paradox at the heart of the European project. The European Union's raison d'être is to protect democracy in Europe. Yet over the last couple of decades it has overseen—or even became complicit in—the erosion of democracy in a number of its member states. The surprising camaraderie between Juncker and Orbán illustrates a strangely symbiotic relationship between technocracy and populism. The two leaders were able to feed off each other. This is not to say that Juncker was ever a mere technocrat, just as dismissing Orbán's phenomenal political success simply as populism is an incomplete account at best. But what they came to represent in the eyes of their allies and opponents was respectively technocratic governance and populist rebellion: 'post-political juristocracy on the one side and democratatorship à la Orbán on the other' (Manow 2020: 18).[4]

To describe Juncker as a technocrat at all is in fact something of a misnomer. The former Prime Minister of Luxembourg was a successful politician for many years prior to his EU career, and in his role as the EU Commission President he proved a formidable *political* actor. This is not to ignore Juncker's lack of popularity, missteps, policy failures and even his controversial stewardship of Luxembourg's fiscal regime (Faiola 2014). Evaluating his three-decades-long feat of political survival in Luxembourg (for eighteen years of which he was Prime Minister), a journalistic sketch referred to him as a 'man with many talents but without qualities' (Schmit, Stoldt and Thomas 2012), and predicted a quick end to his career. Instead, he became a veritable 'Homo Europus' (Mulder 2019), taking his survival skills to a higher European level. It was under Juncker's leadership that the British voted to leave the EU. And as President of the EU Commission, Juncker also oversaw the (mis-)management of both the euro and the refugee crises. Yet the problem was not Juncker as a person, but rather what the Luxembourger came to personify—the mode of supranational governance that bounced between technocracy and the politics of the exception.

Reflecting the EU's intricate system of governance, the role of the EU Commissioners is somewhat ambiguous. They are not meant to act as politicians, but neither are they merely civil servants. An example of this ambiguous role is the recent attempt at 'politicising' the Commission. Its aim has been to improve the quality of the EU's democracy via the so-called *Spitzenkandidaten* process, in which the European Parliament was to have a decisive voice in the selection of the Commission President. Yet, the European Commission, in its position as the 'Guardian of the Treaties' is also meant to fulfil the role of an impartial arbiter between all member states, regardless of which political party rules them. Not surprisingly then, 'Juncker's political Commission' of 2014–19 was a mixed blessing (Dawson 2019). In fact, it can be argued that the limited success of this approach—empowering the Commission President as a *Spitzenkandidat*—exposed the limits of the idea that the EU should be democratised by further empowerment of the European Parliament and its transnational party system. If anything, strengthening the role of the Commission might unwittingly accelerate the process of 'the de-institutinalisation of power' (White 2021: 2), the result of which would be less, rather than more democratic accountability. As Jonathan White argued, Juncker's governing style exemplifies the tendency within the contemporary EU, which responded to numerous emergencies by individuals subordinating and remaking institutions to serve higher ends—such as the preservation of European unity. In other words, rather than taking his authority from the office, Juncker 'was an individual asserting his personal authority to redefine and reshape what the office entailed' (White 2021: 11). Ursula von der Leyen might not be as charismatic as her predecessor, nor was she ever a *Spitzenkandidat*, but like Juncker she too had strong personal ambitions. Following on from his 'political Commission', she promised to lead a 'geopolitical' one.

Juncker also articulated a classic defence of technocratic rationality removed from parliamentary scrutiny when he explained, 'we all know what to do, we just don't know how to get re-elected after we've done it'. Amongst EU officials and scholars, this notion became known as the 'Juncker Curse' (Copsey 2015: 147). Following this logic, Juncker defended the EU's decision-making mechanisms that were often opaque and lacking sufficient democratic accountability. Doing so, he echoed the logic of what is known as the 'Monnet method', which is embraced by proponents of functionalist theories of European integration, and criticised by more sceptical voices as 'integration through stealth' (Majone 2005): 'We decide on something, leave it lying around, and wait and see what happens. If no one kicks up a fuss, because most people don't understand what has been decided, we continue step by step until there is no turning back' (cited in De Vries 2018: 56).

The downside of this approach is the erosion of trust in both EU and national political institutions and their representatives. The more competencies the EU acquired affecting various aspects of citizen's lives, the harder it got to pursue this mode of integration. Particularly over the last couple of decades, the process of European integration had been punctuated by numerous episodes of people 'kicking up a fuss'. In order to pre-empt such responses, Juncker went so far as to justify lying in the pursuit of major policy goals, stating that 'if things get serious, you have to know how to lie' (Hewitt 2014). This might come as a surprise to observers of contemporary politics who consider lies to be an indispensable part of the populist playbook. This takes us back to Hungary, where a Prime Minister confessed to his party faithful:

> There's not much choice. There's not much because we screwed up. Not a little, but badly. No country in Europe has been as dim-witted as we have. There's an explanation. Obviously we lied throughout the last year-and-a-half or two. I nearly died when for a year-and-a-half I had to pretend to govern. Instead, we lied morning, noon and night.[5]

This frank speech was later leaked to the press, leading to anti-government protests and clashes with the police that left more than a hundred people wounded. Yet the target of people's anger was not Orbán, the self-proclaimed adherent of illiberal democracy, but rather his liberal, pro-European predecessor Ferenc Gyurcsány, whose government paved the way for the Fidesz landslide victory, enabling the ensuing consolidation of Orbán's rule. What Gyurcsány represents in the context of post-1989 democratic transformation in Central and Eastern Europe is the failure of pro-European, liberal elites to gain sufficient public support for economic and political reforms (as I discuss further in Chapter 5). The governing elites' reliance on technocratic rationality backfired, leaving many people across the region feeling that *their* revolutions were 'stolen' (Krapfl 2013). What was particularly disconcerting was the ability of many former communists to reinvent themselves as passionate adherents of free market liberalism and European integration. They succeeded in transforming their pre-1989 political capital into considerable private wealth (Tucker 2015), which in turn endowed them with more political power. The widespread perception that politicians of all stripes were corrupt was thus not without justification. This is an aspect of populist rebellions in new member states that tends to be overlooked. In Hungary, following Gyurcsány's fall from grace, Orbán's party won the elections to the European Parliament in 2009, and national parliamentary elections in 2010. With his popularity unabated at the time of writing, Orbán is arguably one of the few remaining politicians who has shaped European politics for more than two decades (and in this respect, is on the path to overtake both Angela Merkel and Juncker). This is not to ignore the divisive nature of Orbán's policies, or the nefarious methods he used to pursue them. Yet what is particularly interesting about his spectacular success in Hungary for the present book, is the extent to which it reveals democratic dysfunction across Europe.

The Crisis of Representative Democracy and the Return of the Political

In response to a number of pressing challenges, particularly over the last decade or so, the European Union has unwittingly exacerbated the crisis of representative democracy. As 'emergency Europe' (White 2015) has become the new normal of this experimental polity, unsettling the existing governing structures, the theoretical frameworks underpinning the European project ought to be questioned as well. To do so, I turn to political and legal thinkers including Hans Kelsen, Carl Schmitt and Hannah Arendt, who confronted a more dramatic and altogether more serious challenge to democracy: the constitutional breakdown of the Weimar Republic followed by the rise of Nazi Germany and the devastating impact of the Second World War. While the concept of popular sovereignty was at the centre of debates about democracy in the first half of the twentieth century, more recently its usefulness has been questioned. Ironically, discussions about sovereignty were declared retrograde just at the time when the process of European integration was entering a phase that would prove their relevance.

With the privilege of hindsight, one could say that the start of the new millennium marked the moment of peak globalisation, which was in Europe further reinforced by intensified processes of economic and political integration. While the EU scholarship was then dominated by claims about Europe leaving concerns with popular sovereignty behind, some major innovations at the EU level, such as the creation of the Economic and Monetary Union (EMU), exacerbated the perceived loss of control. The global financial crisis (GFC) of 2008, for which Europe was ill prepared, acted as a catalyst for a decade of crises from which the European Union is yet to recover. These upheavals led to a backlash against a more cosmopolitan Europe, and to the reassertion of sovereignty at a national level. Brexit was but one example—if a particularly spectacular one—of this trend. The rise of 'sovereignist' political leadership in Hungary and Poland, and the ongoing strength of nationalist mobilisation across Europe, including within large, founding member states such as Italy and France, suggest that nationalism as a political force is here to stay. As Bernard Yack pithily observed, 'the age of liberal democracy is also the age of nationalism' (2003: 29). Yack's argument about politics in general applies equally to the EU: 'liberal politics rests on a familiar but rarely analyzed image of political community, one that tends to nationalize our understanding of politics and politicize our understanding of nationality' (ibid. 31).

To take this argument a step further, I suggest that the process of democratising the EU's politics unwittingly nationalises it. On this view, increased national mobilisation is not, per se, undermining democracy in Europe, but is rather a response to attempts at its democratisation. In fact, Yack's key argument is that an important source 'of the politicization of national loyalties in the modern world seems to be an idea that most liberals continue to hold both dear and indispensable to a decent political order: the principle of popular sovereignty' (2003: 50). This claim is no longer all that controversial within broader discussions of political history (Roshwald 2006) and contemporary political theory (Tamir 1993, 2019; Miller 1995, 2016; Stilz 2019). Yet it continues to be viewed with suspicion within EU studies, where popular sovereignty is seen as 'the source of the ills that befell Europe in the twentieth century' (Lev 2017: 208), with the EU being presented as a successful example of a 'post-sovereign' polity.[6] A good illustration of this view is Jan-Werner Müller's series of rhetorical questions:

> [D]oes European integration, in fact, prove how useless the Schmittian intellectual tool kit has become, and, in particular, that 'Schmittian sovereignty' remains caught in existentialist, concretist ways of thinking, which have long lost touch with the intricate 'legitimation through procedure' or the legitimation through prosperity which some see at the heart of the EU? Has functionalist integration, a kind of 'polity-building by stealth,' by 'neutralizing' the 'primacy of the political,' disproved Schmitt's suspicion of the liberal order to sustain itself through purely economic means? Has Schmittian unitary and decisionist sovereignty, which always asks for the identification of the final arbiter, been extinguished in favor of 'pooled sovereignty' and a kind of subtle sovereignty by 'mutual recognition, continuity and consent'? (2000: 1779)

To be blunt, my answers are no, no and no. First, legitimation through procedures might work in normal times, but Europe has had very little normality over the last three decades. Second, I contest the view that a liberal order could 'sustain itself through purely economic means'. What the recent European developments have shown instead are the limitations of 'polity-building by stealth'. Attempts to overcome political conflicts via 'neutralisation' did not help European democracies, which leads me to my third 'no' regarding 'pooled sovereignty'—a conceptual tool that tends to obscure power, unwittingly exacerbating the problem of democratic accountability. As Yack put it, sovereign control is exclusive—'if one community possesses it, another cannot'. In other words, the sovereign is the one who has the final say on any given territory. Thus, sovereignty that is pooled or joint 'is either a metaphor or a contradiction in terms' (Yack 2003: 43).

In what follows, I will first sketch a somewhat schematic genealogy of the kind of thinking that Müller's praise of 'post-sovereign' polity exemplifies (Rousseau, Kelsen, Kojève) and foreground my further arguments with a brief discussion of opposing thinkers (Schmitt, Arendt).

The desire to neutralise the 'primacy of the political', which can be viewed as part of the EU's DNA, has a long pedigree. It is linked to the idea that political conflicts could and ought to be overcome by reason, which can be traced back to a particular strand of the Enlightenment represented by the likes of Jean-Jacques Rousseau, and restated more recently by John Rawls and Jürgen Habermas. Against the premise that 'might makes right', commonly associated with Hugo Grotius and Thomas Hobbes (and later revived by, e. g., Schmitt), Rousseau constructs a political order based on a social contract. Rousseau's bold blueprint in effect reverses the earlier notion, suggesting that *right* makes might. The social contract is just and legitimate because it relies on citizens' mutual acceptance of their shared interests, embodied in what Rousseau calls *volonté générale*—'the general will'. This is not to be confused with the will of a majority, as people can be easily deceived about what is good for them, while 'the general will is always in the right, and always tends to the public welfare' (Rousseau [1762] 1994: 66). It follows then, that true freedom consists in people's compliance with the general will. By contrast, those individuals who are not sufficiently enlightened to internalise the wisdom of the general will and who defy its demands are enslaved by their selfish instincts. They shall be 'forced to be free' (ibid. 58). In other words, they ought to be liberated from the influence of their ill-informed private will. Clearly, what Rousseau envisaged is rather different from contemporary notions of liberty, in which freedom also entails the freedom to be left alone. In line with this, Rousseau did not believe in the possibility, or even desirability of political representation. His package was all or nothing, and his conception of sovereignty somewhat circular: 'simply by virtue of its existence, the sovereign is always what it should be' (ibid. 58).

Perpetual European Union

However impractical *The Social Contract* might appear today, Rousseau already understood that his blueprint could only work on a relatively small scale. How to apply the same logic to the relationship between sovereigns was far trickier. On the surface, it seems obvious that cooperation would be in their mutual rational interests. This assumption underpins a number of ambitious designs for lasting peace. As early as 1712, Abbé de Saint-Pierre (1658–1743) advanced a project 'to render Peace perpetual in Europe', proposing 'a Treaty to establish a perpetual European Union' (cited in Heuser 2019: 132–3). Rousseau considered its underlying logic compelling, writing that it would be enough to 'realize this commonwealth of Europe for a single day' to make it last forever; 'so fully would experience convince men that their own gain is to be found in the good of all' (Rousseau [1756] 1991: 88–9). Yet however logical this scheme was, Rousseau was profoundly sceptical about its realisability. He anticipated Georg Wilhelm Friedrich Hegel's criticism of contractual theories applied to international relations. The rights of nations, Hegel argued in the *Philosophy of Right* (PR), 'have reality not in a general will, which is constituted as a superior power, but in their particular wills' (cited in Glendinning 2014; compare Hegel [1821] 1989: 499–500, §333). Along similar lines, Rousseau criticised Saint-Pierre's 'perpetual European Union', describing his plan 'as ineffectual for founding it and unnecessary for maintaining it'. Foreshadowing the problems of EU democratic legitimacy that cannot rely simply on 'delivering the goods', Rousseau observed that

> though the advantages resulting to commerce from a general and lasting peace are in themselves certain and indisputable, still, being common to all states, they will be appreciated by none. For such advantages make themselves felt only by contrast, and he who wishes to increase his relative power is bound to seek only such gains as are exclusive. ([1756] 1991: 93)

9

Rousseau's pessimism was reinforced by his view that rulers seldom acted in the interest of the community, motivated as they are by their insatiable desire for power. In fact, he believed the main impediment to the attainment of perpetual peace would be violent resistance from existing rulers. 'No federation could ever be established except by a revolution', concludes Rousseau, and because of that it is not clear whether 'the League of Europe is a thing more to be desired or feared' ([1756] 1991: 100).[7]

It was Immanuel Kant who sought to address a number of the problems Rousseau identified. Kant's thinking on this question developed over a long period of time and across a number of writings, culminating in his famous 'philosophical sketch' of 1795, *Zum ewigen Frieden* ('To Eternal Peace'), commonly mistranslated as *Perpetual Peace* (see Behnke 2008). What is often also lost in translation is the extent to which Kant as a *political* philosopher was pragmatic in advancing abstract ideals primarily as regulatory principles. Thus *To Eternal Peace* should not be read as prognostication but rather as an appeal to overcome our natural proclivity to strife, both at the individual and the collective level. Kant's project was predicated on the idea that a community of well-governed republics would be disinclined to seek military adventures, because their publics would know how likely they were to suffer in a war. Yet Kant too was wary of its feasibility, warning against the danger of both excessive centralisation as well as fragmentation. In line with this, he opposed the centralisation of coercive powers at the supranational level, expecting instead that enough unity would be achieved through the voluntary cooperation of participating states. Rather than suggesting that a 'world state is inevitable' (Wendt 2003), Kant advocated a 'federation of free states' ([1795] 1992: 64).[8]

Kant can in fact be seen as a liberal nationalist. He praised nature for dividing mankind into nations, which differ in their languages as well as religions. Such diversity would prevent them from melting into one large and unwieldy *Universalmonarchie* ('universal monarchy', Kant [1795] 1992: 80). Though the aspiration for the creation of a *Völkerstaat* ('a universal state') that would 'ultimately include all the nations of the world' seems logical, what is achievable in practice is a *Völkerbund* ('a federation of nations'), that is 'an alliance which averts war' without compromising the sovereignty of its members (ibid. 68). Granted, Kant acknowledges that such an arrangement is fragile. Yet the alternative is even less appealing. In other words, though this state of affairs is far from perfect, it is preferable to a universal state, in which laws would 'progressively lose their impact as the government increases its range, and a soulless despotism, after crushing the germs of goodness, will finally lapse into anarchy' (cited in Scruton 2006: 22). Pace Hegel, Kelsen and Kojève (discussed below), a nuanced reading of Kant thus suggests that the endpoint of history remains indeterminate. A peaceful world is something worth striving for, rather than an inevitable outcome of all human striving. As Hannah Arendt observed, 'In Kant, progress is perpetual; there is never an end to it. Hence, there is no end to history' (1982: 57).

Peace through Law

Fast forward to the twentieth century, where designs for eternal peace appeared both highly desirable and yet more elusive than ever. Two thinkers in particular expanded on the legacies of Rousseau, Kant and Hegel, reasserting the possibility of 'right making might': Hans Kelsen, a prolific Austrian jurist and legal philosopher, and Alexandre Kojève, a Russian-born French political philosopher. Kelsen was Schmitt's most formidable opponent, and remains to this day one of the founding figures of international law as we know it. Building on Kant, Kelsen conceives of legal theory as emanating from 'the supreme universal reason', which gives it objectivity that the consideration of 'only ephemeral and temporary phenomenal forms' (Kelsen 1928: 316; compare Zolo 1998: 308), whether they be persons or states, could not achieve. This enables Kelsen to construct a perfectly coherent legal system underpinned by the *Grundnorm* (basic norm), from which all other laws are ultimately derived and to which they are all subordinated. It follows then that all legal systems must be in perfect unity with each other, organised as they are in a clearly established hierarchical order, at the apex of which is the international law. The idea of national sovereignty, Kelsen posits, must be 'radically suppressed' (1928: 320). Just as national legal systems overcame the emphasis on individual sovereignty in the condition of the state of nature, in which everyone was left to fend for themselves, a truly international or, better said, a 'world-legal system' must overcome 'the dogma of state sovereignty' to achieve 'civitas maxima', a truly cosmopolitan legal order encompassing all humanity. Published originally in 1920, *The Problem of Sovereignty and the Theory of International Law* concludes on an optimistic note, with Kelsen arguing that 'it is only temporarily, by no means forever, that contemporary humanity is divided into states' (1928: 319); and envisaging the emergence of a 'world state', the constitution of which must be the aim of all political ambitions (ibid. 320).

Kelsen continued to consider the challenges of creating 'peace through law' (Kelsen 1944) for the rest of his luminous career. Reflecting on the failure of the League of Nations more than two decades after the publication of *The Problem of Sovereignty*, he surmised that the main weakness of the League was its reliance on politics instead of law. The institutional set up, with the Council being the most powerful body, simply replicated the shortcomings of the international system, which was erroneously built around the principle of state sovereignty. To overcome this problem, a powerful and independent court should have presided over all nation states, leading to a quasi-federation that would eventually result in a world state. Importantly, this world state in the making would monopolise the legitimate use of violence. To fully function, it would eventually need to have the ability to impose punitive measures. This would include the deployment of an international police force. Kelsen even endorsed the idea of a 'just war', that might be legitimately waged against states transgressing against the existing order. Prior to the attainment of this ultimate goal of the world state, the victorious great powers that were emerging at the end of the Second World War were to be guarantors of international law; they would be 'the power behind the law' (Kelsen 1944: 66).

There is an obvious inherent contradiction in Kelsen's scheme. On the one hand, consistent with his idea of judicial cosmopolitanism, individuals are to be considered subjects of international law. Yet Kelsen's argument that 'war can be a just sanction of international law against states (and their citizens) who have wrongfully used force' amounts to an endorsement of the principle of collective responsibility, because the targets of such a war might include 'even victims of the totalitarian power of the domestic political *élite* that unleashed it' (Zolo 1998: 316). Moreover, Kelsen's blueprint unwittingly cemented global imbalances by privileging major powers, which were then the US, UK, China and the Soviet Union, thus enabling 'the justification of the use of force by powerful imperialist states' (Chimni 2015: 260). As Danilo Zolo observes, 'it is undoubtedly paradoxical for an author who lays claim to pacifist and anti-imperialist ideals—and makes peace the ultimate end of law—to assume (just) war as the condition for the legal nature of the international system' (1998: 315). None of these criticisms should obscure the fact that Kelsen was a lifelong advocate for democracy underpinned by a robust rule of law state. Though his audacious prediction about the emergence of a 'universal human community of human beings' no longer sounds all that convincing, his writings about democracy and international law retain relevance to this day (see also Chapter 3).

The EU as a Kelsenian Project

Considering his impeccable democratic credentials, immense erudition and the sheer volume of his scholarly output, it is odd to see Kelsen's political thinking largely ignored in the aftermath of the Second World War, especially in Germany (Jestaedt and Lepsius 2006: ix–xi).[9] By contrast, Carl Schmitt's ideas were arguably far more influential, his tarnished reputation as a 'crown jurist of the Third Reich' notwithstanding. And yet it was Kelsen's idea of 'peace through law' that appeared vindicated through the process of European integration. In other words, what Kelsen advocated for the world was enacted after the Second World War within Europe: 'integration through law'. As the first President of the European Commission, Walter Hallstein, argued in his book *Der unvollendete Bundesstaat* ('The Incomplete Federal State'):

> The community is a creation [*Schöpfung*] of law. That is the decidedly new development which marks it out from previous attempts to unite Europe. The method employed is neither

violence nor subjection but a spiritual, a cultural force: law. *The majesty of law is to create what blood and iron could not achieve for centuries.* (Hallstein 1969: 33; my emphasis)

On this reading, more than anything else it is the law that holds Europe together, an idea that is captured neatly in the German term *Rechtsgemeinschaft* (Community of Law).[10] Hallstein, even more than Kelsen, was deeply suspicious of nation states. The system of sovereign nation states, argued Hallstein, had lost its validity because 'it failed the only test that would have justified its continuance into our century' (1973: 20). He believed the answer must be found in integration instead of national sovereignty, with an individual rather than a state at its centre (Pernice 2001: 2). The ingenious concept that Hallstein is said to have invented to deal with the problem of national sovereignty is the *Europäische Rechtsgemeinschaft* (European Community of Law), which is viewed as a distinct German contribution to the European project (Bogdandy 2017: 1–2; compare Pernice 2001: 2). The method of 'integration through law' worked fairly well, particularly in the first couple of decades of European integration, even in times of serious political conflict between member states that continued to defend what they perceived as their national interests.

To this day, Europe is shaped by ongoing tensions between two tendencies: efforts to maintain the independence of participating member states on the one hand, and the striving for a truly united, transnational polity on the other. The intermittent result of this process was aptly described as 'the European rescue of the nation-state' by an influential eponymous study, which sought to challenge the dominant, teleological view of post-Second World War history, 'that predicted that integration would continue, because the nation-state would prove increasingly unable to cope with the trend of modern economic development' (Milward 2000: 428).

Paradigmatic in this respect was 'the empty chair crisis' of 1965–6, which marked an attempt to defy the seemingly ineluctable process towards more supranationalism. The crisis was triggered by French President Charles de Gaulle, who resented Hallstein's attempts to create a truly federal Europe. De Gaulle's uncompromising position represented the first major setback to the project, and its meaning continues to be debated within EU studies. The causes for the crisis were manifold. In January 1963, President de Gaulle defied all the other member states by vetoing the UK's first application for membership, driven by his desire to keep Europe more European (and by extension, more French). Two years later, a major conflict erupted, primarily involving France and West Germany. At issue were the modalities of the financing of the Common Agricultural Policy, from which France had benefited more than other member states (Bajon 2018). The point of contention was not merely technical, however. In fact, the conflict illuminates the fundamental underlying problem that Europe continues to struggle with: whether the project is best conceived of as a Europe of nation states, a 'United States of Europe', or something entirely new—an *objet politique non identifié* ('an unidentifiable political object'), as Jacques Delors, Commission President from 1985 to 1995, would describe it later.

Hallstein did not merely believe that nation states were obsolete, he also acted on this belief. He keenly observed scholarly debates about the nature of European integration, which were then dominated by neofunctionalism, a theory developed primarily by two influential US scholars, Ernst B. Haas, author of *The Uniting of Europe* (1958), and Leon Lindberg. At the heart of the theory is the functional logic of 'spillover', which explains a steady and gradual pull towards an 'ever-closer union'. This would continue empowering supranational institutions at the expense of smaller governing units, including nation states. As Lindberg explained, 'the initial task and grant of power to the central institutions creates a situation or series of situations that can be dealt with only by further expanding the task and the grant of powers' (cited in White 2003: 119). A by-product of this process would be the further empowerment of supranational, technocratic governing structures such as the European Commission. This theory ended up both describing and—even if only unwittingly—*prescribing* further political developments.[11] As Jonathan White has demonstrated, Hallstein embraced both Haas' and Lindberg's insights. Following the neofunctionalist logic, he saw himself on the winning side of history, conceiving of the 'integration process as in some sense inevitable', based on the understanding of the 'spill-over' concept as 'inherently unidirectional' (White 2003:

120). However, Hallstein's excessive confidence in the rightness of his position led to a misguided negotiating strategy that alienated the French President and resulted in a paralysis of the European Council for six months, leading further to the derailment of the construction of a federal Europe.[12]

Not surprisingly then, most conventional accounts depict President de Gaulle as a veritable villain in relation to European integration. He was explicit about his opposition to the Commission as 'a technocracy, for the most part foreign, destined to infringe upon France's democracy' (de Gaulle, 1965: 1), and ridiculed those who, like Hallstein, 'dreamt' of a European federal state based on 'abusive and fanciful myths' (de Gaulle 1965: 4; see also Gillingham 2003: 70). The conflict was eventually settled by a compromise reached in Luxembourg in January 1966, which amounted to giving all member states a right to veto those initiatives that were seen as contradicting their vital national interests (however these might be defined). Parenthetically, this was also such a setback to neofunctionalism that Haas himself declared the theory obsolescent (Haas 1976; see also Niemann, Lefkofridi and Schmitter 2019: 45). De Gaulle was no fan of the UK as a member of the community—he rejected its application twice—but he was right to predict that Britain would only accept a community in which member states and not its supranational institutions had the final say. As de Gaulle put it at a Paris press conference on 9 September 1965: 'This plan alone seems to France to be consistent with what the nations of our continent actually are. It alone could one day make possible the adherence of countries such as Britain or Spain which, like ours, could in no way accept the loss of sovereignty' (1965: 2).

Once the possibility of a veto was gone (which occurred largely through the Single European Act in 1986 and the Maastricht Treaty in 1992), Brexit appeared to be the only option left to regain that control (as discussed further in Chapter 3). Like a number of British leaders after him, de Gaulle stood for a 'Europe of the fatherlands', but he was not opposed to European integration as such. His was a dynamic concept of European integration, 'markedly different from the technocratic model of supranational economic union', aiming at the creation of a 'Europe from the Atlantic to the Urals' (Bajon 2018).

The long-term impact of the 'empty chair crisis' remains contested. For Andrew Moravcsik, for example, it is 'striking how *little* of what de Gaulle sought he achieved and thus how little the crisis diverted the longer-term evolution of the EC' (1998: 196). By contrast, Desmond Dinan considered that the French President emerged victorious in 1966, with the crisis undermining both 'Hallstein's credibility and the Commission's confidence' (2005: 51). John Gillingham advanced a more balanced assessment by pointing out that 'part of Hallstein's work would stand. His legacies would be the Eurocracy and, of transcendent and increasing importance, a new tradition of European constitutional law' (2003: 71). In fact, as Joseph Weiler observed, it was precisely the ability of member states to veto proposals they considered incompatible with their national interests that led them to tolerate 'integration through law' pursued primarily by the European Court of Justice: 'The integrating federal *legal* development was a response and reaction to a disintegrating confederal *political* development' (Weiler 1991: 2425). Adapting Albert O. Hirschman's influential study, *Exit, Voice and Loyalty* (1970), Weiler argued that law and politics acted in tandem, resulting in an equilibrium that created a de facto constitution for Europe. A number of key decisions of the European Community Court of Justice in 1963–4 foreclosed the possibility of 'selective exit' for members of the community, in particular by instituting the doctrine of direct effect (Van Gend en Loos case) and the principle of supremacy (the case of Costa v. ENEL). The willingness of states to accept these radical innovations, which transformed Europe into a quasi-federal legal order, could only be understood against the background of their increased 'voice'—the right of veto—which they established through the Luxembourg compromise (Weiler 1990). The closure of exit and the increase of voice were thus in a symbiotic relationship: 'If Exit is foreclosed, the need for Voice increases' (Weiler 1990: 22). The third aspect, the question of loyalty,[13] becomes particularly important as the possibility of vetoing European decisions was eroded in the Single European Act of 1986, which introduced qualified majority voting. In its totality, this transformation of Europe, on Weiler's 1994 reading, amounted to 'a quiet revolution'.

17

At any rate, Hallstein's notion of the 'majesty of law' appeared to have vindicated the idea of 'right making might' in the aftermath of the Second World War. As envisaged by Kelsen in his design for the world, the Court of Justice rather than the Council became the most powerful body pushing the integrationist agenda forward. In a famous description, it was the court 'tucked away in the fairyland Duchy of Luxembourg and blessed … with benign neglect by the powers that be' which 'fashioned a constitutional framework for a federal-type structure in Europe' (Stein 1981: 1). As the court attained a quasi-heroic status—'an actor with a powerful vision and remarkable influence' (Weiler 1994: 531)—its role became both more visible and more controversial. The revolution might have been quiet, but once its impact was felt, Europe faced repeated attempts to undo it.

In fact, recent historical scholarship suggests that national acceptance of the European Court of Justice (ECJ) and its jurisdiction was not as pronounced as the 'integration through law' (ITL) paradigm suggested. This is not to deny that the narrative remains popular, particularly amongst EU legal scholars, very much in defiance of new empirical findings that have 'largely debunked its core elements' (Rasmussen 2021: 927). While ITL celebrates Europe's constitutionalisation, driven by the bold and imaginative decisions of its top court, it understates the resistance of 'Member State governments, administrations and courts' (Rasmussen and Martinsen 2019: 251), which vigorously opposed major constitutional doctrines already in the 1960s and 1970s, even though they proved unable to stop them. Part of the problem is, as Morten Rasmussen noted, that the likes of Eric Stein and Joseph Weiler were not only 'among the most sophisticated and brilliant scholars of the field, but they were also actors in their own right' (Rasmussen 2021: 927). Though academics by vocation, Stein and Weiler 'played an important role in advising the European institutions and cementing the constitutional discourse used by the supranational institutions' (ibid.). Thus, the ITL paradigm did not merely reflect the changing nature of Europe's political transformation, but decisively contributed to its creation. As Rasmussen and Martinsen observe,

At first (in the 1960s and 1970s), the discipline of European law seemingly colluded with the ECJ's efforts to reject accusations of activism by focusing scholarly energy on formalist analyses of European law, employing the terminology of the 'new legal order' and generally sidestepping discussions on the nature of European law. (2019: 262)

More recent developments threaten to undermine both the status of the court and the ITL paradigm further. Revealing in this context was the decision of the Polish Constitutional Tribunal in October 2021, which questioned the principle of supremacy by declaring the ECJ's interpretation of several articles of the European Treaties to be incompatible with the Polish constitution. The decision was hugely controversial, marking a low point in the ongoing dispute between the EU and Poland over its judicial reforms, which the Polish government had pursued since 2015. First, the legitimacy of the Constitutional Tribunal is dubious, owing to irregularities that occurred in the appointment of its judges, which compromised its political independence. Critics of the conservative Polish government led by the Law and Justice party (Prawo i Sprawiedliwość, PiS) maintained that the true aim of judicial reforms was the subjugation of the independent judiciary. Second, the substance of the decision was considered indefensible and based on misguided assumptions about both the Polish written constitution and the EU's de facto constitutional order. In response to these allegations, the Polish government maintained that judicial reforms were not within EU competences and emphasised its conflicting view on sovereignty. Defending the Polish position, Prime Minister Mateusz Morawiecki was defiant, arguing that 'the supremacy of national constitutions is in fact principle of the primacy of state democracy over EU institutions' (Morawiecki 2021b). Morawiecki might have had neither de Gaulle's charisma, nor his authority, but he echoed his arguments. As de Gaulle demonstrated through his intransigence in 1965, member states rather than any European institution were ultimately in charge. In a similar way, the Polish PM proclaimed: 'Today we answer the question whether the nations and citizens are to remain European sovereigns, or EU institutions are to become the sovereigns' (Morawiecki 2021b). Though Morawiecki's bravado may have overstated his power, the challenge he represents is very real. If the EU is to remain truthful to its Kelsenian legacy, the primacy of EU law must be reaffirmed and the Polish insubordination quashed. Whether and how this can be achieved is discussed in the following chapters.

The European Union as the End of History

It was Alexandre Kojève, rather than Kelsen or Hallstein, who fully grasped the world significance of Europe's transformation. Building on a Hegelian philosophy of history, Kojève postulated the universal and homogeneous state as its endpoint. Kojève's theory offers a solution to Kant's account of 'eternal peace'. On Kojève's reading, the Kantian project is limited because it fails to explain why states would be willing to surrender their sovereignty, given their fears surrounding security threats from other states. In other words: any hope for a universal, lasting peace could only be realised if all states were joined at once. But until and unless that is the case, why would they do such a thing? The answer is to be found in integration via *droit*—a French concept that can mean both 'right' and 'law' (Howse and Frost 2000: xiii; Kojève 2000: 326–7). As Kojève explained in a letter to Leo Strauss in 1952:

> If the Westerners remain capitalist (that is also to say *nationalist*), they will be defeated by Russia, and that is how the End-State will come about. If, however, they 'integrate' their economies and politics (they are now on the way of doing so) then they will defeat Russia. And that is how the End-State will be reached (the same Universal and Homogeneous State). But in the first case it will be spoken about in 'Russian' … and in the second case—in 'European'. (Strauss and Kojève 2013: 256; my emphasis)

Kojève thought this endpoint was a good thing, and worked towards its realisation by becoming a highly effective and valued French bureaucrat who advanced the cause of Europe's unity and inspired many others (including Robert Marjolin, one of the 'architects of the euro', see Chapter 2).[14] Though he was convinced that the 'period of *national* political realities is over', Kojève acknowledged that the 'era where all of *humanity* together will be a political reality still remains in the distant future' ([1945] 2004). Anticipating contemporary arguments about the EU as an intermittent step towards global unity, Kojève wrote about his period as 'the epoch of *Empires*, which is to say of *transnational* political unities, but formed by *affiliated* nations' ([1945] 2004; see also Chapter 3).

By 1989, if we are to trust Francis Fukuyama and his provocative thesis about 'The End of History', it became clear that 'the End-State' was to be European. Adapting and restating Kojève's philosophy of history, Fukuyama declared 'the triumph of the West' had been caused by 'the total exhaustion of viable systematic alternatives to Western liberalism' (Fukuyama 1989: 3). Though Fukuyama's essay was more often criticised than praised, his core thesis has been echoed in numerous accounts of post-1989 European history. Time and again, political thinkers deployed a teleological reading of European integration in order to strengthen the pragmatic credentials of their lofty theories. Writing in the immediate aftermath of German unification in 1990, for example, Habermas bemoaned the fact that 'the democratic processes constituted at the level of the nation state lag[ged] hopelessly behind the economic integration taking place at a supranational level', arguing that 'democratic citizenship need not be rooted in the national identity of a people' (cited in Outhwaite 2021: 33). In the European project, Habermas believed he could glimpse a pre-configuration of what he called '*Weltinnenpolitik*, global domestic politics' (ibid. 49). In a similar way, Alexander Wendt pointed at Europe to demonstrate the viability of his bold proposition that a world state was inevitable. In fleshing out what shape such a state might take, Wendt argued that his blueprint did not require the creation of 'a single UN army', a centralised 'world government' or the abandonment of the principle of subsidiarity. To be sure, Wendt assumes that it would be necessary to collectivise 'organized violence', which would underpin its 'common power, legitimacy, sovereignty and agency'; but other than that, the world state can have many forms. 'The EU is already not far from meeting these requirements on a regional level', writes Wendt. 'Were a "completed" EU to be globalized it would be a world state' (Wendt 2003: 506).

Viewing the EU as an avant-garde of a peaceful world to come is also the leitmotif of Ulrich Beck's book, *Cosmopolitan Vision*, which he believed had 'left the realm of philosophical castles in the air and ... entered reality' (2006: 2). Beck regarded the European Union as a revolutionary project that taught its member states that 'their power is not diminished but increased by renouncing national sovereignty'. Through this experience, Europe exerts 'a new influence on the world stage' as an ultimate peace project (Beck 2006: 175).[15] And Europe can even be seen as a harbinger of a world without borders, exemplifying, in the view of Joseph H. Carens, the fallacy of the assumption that 'open borders would be intrinsically incompatible with state sovereignty' (2015: 270). For who could 'seriously doubt that the European states are still real states today with most of the components of state sovereignty', despite the fact that EU citizens are largely free to move, asked Carens rhetorically (2015: 272). Such accounts are predicated on the assumption that Europe represents not only 'the most ambitious' but also the 'most *successful* example of peaceful international cooperation in world history' (Moravcsik 2001: 114; my emphasis). Which takes us back to the series of questions Jan-Werner Müller raised about the European project invalidating Schmittian perspectives on contemporary politics.

The End of History as the End of the Political

'Can one say, then, to put it crudely, that if Europe works, Schmitt is wrong?' asked Müller (2000: 1779). Two decades later, it makes sense to reverse that premise. The less well the EU works, the more fruitful it is to deploy Schmitt to understand it. There are three major aspects of Schmitt's oeuvre relevant to Europe's current predicament. First, there is 'the concept of the political' (Schmitt [1928] 2007), informed by Schmitt's critique of depoliticisation, which is manifested in the EU's reliance on the functionalist logic of 'integration through stealth'. With a growing emphasis on 'a Europe of values',[16] it is useful to recall Schmitt's early concern about the importance of a foundational idea for a polity: 'No political system can survive even a generation with only the naked techniques of holding power. To the political belongs the idea, because there is no politics without authority and no authority without an ethos of belief' (Schmitt [1923] 1996: 17).

Second, there are Schmitt's writings on *Grossraum* ('great space'), which prefigure argumentative strategies in favour of spatial orders (*Nomos*) transcending the territorial limits of nation states. Third, there is the famous question of 'Who decides?', which Schmitt considers to be the defining feature of sovereignty. In times of crisis the question of who is in charge becomes particularly pressing. Evading the issue of 'the identification of the final arbiter' (Müller 2000: 1779) amounts to an avoidance of democratic accountability. Far from being obsolete, 'Schmittian sovereignty' is as relevant as ever; the question is where to locate it.

While Schmittian perspectives are useful in diagnosing the EU's many ills, when it comes to seeking solutions the picture becomes muddled. A note of caution is thus in order. What follows should not be read as an exegesis of Schmitt's political thought, which would need to address the relationship of his political thinking to his political actions. For obvious reasons Schmitt remains a divisive figure. His anti-Semitism and his open support of Nazism are well documented. There are perhaps as many scholars blinded by Schmitt's brilliance notwithstanding his appalling political judgments, as there are those who are blind to his brilliance because of his misjudgments. Yet it is possible to be both incisive as an analyst and awful as an actor. I thus follow the lead of the 'worldly philosopher' Hirschman, who sensed 'an odd convergence' of his thought with Schmitt's. 'I think he was right', Hirschman wrote, 'in looking toward more exceptional situations and toward the capacity to seize them via "decisionism" as the avenue to escape from "the laws of motion" of both Marxist and non-Marxist (Weberian) social scientists' (cited in Adelman 2013: 625).

Schmitt's preoccupation with the nature of the political and the threat of technocracy immanent in the ongoing process of depoliticisation, was shared by a number of influential thinkers spanning ideological divides, such as Leo Strauss, Reinhart Koselleck, Hannah Arendt and Jan Patočka. Contra Kojève, they did not seek to hasten 'the end of history', because they believed that it would also bring about the end of the political. This basic insight has significant bearing on Europe's aims and the means to achieve those aims. 'The world's Utopian unity', wrote Koselleck in *Critique and Crisis*, 'reproduces its fission' ([1959] 1988: 6). In a similar vein, Arendt warned against 'the danger inherent in the new reality of mankind [which] seems to be that this unity, based on the technical means of communication and violence, destroys all national traditions and buries the authentic origins of all human existence' (1968: 87). Arendt might have been described as a 'thinking pariah' (Pinkoski 2019), but she understood the importance of political communities and offered as eloquent a defence of liberal nationalism as any. 'Nobody can be a citizen of the world as he is the citizen of his country', she wrote in a critical appreciation of Karl Jaspers, which deserves to be quoted at length:

> A citizen is by definition a citizen among citizens of a country among countries. His rights and duties must be defined and limited, not only by those of fellow citizens, but also by the boundaries of a territory. Philosophy may conceive of the earth as the homeland of mankind and of one unwritten law, eternal and valid for all. Politics deals with men, nationals of many countries and heirs to many pasts; its laws are positively established fences which hedge in, protect, and limit the space in which freedom is not a concept, but a living, political reality. The establishment of one sovereign world state, far from being the prerequisite for world citizenship, would be the end of all citizenship. It would not be the climax of world politics, but quite literally its end. (1968: 81–2)

The idea of 'a politics-less final condition of humanity', as Arendt put it bluntly, 'is not at all utopian. It is simply appalling' (2005: 153). In his 1929 essay about the essence and value of democracy, even Kelsen acknowledged that a certain level of cultural homogeneity and a shared language are important preconditions for democracy to work (Kelsen [1929] 2019). Granted, the European Union cannot be compared with 'one sovereign world state', but whether and how it can either accommodate or recreate 'the space in which freedom is not a concept, but a living, political reality' remains an open question. While the EU prides itself on being 'an area for freedom, security and justice', a decade of crisis has exposed serious tensions between these demands. Celebratory accounts of the EU as 'the first truly postmodern international political form' (Ruggie 1993: 140), which attempted to 'reinvent itself beyond territoriality and outside of fixed frontiers' (Maier 2002: 13), proved premature. The 'unbundling of territoriality' (Ruggie 1993: 171) also militated against the EU's ability to respond to external challenges—whether it was Russia's neo-imperialist ambitions in Ukraine, or the influx of refugees from the Middle East. More recently, Europe's reluctance to impose strict border controls both internally and towards the outside world became a liability during the Covid-19 pandemic. At any rate, Europeans do not have the luxury of living in a 'politics-less' world.

However much Schmitt shared Arendt's view about the threat of depoliticisation, he was less sanguine about the viability of nation states. As he wrote in a 1955 letter to Kojève, 'it is all over with the "state," that is true; this mortal God is dead' (cited in De Vries 2001: 101). In the same year, a bestselling German author and journalist echoed a similar sentiment. Invoking Hegelian ideas of world history 'swinging from one extreme to another', Ferdinand Fried pondered the future of European integration in response to the Messina Conference:

> Following the hopeless fragmentation of the old Europe into so many separate nation states, which then fought bitterly among themselves for hegemony, the recent catastrophe has resulted in the counter-concept of a united Europe, a European Union. No less a figure than Churchill endorsed it, in his famous speech at Fulton; the American Secretary of State, George Marshall, tried to enforce it with his Marshall Plan; and eventually Robert Schuman and Jean Monnet sought to make it a partial reality in the form of the European Coal and Steel Community. (Fried 1955)

This ringing endorsement of the European project proved prescient—both in anticipating the success of the Treaty of Rome (signed in 1957), which established the European Economic Community, and even its more recent and ambitious reincarnation the Maastricht Treaty (signed in 1992), which created the European Union. What is curious though is the author himself, Ferdinand Fried. While being strongly influenced by Schmitt in the 1930s, unlike Schmitt, Fried succeeded in transforming himself immediately after the Second World War from a Nazi propagandist into an enthusiastic proponent of European integration.[17] As Joshua Derman observed, while Fried's ideological predispositions were not widely shared by the architects of European unity, 'his enthusiasm for the project illustrates how wartime proponents of "great spaces" could merge into the mainstream of postwar European politics without disavowing their earlier ideas' (2020: 22). This is not to overstate the point that Christian Joerges made about the 'darker legacies of law in Europe' (Joerges and Ghaleigh 2003), but rather to tease out some problems that are inherent in the conceptualisation of Europe as a *Grossraum* of sorts, which by aiming to overcome the limitations of nation states might morph instead into 'a space without a demos' (Preuß 2017: 58).[18]

'Wehrhafte' Demokratie *(Militant Democracy) in Germany and Europe*

There is another more positive aspect of Schmitt's constitutional theory relevant to contemporary democracy in Europe, which is the idea that a viable constitution has to be based on a number of core principles that are in some ways unalterable. This was one of the key lessons of the Weimar Republic, the constitutional order of which was fragile because it attempted to regulate too many aspects of politics at once without establishing a clear hierarchy amongst them. The (West) German post-Second World War constitution represents a fundamental improvement on its Weimar predecessor by postulating an explicit commitment to the basic principles of liberal democracy—the so-called 'eternity clause' (Article 79, paragraph (3) of the Basic Law)—which ensures 'the immunity of certain parts of the constitution from any constitutional amendment' (Preuss 2011: 430). The aim of this provision is to entrench democracy and its commitment to the protection of human dignity in Germany for good.[19] As I will discuss in Chapter 2, this provision complicates matters for EU constitutionalism as it generates tension between German and EU commitments to the rule of law state. What is more, the EU suffers from a problem similar to that identified by Schmitt in the Weimar Republic: over-constitutionalisation (Grimm 2016), which results in a situation in which there appears to be no clear hierarchy between various, at times conflicting, commitments. In fact, the EU's rhetorical pledges to democracy were arguably honoured as much in their breach as in their observance, particularly during the eurozone crisis when Europe's economic constitution led to 'the emergence of a new constitutional constellation' (Joerges 2014: 985), prioritising ordoliberalism rather than liberal democracy (see Chapter 2).

Macron's idea for a 'sovereign Europe' is an attempt to counter this trend (see Chapter 3), but whether and how the EU can be transformed into a serious geopolitical actor remains an open question. At any rate, the EU's track record so far in its dealings with Russia and Ukraine (including the unlawful occupation of Crimea in 2014), and its response to the challenge of a more authoritarian China and Belarus, give little reason for optimism (see Chapter 4). What is more, 'sovereign Europe' has appeared largely missing in action, even in response to autocratic tendencies within the EU. As the Syriza-led government of Greece found to its peril in 2015, challenging the EU's economic orthodoxy can prove to be more costly for the political survival of its leaders than openly 'illiberal' rebellions from new member states, such as Hungary and Poland, against what were widely perceived as Europe's core political values (see Chapter 5). As a result, 'the Greek welfare state was transformed into a warfare state'. Since the government was 'unable to redistribute wealth ... it worked overtime to redistribute blame' (Krastev 2017: 67). Such scenarios were replicated in a number of countries that were at the receiving end of eurozone 'rescue programmes', including Ireland, Portugal and Cyprus. The result has been not merely a lasting damage to national democracies in the affected member states, but also to the democratic credentials of the European Union.

The historic irony is that illiberal leaders have flourished in the countries of Central Europe, not despite their countries' membership in the EU, but to some extent because of it. While the likes of Yanis Varoufakis and Alexis Tsipras (Greece's former Finance Minister and Prime Minister respectively) eventually lost domestic support, the popularity of Orbán in Hungary and the Law and Justice party in Poland has been solidified. Populism found fertile soil in a number of new member states—and a growing resonance outside of them—owing to the sense of powerlessness induced by the previous governments' reliance on the rhetoric of necessity. Against the 'there is no alternative' doctrine (TINA) that became pervasive in the 1990s across both the Western world and the countries that emerged out of the collapse of communism, populists promised to reclaim agency. Defying the discourse of necessity, in which 'executive authority is reduced to something like a conduit of forces beyond its control' (White 2020: 133), populists promised to win back control, and time and again they delivered on that promise.

There is thus a strange symbiosis between the technocratic rationality that the EU deployed in defence of its policies and the enduring appeal of populist challengers in both Western and Eastern Europe. The European project has unwittingly exacerbated the crisis of democratic representation. The process of post-communist transformation in Central and Eastern Europe coincided with the 'hollowing of Western democracy' (Mair 2013). As an ever increasing number of citizens in established democracies felt they were no longer represented by mainstream parties (reflected also in the rapid decline of party memberships), they began to support alternative political forces deemed unacceptable by the mainstream. Democratic choices were thus continuously narrowed in the name of democracy. Paradoxically, the ideal of *wehrhafte* democracy threatened representative democracy. Excluding elements of the people from the polity in order to defend democracy creates dysfunctions even within a well-established order such as the nation state; doing it in a transnational federation in the making—such as the European Union—might prove self-destructive. David Dyzenhaus points to the dangers inherent in the kind of Schmittian 'liberalism with a vengeance', in which the answer to the question 'whether one is part of "the people" and thus entitled to the protections and benefits of the liberal democratic state, including the rule of law' depends on the extent to which one adheres to the principles of liberal democracy (Dyzenhaus 2016: 504). The question of what is applicable to groups within a state applies even more to the nations constituting the EU. How can the EU, we might ask, building on Dyzenhaus, 'respond to anti-liberals and remain true to liberal ideals, including (if this is one such ideal) not forcing people to be liberal in ways that would not be considered legitimate if they were visited on the individuals who make up the people?' (Dyzenhaus 2016: 504). A Europe that 'disciplines and punishes' (Kundnani 2018) is unlikely to appeal to the hearts and minds of European citizens. Instead, it is bound to strengthen both the resolve and the popularity of populist leaders in the countries at the receiving end of the EU's authoritative measures. At any rate, as Philip Manow concludes, 'the populists are not the problem of representative democracy, they just show that it has a problem' (2020: 22–3). They are the symptom, not the cause.

Exit, Voice and Loyalty in Orbán's Hungary

In many ways, Orbán's Hungary has become a mirror image of the more pro-Western European Hungary led by his nominally left-wing, liberal predecessor, Gyurcsány. Undoubtedly, Orbán's government is no less corrupt than Gyurcsány's ever was and, if anything, it may well be even more effective in excluding elements of the population from the polity. A similar dynamic is at play in contemporary Poland. In both countries, both sides of the political spectrum deny the legitimacy of their opponents. Delegitimising one's political opponents as the enemies of the existing political order or of the nation itself might seem a clever political strategy, but it does little to enhance the democracy in whose name that strategy is pursued. It increases political polarisation which in turn reduces the possibilities for compromise. Thus, 'the Polish *Law and Justice* (PiS) party argues that its defeat in the elections would lead to Poland's downfall, while its opponents are convinced that the party continuing to hold onto power would lead to the death of democracy' (Manow 2020: 149).

Once again, the EU appears to be damned if it acts and damned if it refrains from interference. What is more, the EU's freedom of movement unwittingly strengthens the hands of the populist leaders by reducing people's motivation to voice their grievances and improve the quality of democracy in their country. Here again, borderless Europe is part of the problem rather than part of the solution. As Ivan Krastev observed, 'the citizen who decides to leave his country hardly has the reform of the country he has left in mind. He is interested in changing his own lot in life, not the lives of others.' Thus the biggest beneficiaries of intra-EU open borders 'turned out to be the brilliant individual émigrés' and 'the bad eastern European politicians' (Krastev 2017: 53). This echoes Hirschman's logic in *Exit, Voice and Loyalty*: 'the presence of the exit alternative can … tend to *atrophy the development of the art of voice*' (1970: 43). There is an additional twist to this argument owing to the specificity of the EU's supranational governance structures. The EU dimension exacerbates the divide between the 'Somewheres' and the 'Anywheres' (Goodhart 2017), and thus reduces the credibility of those voices who continue to criticise the nativist leaders in their respective homelands from afar. These 'Anywheres' are seen as elitists who have lost touch with 'ordinary' people, while the 'Somewheres' back home are cast as authentic, populist rebels. 'The art of voice' is thus not necessarily atrophied, but rather it is discredited. The critics who left the country to pursue better opportunities abroad can be dismissed as lacking loyalty, a charge that has significant traction with those who remained. New nativist elites can thus cast their opposition against 'Anywheres' as an 'active resistance against the EU' (Ágh 2019: 121), all the while benefiting from significant transfer payments.

Though the EU 'professes a deep commitment to democracy', argues R. Daniel Kelemen, it 'is now providing a hospitable environment for aspiring autocrats' (2020: 482, 494). Why? Kelemen lists three factors underpinning the EU's authoritarian equilibrium: 'partial politicisation, money and migration' (ibid.). First, the EU has been sufficiently politicised at the European level by, for example, endowing supranational party groups with significant powers vis-à-vis other European institutions, such as the European Commission, but it has not been politicised enough for these parties to fear a voters' backlash for their alignment with parties outside the common platform. Second, the EU provides new member states with funding which 'autocratic rulers can use …

to help prop up their regimes' (ibid. 483). Third, and in line with Krastev's observation discussed above, free movement 'facilitates emigration by dissatisfied citizens, which tends to deplete the ranks of the domestic opposition, thereby supporting autocratic regime survival' (ibid.). Though Keleman's analysis is compelling, it is less obvious what remedies, if any, follow from it.

The Political Economy of Populism

The success of populist leaders in Hungary and Poland is at least partly a consequence of the failure of the liberal, pro-EU political elites who preceded them. The EU itself is also implicated in this process. When the answer to most challenges that people encounter tends to be 'more Europe', we shouldn't be surprised that citizens grow distrustful. After all, how could that Europe possibly deliver on all its (often conflicting) promises? That is why Joseph Weiler is right to warn against an EU that is based on '"Telos legitimacy" or "political messianism"', whereby "legitimacy" is gained neither by '"process" nor "output" but by promise—the promise of a "Promised Land"' (2012: 250). One's indignation about the populists and their supporters should not obscure the possibility that at least *some* of their grievances are legitimate. Similarly, it is important to accept that robust debates about the very nature of democracy—both at national and European levels—are a part of legitimate democratic contestation (Manow 2020: 141).

When the charges of populism are used too loosely, a meaningful contest between various versions of democracy ends up being inhibited not just by self-proclaimed 'illiberal' leaders, but also by their opponents. Populism then functions as a conversation stopper, foreclosing debate and hindering serious analysis of the causes of discontent (Manow 2018: 26–9). Revealing in this respect is how often well-meaning criticism of the support for such populist movements is itself anti-democratic in its character. As a Polish sociologist of law observed, 'citizens who express different opinions are treated as politically immature, corrupt, or demoralised by their leaders, and in any case incapable of independent thought' (Czarnota 2020: 44). In line with this, academic literature tends to downplay (or downright ignore) the economic dimension of populism. Just as it makes sense to study populism in the context of 'European culture wars' (Furedi 2018), or from the perspective of conflicting views on the philosophy of history (Legutko 2016), it is important to consider the 'political economy of populism' (Manow 2018). Philip Manow demonstrates how this can be done, tracing both the cultural and economic factors that have led to the illiberal backlash, which manifests itself in differing forms in different parts of Europe. The (perceived) loss of sovereignty over fiscal policies in Southern European countries such as Greece and Spain led to the rise of left-wing populism in the form of Syriza and Podemos respectively. By contrast, the (perceived) loss of sovereign control over borders in Northern countries such as Germany and the Netherlands led to the strengthening of right-wing populist parties, mobilising the electorate with their opposition to migration—think of the Alternative für Deutschland party (AfD), which received a new lease of life after the 2015 migration crisis. Contemporary Hungary and Poland, on the other hand, combine economic policies that could be described as left-populist with a strong anti-migration message characteristic of right-wing populism, reflecting the two factors that Manow assigned to Europe's South and North respectively.

Concluding Remarks

This chapter has traced the twists and turns of post-Second World War European history against the background of the key ideas that have shaped the European project. While confidence in the EU's teleology has waned, its underlying assumptions continue to inform both Europe's political leaders and a great deal of EU scholarship. The EU continues to be seen as a *sui generis* political experiment based on the ideal of shared sovereignty. In line with this, earlier sovereignist critics of the project tend to be dismissed as retrograde or downright anti-European. Yet it should no longer be controversial to argue that the EU we currently have is neither the best nor the only one possible. Europe might have become something very different if the imprint of the likes of Charles de Gaulle had remained stronger than that of the likes of Walter Hallstein and Jacques Delors. The aspiration to create a Europe without borders backfired, posing challenges to democracy both at national and European levels. The attempt to depoliticise conflicts through a federal-like, supranational rule of law state—the *Rechtsstaat*—ended up undermining not just democratic self-government in the constitutive nation states, but the principles of the rule of law themselves.

The series of crises that Europe has experienced, particularly over the last couple of decades, has exposed the limitations of the technocratic mode of governance, which has failed to deliver on the promise of freedom, security and justice. The growing gap between the EU's political rhetoric and its limited capabilities has helped to create a fertile ground for populist leaders who have promised to reclaim control. While the non-violent revolutions of 1989 opened up possibilities for new beginnings, the various iterations of the 'end of history' narrative reinforced the elites' arguments about there being no alternative to the order they pursued—whether they called it post-national and post-sovereign (see Chapter 2), a sovereign Europe (see Chapter 3) or simply just liberal. In fact, the term liberal has also been used to narrow the parameters of political debate. In particular, as discussed in the chapters that follow, liberal precepts in the economic sphere were all too often reduced to normative claims about the minimalist, regulatory role of the state. This is the core premise of ordoliberalism, which became influential first in West Germany after the Second World War, and later via the Maastricht Treaty in Europe at large. In fact, ordoliberalism has become the EU's de facto law of the land (Joerges 2014). With the onset of the eurozone crisis, it served as a justification for an 'emergency Europe' (see Conclusion below) that sought to apply technocratic solutions to problems that were distinctly political. The rhetoric of TINA was applied again at the peak of Europe's refugee crisis in 2015. Finally, the outbreak and the rapid spread of the novel coronavirus in 2020 strengthened the need for scientific expertise, while at the same time exposing its limits. There were no technocratic solutions to the myriad of ethical and political challenges that were presented by the pandemic. What is the right balance, for example, between individual freedom and public safety?

This is the context in which the recent political developments in Central and Eastern Europe ought to be considered, highlighting the twin threat of technocracy and populism (see Chapter 5). Undoubtedly, democratic backsliding in countries like Hungary and Poland has many domestic causes. But it is also a sign of the EU's dysfunction. As Europe after 1989 moved ever further towards a 'political messianic venture *par excellence*' (Weiler 2012: 256), it compromised its own ability to enhance democratic consolidation in the new member states. Paradoxically, the EU's quasi-ideological predisposition and its self-understanding as a de-territorialised polity has also weakened its credibility as a geopolitical actor by exposing the growing gap between the EU's ambitions and its capabilities, whether in relation to Russia, Ukraine and Belarus or China (see Chapter 4). Liberals in Central Europe became so successful in emulating their Western counterparts that they ended up alienating their electoral base. Instead of strengthening democracy in Europe, they may have unwittingly contributed to its decline. This is the liability of Europeanisation, which has been skilfully exploited by those political leaders who defy the West European elite consensus. Viktor Orbán's talk about 'illiberal democracy', for example, is not merely oxymoronic; rather it is a deliberate provocation that amounts to a highly effective political strategy with both domestic and wider European appeal. Jean-Claude Juncker may have been half-right when greeting Orbán as a dictator, but it was at least partly the organisation he represented which facilitated this transformation.

2

A POST-SOVEREIGN EUROPE?

GERMANY, EUROZONE, REFUGEE CRISIS

[T]his time it was Beethoven's cheerful song to joy; millions sank, as Nietzsche describes it, awestruck in the dust, hostile boundaries gone, the gospel of world harmony reconciled and brought together those who were separated; they forgot how to walk and talk and were about to fly off, dancing, up into the air.[1]

Robert Musil, *The Man Without Qualities* (1930)

The European Union means many different things to its many different peoples. Its current hybrid form—neither a full-fledged federal superstate, nor simply an international organisation—comes closest to the ideals of its most powerful member, Germany. This is doubly ironic. First, one of the major rationales for a post-sovereign Europe is that its system of governance ensures no single state, nation or even institution will exercise much power on its own. Second, owing to its historic legacies, size and geographic position, Germany is arguably the least suitable nation to lead. In Hans Kundnani's (2014: 69) apt formulation, Germany's 'post-heroic society' has little aspiration to project power. This is not to deny that the post-1989 Berlin Republic tends to be more assertive, but it seeks to do so via its

35

commitment to multilateralism and to a Europe that is conceived of as post-national. Thomas Mann's famous appeal of 1953 that the aim of postwar reconstruction must be to create a European Germany, rather than a German Europe, has been pursued by politicians of all stripes. Yet, paradoxically, what has emerged over the last decade is a European Germany in an increasingly German Europe.

This chapter will sketch Europe's transformation under Germany's reluctant leadership and point towards its limitations. As Europe's most powerful economy and a major provider of credit, Germany became a dominant player in the eurozone crisis, the first clear signs of which emerged in 2009. As one of both Russia's and Ukraine's main commercial partners, Germany was crucial in shaping the EU-Russia and EU-Ukraine relationship after the Euromaidan revolution in late 2013. As one of the most attractive places for migration, Germany found itself at the centre of the migration crisis in 2015. With the notable exception of Ireland, Germany is also the country most likely to be affected by Brexit. As Germany sought to meet the challenges of the past decade, it unwittingly created new problems. This was partly caused by Germany's unique identity, which has shaped its position in Europe. Consistent with the underlying theme of this book, Germany's role in Europe will be examined via conflicting understandings of sovereignty and democracy, and the way in which they were challenged by the politics of emergency.

There is perhaps no more potent symbol of the German—and European—genius than the Finale of Beethoven's Ninth Symphony, with its jubilant rendition of Friedrich Schiller's 'Ode to Joy', celebrating the universal brotherhood of man. It is also an excellent illustration of both European values and the EU's political ambitions. Musically compelling, the surprising turn in the symphony towards its end is announced by the solo bass vocalist, who sings: 'O friends, no more these sounds continue! Let us raise a song of sympathy, of gladness' (cited in Holbrook and Hirschman 1993: 196). After the 'primeval chaos' and 'apocalyptic discord' that have characterised the first three movements of the symphony (ibid. 196), the listener is treated to an uplifting melody that shutters 'hostile boundaries' and promises an Elysium whose 'magic reunites those whom stern custom has parted' (ibid. 196). It was no accident, then, that the song became an anthem for the European Union, perhaps one of its best-known symbols. And it was no accident that Angela Merkel professed her passion for Beethoven when addressing the European Parliament in July 2020. It was her first trip abroad after a long period of travel restrictions imposed after the outbreak of Covid-19, and it was significant that it led to Brussels, the EU's de facto capital.[2] Speaking on the occasion of Germany's assumption of the EU's rotating presidency, the German Chancellor reminded her audience of the 250th anniversary of Beethoven's birth. As a music lover, Merkel said, she continued to be overwhelmed by the power of his Ninth Symphony. She concluded:

> Every time I listen to it, I discover something new in the music that impresses and moves me—and it's the same with Europe. Europe can be rediscovered again and again. And it still impresses me. So permit me to end today with the hope that the message of this music, the spirit of brotherhood and harmony, may guide us in Europe. What could be a more fitting message than that this Europe is capable of great things if we support each other and stand together? (Merkel 2020)

Though universalist in its aspiration, this is a very 'German' perspective, a call for a Europe 'capable of great things', which would live up to the ideals of the eighteenth-century Enlightenment that Schiller's poem so beautifully articulates. 'Primeval chaos' and 'the apocalyptic discord' in this narrative stand for the nationalistic excesses of the first half of the twentieth century which tore Europe apart, causing unprecedented physical destruction, death and human suffering. To create a better world, in this view, it was necessary to overcome nationalism and embrace a world without divisions. The creation of a borderless and truly united Europe would represent an important step towards just such a world. Yet, Beethoven's 'political fantasy' (Buch 2003) served many causes, not all of them laudable. Artistically brilliant, its political ambition may well be hubristic.[3] In fact, two centuries of Europe's turbulent history—and Germany's place in it—could be sketched by tracing the perceptions and appropriations of Beethoven's Ninth. First performed in Vienna in

1824, Beethoven's most famous work was, as Esteban Buch writes, deployed in support of radically different political projects:

> German nationalists admired the music's heroic power, and nineteenth-century French republicans found in it an expression of 1789's three-word motto, *Liberté, Égalité, Fraternité*. The communists hear in it the gospel of a classless world, Catholics hear the Gospel itself, democrats hear it as the voice of democracy. Hitler celebrated his birthday with the *Ode to Joy*, and yet the same music was used to oppose him, even in his concentration camps. The *Ode to Joy* resounds periodically at the Olympic games, and ... it was the anthem of the racist Republic of Rhodesia. (2003: 5)

The history of the reception of Beethoven's Ninth prefigures to some extent Germany's current dilemmas in the EU, caught as it is between noble aspirations to lead Europe into a better future and an awareness of historic legacies that continue to inform its reluctance to exercise leadership. Ironically, though Schiller's lyrics perfectly express the EU's ambition, the European anthem has no words—a Europe of twenty-seven nations with twenty-four official languages could hardly have endorsed original German lyrics. This compromise might be seen as an admission of failure, with the adaptation degrading the original work into 'a truly bastard child of the Enlightenment: a song without words; hope without a text' (Clark 1997: 801),[4] or, alternatively, its very ambiguity can be celebrated as the expression of 'an evolving collective European identity' (Katzenstein 1997: 24). Foreshadowing Merkel's argument about rediscovering Europe 'again and again', Peter J. Katzenstein compared Beethoven's repeated reworkings of the Ninth Symphony's ending with 'European states continuously reworking a collective identity', as they develop a unique post-national polity that is 'not a democratic state-in-becoming' but a system of multilevel governance (Katzenstein 1997: 24). In a similar vein, as we learn from an EU official website, the anthem is not meant to replace the member states' own national anthems, but rather 'to celebrate the values they share'. The anthem, just like the European Parliament, is a symbol of a state, but with a difference.[5]

The very fact that Merkel ended up becoming German Chancellor can be linked to another appropriation of Beethoven's Ninth Symphony. On Christmas Day 1989, a multinational orchestra combining musicians from the two Germanys, the Soviet Union, France and England celebrated the demise of communism in Central and Eastern Europe. On that occasion, even Schiller's lyrics played a role—their symbolic power reinforced through a decision of the American conductor Leonard Bernstein. Bernstein took the liberty of altering a crucial line in the Ode, substituting the word *Freiheit* (freedom) for *Freude* (joy). Bernstein's *Ode to Freedom* seemed a fitting tribute to the end of the Cold War, which had its most tangible manifestation in the demise of the Berlin Wall that had occurred just a few weeks earlier, on 9 November 1989. Merkel was still a very junior politician from East Germany then, and was yet to be catapulted to power by her mentor, the Chancellor of German unity, Helmut Kohl.

It was the prospect of German unification that accelerated the plans for the Economic and Monetary Union. The introduction of the euro was seen as the answer to the widespread concern about Germany becoming too powerful—an old problem often referred to as the 'German question'. Kohl's commitment to the single European currency was to ensure that the country would remain embedded within European institutions. Whatever disagreements the French President François Mitterrand and the German Chancellor might have had, they both agreed that 'the German question is a European question'. It is ironic then that a project—the euro—that was meant to cement European unity and make Germany more European resulted in a Europe that is both increasingly fragmented and more 'German' than either leader could have imagined. It is to a large extent thanks to the eurozone crisis that Merkel was to become 'the world's most powerful woman', as *Time* magazine put it.[6] A Danish academic was even more effusive in his praise of the then German Chancellor, invoking the famous encounter between Hegel and Napoleon to reflect on her world-historic importance. Just as Hegel saw Napoleon, riding through the German city of Jena in 1806, as 'the soul of the world mounted on a horse', Matthew Qvortrup 'saw "the world spirit" [*Weltgeist*] in the shape of a middle-aged woman in a purple pantsuit at an EU summit' (2016: 330). 'Whether we like it or not', Qvortrup observed, 'we live in the world of Angela Merkel' (ibid. 331).

If Merkel unwittingly became the EU's Napoleon, what was its French Revolution? It was the Maastricht Treaty of 1992, I suggest, which was to represent 'a quantum leap' (Delors 1989) towards European unity, moving it closer towards the ideal of a federation. Clearly, there was nothing resembling the Battle of Jena, but the difficulties of ratification were numerous, and they foreshadowed many problems that Europe still faces. Taking advantage of the momentous developments unleashed by the 1989 non-violent revolutions that ended Europe's Cold War divisions, the Maastricht Treaty created the European Union largely as we know it today, including giving it its current name and its own legal entity. In addition to the single European currency, the Treaty on European Union (as it is also known) created the European citizenship. Both of these innovations were designed to ensure that the ideal of a borderless Europe would become a practical reality. At the same time, Maastricht represents the conflict between Europe's ambition and its limits—the obdurate political reality of many people not wanting to be co-opted into a Europe that would be as tightly unified as the name suggests. To be sure, the Treaty makes a strong commitment to subsidiarity, but that is difficult to square with the legal and institutional framework that was considered necessary for the viability of the Economic and Monetary Union. At any rate, Maastricht further expanded a number of attributes that make the EU look like a state, even if they are conceived in a peculiar way, reflecting its unique, experimental nature.[7]

The question that the Treaty on European Union evades is the one of popular sovereignty. Does Europe have a people? If not, can it forge one? And why does it matter? A possible answer is that Europe would hardly be 'capable of great things' unless its peoples 'support each other and stand together' (Merkel 2020). In other words, unless European citizens become *a* people. With a similar emphasis on greatness, the then President of the European Commission, Jacques Delors, argued in 1989 that 'history is only interested in the far-sighted and those who think big'. Was Maastricht big enough?

For the proponents of an 'ever-closer union', the Treaty did not go far enough. It created 'a Europe of bits and pieces' (Curtin 1993), generating dysfunctions that proved difficult to remedy for decades to come. As noted above, the very term 'Union' suggests a greater degree of unity than the Treaty was able to deliver. This is particularly true in the area of Foreign Affairs and Security Policy, which requires unanimity and thus remains under the control of sovereign member states. In other areas, concessions were made to individual member states opposed to the federal ambitions of the Treaty, such as Denmark and the UK, which secured an opt-out from the Euro. But even the euro itself—arguably the EU's most ambitious project to date—was conceived as a halfway house. This is in fact something that was understood from the very beginning.

Notwithstanding their many differences, the architects of the euro shared the view that the Economic and Monetary Union was an incomplete project. They fell into two major camps, both of which assumed that the success of the single European currency required greater political integration. They differed mainly in their views on the sequencing of the events. The so-called 'monetarists', who thought of the euro 'as a tool to challenge national sovereignty while waiting for some kind of political union' (Dyson and Maes 2016: 193), believed that the introduction of the euro would eventually lead to further political integration, strengthening the Union as a result. Amongst the monetarists were passionate advocates of a post-national Europe such as Robert Triffin, Robert Marjolin and Tommaso Padoa-Schioppa. By contrast, the 'economists', such as Hans Tietmeyer and Karl Otto Pöhl, were convinced that for the project to work, both economic convergence and political unity must precede the creation of the single European currency. The first approach was particularly popular in France, while the second found more adherents in Germany. The 'monetarists' prevailed, but the concerns of the 'economists' shaped the eurozone's institutional architecture too—arguably combining the worst of both worlds. The European Central Bank (ECB) largely emulated the governing principles of the German Bundesbank, with a particular emphasis on price stability and political independence—principles that worked well in Germany but were to become a serious liability for the eurozone.[8] The decision to base the ECB in Frankfurt further strengthened the continuity between the German and the European Central Bank. Ultimately, the single European currency was the result of a contest of ideas as much as the power struggle between France and Germany.

The question that is more fundamental, yet that was seldom raised by scholars sympathetic to the European project, is whether the euro should have been introduced in the first place. While a number of economists considered the project to have been misguided from the outset, no major scholars of European integration questioned its wisdom.[9] Milton Friedman (1997), for example, wrote presciently that the euro would 'prove a barrier to the achievement of political unity', because unlike the United States, Europe consisted of nations 'whose residents speak different languages, have different customs, and have far greater loyalty and attachment to their own country than to the common market or to the idea of "Europe"'. Expanding on this, one could argue that the Treaty on European Union represented a step too far. It is worth recalling that its initial success was not preordained. The Treaty was first defeated in the Danish referendum, exposing the extent of public resistance, and the subsequent endorsement in the French referendum occurred with the thinnest of margins (50.8 per cent to 49.2 per cent). While the debate in France was focused less on economics and more on 'sovereignty and identity' (Schmidt 2020: 94), the euro was later to be perceived as undermining both. In the United Kingdom, Margaret Thatcher was fundamentally opposed to what she perceived as Brussels' federalist ambitions, but rather than succeeding in reversing the seemingly irresistible movement of European politics, she lost the support of her own party and her position as British Prime Minister. Thatcher's defeat reinforced the fundamental divide within the British Conservative Party towards Europe which has shaped UK and EU relations ever since, and that would eventually lead to Brexit (see Chapter 3). Though Germans were not keen to part company with their 'beloved German mark',[10] there was no widespread public opposition to the introduction of the euro or to other federalist aspects of the Maastricht Treaty. More than sixty prominent German economists warned that monetary unity would lead to political disunity, but such dissenting voices had little impact (Plickert 2017).

However, while Germany's political leaders from Kohl to Merkel appeared to be comfortable with the idea of their country sharing sovereignty with Europe, there have always been many who continued to think of Germany as a nation state and the EU as a community consisting of sovereign states. Significantly, this has been the opinion of the German Federal Constitutional Court (Bundesverfassungsgericht, BVerfG), which ruled against the assumption that Europe was becoming a quasi-federal state to which Germany would have been subordinated. Responding to a number of complaints filed against the Maastricht Treaty, the court asserted that the EU is a *Staatenverbund* (that is, a community of states, echoing Kant's idea of *Völkerbund*) rather than a *Bundesstaat* (a federal state, contra, e.g., Hallstein, see Chapter 1). This distinction is important because it explicitly addresses the question about the locus of sovereignty. In other words, the Maastricht Judgment did not merely describe the nature and form of European integration but also prescribed its limits. Closely related to this, in legal terms, is the issue of *competence-competence* (MacCormick 1995: 260), which is about determining who has the final say in the case of conflict between the participating states and the centre. The German dichotomy—between the *Staatenbund* (from which the term *Staatenverbund* is derived) and the *Bundesstaat*—delivers a clear answer: while the federal state decides in the case of the *Bundesstaat*, the participating member states have the final say in the *Staatenbund* (Kahl 1994: 243–4). Consistent with this, the German court asserted that the political legitimacy of the European Union is ultimately derived from democratically constituted member states, which in turn embody the sovereign will of the *peoples* of Europe. The emergence of a European democracy would only be made possible by the existence of *a* European people, which appears to be an unattainable goal. In sum, the EU is not a state, and should not become one.

The decision was both surprising and controversial. It was surprising because (West) Germany was from the outset very pro-integrationist, as is reflected even in the German constitution, which envisages the possibility of Germany becoming part of a European federation proper. The decision was controversial because it flew in the face of the growing consensus about the unique nature of the EU amongst legal scholars, the vast majority of whom considered the categories of the state, nation and sovereignty obsolete at best, and dangerous at worst. Moreover, because of its political history, Germany had committed itself to work towards 'a united Europe' in its constitution from 1949, which contained a specific article (Article 24) empowering the German parliament to authorise the 'transfer of sovereign powers' (Übertragung von Hoheitsrechten) to international institutions such as the EU.[11] Germany also had to learn to live with the reality of *not* being fully sovereign in the aftermath of the Second World War, having regained its formal status as an independent nation only a few weeks before its unification on 3 October 1990.

Weiler's verdict on the 'Maastricht decision' of the German Constitutional Court was damning. He found the decision 'sad, even pathetic' and 'embarrassing' (1995: 222). The decision was sad, Weiler wrote, because by emphasising the importance of *demos*, it was redolent of a discredited conception of a polity based on Schmittian 'Blood (*Volk*) and Soil (*Staat*)'. It was pathetic, because it attempted to impose that retrograde view as a 'telos which [was] alien to the foundational purposes of European integration' (ibid. 224). Instead of taking the opportunity to '[rethink] in creative ways the concept of polity and membership', Weiler argued that the court sought to restate 'the tired old ideas of an ethno-culturally homogenous *Volk* and the unholy Trinity of *Volk-Staat-Staatsangehöriger* [nation-state-citizen] as the exclusive basis for democratic authority and legitimate rule-making' (ibid. 223). And as the court was ashamed to acknowledge Schmitt as the true inspiration for these antiquated notions, Weiler alleges that the judges instead cited Herman Heller, the Jewish, Socialist, anti-fascist Schmitt critic. Finally, the decision was embarrassing, because it amounted to the court embracing the EU's political order as it was, overlooking its democratic deficit and missing an opportunity to articulate possible remedies. Challenging the court's reasoning, Weiler asked:

> Is it mandated that demos in general and the European demos in particular be understood exclusively in the organic cultural

homogeneous terms which the German Federal Constitutional Court has adopted in its own self-understanding? Can there not be other understandings of demos which might lead to different conceptualisations and potentialities for Europe? (1995: 240)

Not surprisingly, Weiler answered his rhetorical questions affirmatively and sketched his own vision of a polity that is 'not statal in character' and thus not 'enslaved to the concepts of *Volk*, *Staat* and *Staatsangehöriger*' (1995: 244). Instead, Weiler urges us to think of a Supranational Europe which aims not to replace its constitutive member states, but to transform them in a way that makes them less centred on narrowly conceived national interests. Jürgen Habermas echoes this argument with his vision of a 'postnational' Europe, which need not be 'mentally rooted in "the nation" as a pre-political community of shared destiny' (2001: 76). Importantly, such a Europe is not to be confused with the more clearly centralising project of the 'United States of Europe' (Weiler 1995: 248; Habermas 2015: 14). Similarly, Habermas dismisses the reasoning of the German Constitutional Court as a 'false alternative' between a *Staatenbund* (confederation) and a *Bundesstaat* (federal European state), advocating instead 'a *supranational*, yet *democratic*, polity' (2015: 14). 'In this polity, and to this demos', Weiler argues, 'one cardinal value is precisely that there will not be a drive towards, or an acceptance of, an over-arching organic-cultural identity' (1995: 254). And just as European identity would merely complement national identities, European citizenship enhances and extends the range of rights and allegiances rather than replacing them with new ones. Rather than being destabilising, people's membership in 'multiple demoi' (ibid. 252) would give rise to 'critical citizenship'. This would move Europe closer to the enlightened, Kantian ideal, which 'diminishes the importance of the statal aspects of nationality' (ibid. 250). Weiler concludes on an optimistic note, arguing that

> in the realm of the political, the special virtue of contemporaneous membership in an organic national-cultural demos and in a supranational civic, value-driven demos is in the effect which such double membership might have on taming the great appeal, even craving, for belonging and destiny in this world which

nationalism continues to offer but which can easily degenerate to intolerance and xenophobia. (ibid. 256)

Three decades later, it is questionable whether the advances brought about by the institutional and political innovations of Maastricht in fact decreased 'intolerance and xenophobia' in Europe. Moreover, defying a great deal of EU legal scholarship, in 2020 the German court returned to its Maastricht Treaty reasoning in its decision on the ECB's Public Sector Purchase Programme (PSPP) for bond buying. Not surprisingly, the judgment elicited similar criticisms. Observers outside of Germany in particular were incensed by this 'act of constitutional rebellion' (Sarmiento and Utrilla 2020). The court was accused of having 'launched a legal missile into the heart of the EU' (Wolf 2020) and of 'plunging Europe into a constitutional crisis' (Fabbrini and Kelemen 2020). While critics of the BVerfG's judgment continue to view the EU as a quasi-federation that should not be destabilised by its subordinate units, its defenders aver that the EU's powers are conditional on its member states' assent. As the former German constitutional judge Dieter Grimm wrote, 'for the Federal Constitutional Court, it is key that the European Union is a union of sovereign states, which make up its foundation, and that it must respect their identities, which are reflected primarily in their national constitutions' (2020: 945).

From Constitutional Patriotism to the Single European Currency

At any rate, the conflict is far from settled. In my view, Weiler's criticism does not do justice to the Maastricht decision or, in fact, to the Schmittian conception of the demos. While Schmitt opposed both representative democracy and liberalism, his conception of the demos was broader than Weiler allows for. In his 1928 *Constitutional Theory*, for example, Schmitt listed a number of elements that could

> contribute to the unity of the nation and to the consciousness of this unity, such as common language, common historical destiny, traditions and remembrances, and common political goals and hopes. The language is a very important factor in this, yet it is not by itself determinative. What is definitive is the commonality

of historical life, conscious willing of this commonality, great events and goals. (Schmitt [1928] 2008a: 262)

Clearly, this account can be deployed as much to advocate ethnic purity (as Schmitt himself disgracefully did in 1936)[12] as to defend Europe as a political project based on 'common political goals and hopes', compatible with, amongst others, Habermas' vision of 'constitutional patriotism' or Merkel's determination to work towards a Europe 'capable of great things', one in which 'we Europeans have our destiny in our hands' (Merkel cited in Middelaar 2019: 129). Even Habermas invoked 'the commonality of historical life' (Schmitt [1928] 2008a) to justify why 'we' (as Germans and Europeans) have obligations to live up to the virtues of constitutional patriotism. In other words, Habermas too is aware of the sociological fact of demos as a historical community of descent, which he initially articulated in the context of the German *Historikerstreit*:

> Our own life is linked to the life context in which Auschwitz was possible not by contingent circumstances but intrinsically. Our form of life is connected with that of our parents and grandparents through a web of familial, local, political, and intellectual traditions that is difficult to disentangle—that is, through a historical milieu that made us what and who we are today. None of us can escape this milieu because our identities, both as individuals and Germans, are indissolubly interwoven with it. (Habermas cited in Markell 2000: 53).

Inescapable identities impose on us inescapable obligations. After 1989, and in the context of the negotiations that would lead to the failed Constitutional Treaty of the European Union, Habermas extended this narrative to advocate 'identity-formation beyond national boundaries' (Habermas 2001a: 16). Constitutional patriotism was no longer to be applied merely to the Federal Republic of Germany, but was to become the crucial element in the creation of a European postnational democracy. Europe's transition towards this qualitatively new democratic polity, Habermas believed, could be eased by a shared self-understanding of people from across Europe. The people merely needed to draw the correct lesson from their histories and think of themselves as 'the sons, daughters, and grandchildren of a barbaric nationalism' (Habermas 2001b: 103). This would give rise to a transnational, European-wide public sphere, overcoming the confines of nation states. As I will argue below (and in Chapter 3), this vision for Europe is both theoretically misguided and politically self-defeating. Ironically, Habermas' reasoning is also somewhat parochial as it seeks to extrapolate a universal moral prescription from a unique German historic experience. Not many people in Poland or the UK, for example, are likely to think of themselves as the 'grandchildren of a barbaric nationalism', considering that their forebears' generation was instrumental in defeating Nazi Germany, demonstrating the power of *liberal* nationalism (Auer 2004a).

At any rate, far from advocating the restoration of a racially defined state (as insinuated by Weiler), the German court sought to constrain Europe's ambition to assume a number of state-like functions that would no longer be anchored in popular sovereignty. In fact, Weiler's detailed, extensive and highly influential critique of the Maastricht Treaty decision largely ignores the fundamental question that the court sought to address—the location of sovereignty. The other conspicuously absent subject is the single European currency—a curious omission considering how central the treaty was for the creation of the Economic and Monetary Union. Be that as it may, Weiler's justification of a 'supranational European polity' is echoed by similar accounts deployed in defence of the euro. For example, just as Weiler spoke in favour of 'the view that would decouple *Volk* from Demos and Demos from State', Wim Duisenberg, the first president of the European Central Bank, praised the novelty of the euro as 'the first currency that has not only severed its link to gold, but also its link to the nation state' (cited in Marsh 2009: 12). Both of these major projects introduced by Maastricht, EU citizenship and the euro, were premised on the idea that it was both possible and desirable to transcend nationhood.

What Weiler and Duisenberg celebrated as the EU's unique virtue—its indeterminate character beyond the confines of a nation state—turned out to be a major liability, particularly in the decade of crises. With the eurozone crisis going back to 2010, the refugee crisis that culminated in 2015, the crisis of the EU-Russia relationship going back to the Ukrainian Maidan revolution of 2013–14, to the Covid-19 crisis in 2020, the EU has struggled to live up to the expectations it raised both in relation to its own people and neighbouring countries. This is not an accident. What neither of the accounts of a post-national or supranational Europe tell us is what is to happen in the case of the exception. The question of who decides on the emergency is, after all, the very question about sovereignty which these theories declared obsolete. As we shall see, this omission is not only a serious weakness of the dominant approaches to the study of European integration, but a problem of the EU as a political system. The increasing constitutionalisation of many areas of European politics which would normally remain open to political contestation has resulted in a situation where changes can only be implemented by a new EU treaty (which would be very difficult to negotiate and ratify by all twenty-seven member states), or by ad hoc agreements on particular issues between member states, which are oftentimes reached to bypass, or defy, the existing constitutional order. Thus, instead of European integration advancing through law as envisaged by Hallstein, more recently integration has proceeded through 'the disintegration of law' (Scicluna 2018). Unconventional steps have been followed by unconventional justifications. Defending the measures pursued during the eurozone crisis, which appeared to be in breach of the Maastricht Treaty, Middelaar argued that in an emergency situation, 'breaking with the rules could actually equate to being true to the contract' (2019: 40).

While the European Union as a community of law was being undermined by 'the triumph of expediency over democratic legitimacy' (Scicluna 2019), political leaders continued to stress the importance of rules. Consequently, the EU ended up oscillating between two modes of governance underpinned by two conflicting rationales: the politics of emergency and the technocratic reliance on depoliticised rules. Perhaps nobody embodied these two contradictory impulses better than 'Europe's most influential leader', Chancellor Merkel (Qvortrup 2016). To a number of her critics, Merkel was less a principled politician[13] than one who had 'perfected the art of staying in power by means of unpredictable changes of course' (Streeck 2016a: 8). Instead of shaping public opinion and leading, Robin Alexander (2017) has argued, she merely reacted to ever changing public moods.[14] Yet the problem is not Merkel and her governing style, which aimed to avoid politics whenever possible (see Müller 2018). Rather it is the EU as a whole which has been repeatedly caught between technocracy and the politics of the exception. Merkel's approach seemed a perfect fit for the EU institutions and its methods of working and thinking, which are 'designed to smother political passions with a web of rules: depoliticisation' (Middelaar 2019: vii). Furthermore, rather than strengthening the sense of European unity, leading to 'a supranational civic, value-driven demos' (Weiler 1995: 256), the numerous crises of the past decades have led to a resurgence of national attachments. This became particularly visible in the early stages of the Covid-19 outbreak, when the decisive actions early on were taken largely at the level of nation states.

Post-Sovereign EU in Times of Pandemic

Having been told for decades how much the EU mattered to their daily lives, Europeans might have been forgiven for thinking that the EU would step in when their very lives were being threatened. 'No form of order, no reasonable legitimacy or legality can exist without protection and obedience' wrote Schmitt, asserting (leaning on Hobbes) that 'the *protego ergo obligo* is the *cogito ergo sum* of the state' ([1928] 2007: 52). As discussed, the EU is different. Yet, it was of little comfort to people in northern Italy, for example, to discover in early 2020 that as EU citizens they belonged to an experimental polity that was *not* a state. Even if Covid-19 does not end up becoming a 'deglobalisation virus' (Goodhart 2020), the pandemic has certainly highlighted the importance of nation states. It was nation states that had the capacity to act swiftly and decisively to combat the spread of the disease. They declared emergencies, closed borders, boosted health services and introduced massive compensation packages for individuals and companies whose incomes had collapsed owing to the pandemic. These were vital measures, some of which the EU agreed to contribute to eventually, but only after many months of arduous negotiations.

In a clumsy effort to tap into social media, the EU Commission delegation in France designed a Twitter meme featuring two angry men yelling at each other about the EU *not* having done enough during the Covid-19 outbreak. '*La santé n'est pas une compétence de l'Union européenne*'—'Health is not a competence of the European Union' is the correct answer to such allegations,[15] but unlikely to satisfy many people who expected more from '*l'Europe qui protégé*'—'a Europe that protects'—as the popular EU slogan promises. The fictional dialogue concludes by pointing out the logical inconsistency of arguing that Europe failed while at the same opposing it, rather than advocating its further empowerment with new competencies. Yet this claim would only be credible if Europe was indeed the political and geographic unit best suited to manage such a crisis. That is far from self-evident. Europeanising public health to the extent that would be adequate to the severity of the challenge posed by Covid-19 would require an unattainable level of transnational solidarity and convergence of national healthcare provisions.

As it was, the mishandling of the Covid-19 pandemic exposed the deficiency of political decision-making processes at both national and European levels. As in previous crises, the question about the most appropriate level for a decision to take place—whether it be local, national or European—exposed the inadequacy of existing governing structures. This is what I have described elsewhere as the 'EU's sovereignty paradox' (Auer and Scicluna 2021: 29): member states have ceded too much control to the supranational level to be able to set effective policies in vital areas independently of each other and of the Union institutions. At the same time, they retain enough initiative to resist compromise and thwart common solutions. As we will see, this is a common pattern to all major challenges Europe has faced in its crisis decade.

Exemplary of this problem was also the second stage of the pandemic management. European leaders were determined to avoid the mistakes of their initial response—Europe was to act in a more united fashion. This was the reasoning that informed the decision to task the European Commission with the procurement of vaccines. The assumption was that a larger political unit—the EU—would be in a stronger negotiating position when dealing with large, multinational pharmaceutical companies, and would secure better deals for EU citizens. It did not quite work out that way. Instead, the EU's vaccine procurement scheme has demonstrated that the EU lacks the legitimacy—and arguably also the capacity—to take bold steps early on. Compared to the UK, the Commission signed contracts with vaccine manufacturers later, while the European Medicines Agency has been significantly slower than its UK counterpart to approve vaccines. The EU strategy proved misguided and costly, resulting in significant delays to the vaccination rollout, which led in turn to further delays to the reopening of economies in continental Europe. Unexpectedly, the UK's decision to opt out from the EU's vaccination strategy turned out to be the first tangible Brexit dividend.

Revealing in our context is the discrepancy between the high-minded motives that underpinned the EU's vaccination policies and the results they led to. Amongst their key aims was to avoid vaccine nationalism and reinforce European solidarity, all the while enabling Europe to live up to its responsibility as a good global citizen by assisting global vaccination efforts. Yet faced with an acute shortage of vaccines combined with a rapid growth of infections in early 2021, national governments felt compelled to pursue their own strategies, seeking side agreements with vaccine manufacturers in Europe as well as China and Russia. The Commission, in turn, threatened to impose export bans on vaccines produced within the EU (Mussler 2021).

The Euro as a Currency in Search of a State

Measured against its stated goals, the Economic and Monetary Union has failed. Its primary aim was to bring both European nations and EU citizens closer together; instead it strengthened centrifugal tendencies by exacerbating the divisions between the EU's member states. It was meant to anchor Germany ever more firmly in Europe; instead it reinforced Germany's (reluctant) hegemony. It was meant to contribute to a convergence of economic conditions between Europe's economic centre and its peripheries; instead it threatens to cement these discrepancies. Wolfgang Streeck's verdict, reached at the height of the eurozone crisis, is likely to remain valid for some time to come. '"United Europe" has never been so disunited in the last half-century as it is today', he wrote, observing that 'at the level of the lifeworlds of citizens, nationalistic cliches and national identifications have returned with a vengeance' (2014: 213). In contrast, Habermas continues to believe that the only serious problem the eurozone has faced so far has been the German reluctance to accept responsibility for the completion of the Economic and Monetary Union, which he sees as being made possible by the upheavals caused by the pandemic. The EU recovery fund, which was the result of a compromise reached chiefly between Merkel and Macron, appears to have broken with the German taboo of 'Eurobonds'. Almost exactly three decades after German unification, Habermas (2020) argues, the German government can at long last pursue its true purpose 'by gathering together our national forces for the decisive step in integrating Europe'.

The fund is new, but the trope of integration through crisis is as old as the project of European unification. This mode of integration has its limitations, as does the novel instrument of EU-wide state financing. To start with, as a number of economists have pointed out, the recovery fund might appear to be large in total but is small in relative terms considering the extent of the economic slowdown, the impact of which has been exacerbated by unsustainably high levels of sovereign debt in Europe's peripheries. Second, and more importantly, mutualising debt alone is not a satisfactory political solution to the eurozone's many problems. Particularly problematic is the way this policy was adopted. It came about after a decade of arduous negotiations, in which the 'frugal' nations in the North were pitted against the 'spendthrift' nations in the South, reinforcing nationalist stereotypes. It occurred in defiance of an explicit promise to German voters, who were assured time and again by their political leaders that the EU would *not* become a transfer union. This was something that was explicitly prohibited by the Maastricht Treaty, notwithstanding the widespread understanding amongst many economists (particularly outside Germany) that transfers were indispensable for the functioning of a currency union, particularly considering the vast discrepancies between the levels of economic development amongst (and within) participating states. While the prospects for a genuine reform of the dysfunctional Economic and Monetary Union remain elusive, EU leaders continue to rely on the dubious method of 'governing by rules and ruling by numbers' (Schmidt 2020), which lacks democratic legitimacy.

The agreement between Macron and Merkel reached in 2020 is unlikely to end the 'battle of ideas' which have shaped both the euro's creation and the EU's crisis management. Throughout the long decade of crisis, both France and Germany have continued 'digging trenches around established intellectual and theoretical propositions', making the French 'even more French and Germans even more German' (Brunnermeier et al. 2016: 7). While the French from the outset favoured a more politicised approach to the single currency, including by complementing its introduction with a *gouvernement économique*, the Germans successfully blocked these efforts and ensured the ECB's independence. This is not to ignore the fact that German advocacy of an apolitical and technocratic central bank was itself a political stance that reflected a particular political culture. Though such a preference was understandable 'given the country's experiences with two monetary devaluations', it does not follow 'that this kind of setup is an inevitable necessity that precedes all politics like a kind of mathematical imperative' (Böckenförde 2017: 355). In fact the irony is that at the height of the eurozone crisis the German government behaved in ways that exposed it to charges of being concurrently both too German and not German enough. Merkel and her then Finance Minister, Wolfgang Schäuble, were criticised for their dogmatic adherence to (ordoliberal) rules. At the same time they were seen as betraying those very same rules, particularly by many German observers. It is worth recalling that the emergence of the AfD was initially triggered by Merkel's insistence that there was 'no alternative' to her eurozone policies—a position that was at times as unpopular outside Germany as within it, albeit for very different reasons.

The German government's eurocrisis policy was underpinned alternately by the logic of technocratic rationality and the politics of emergency. Technocracy was Merkel's preferred way of governing, and all who disagreed with her solutions showed themselves to be bad Europeans and 'bad Germans to boot, because the definition of a good German is being enthusiastic about European integration' (Müller 2018). Yet time and again, the German government also supported exceptional measures. The ECB, for example, has formally maintained both its political independence and its focus on monetary stability. However, with the implicit backing of the German government, Mario Draghi's unconventional monetary policies greatly enhanced its power. Under his leadership, the ECB morphed into a decisive *political* actor that operates outside political control. As Hans-Werner Sinn has documented, the ECB has adopted a number of unconventional tools, such as the Outright Monetary Transactions instrument which enabled it to bypass the Maastricht Treaty prohibition of state financing, moving the EU ever closer towards 'a joint-liability union'. Rather than enhancing Europe's unity, Sinn argued, this debt mutualisation by stealth 'is likely to lead to deep divisions in Europe'. This path, he wrote,

> does not lead to the establishment of a federal state in the real sense of the word, i.e. to a union of equals who by their own will, decide to come together and provide mutual assistance. Instead it leads, if anywhere at all, to a unitary state that will come into being through a disregard of the wishes of the population and through the actions forced upon them by a technocratic body that acts wholly independently and that pre-determines parliaments' subsequent decisions. (Sinn 2014: 356)

The difficulties faced by a currency union that supranationalised monetary policy while keeping fiscal policies in the hands of member states were entirely predictable and, indeed, were predicted. Ernst-Wolfgang Böckenförde, for example, cited the 1993 Maastricht decision (to which he also contributed), which posited that the creation of the currency union without the concomitant creation of the political union 'is a political decision that will need to be owned by relevant political institutions'. If problems occur in the absence of a political union, Böckenförde argued, 'there will be a need for a renewed *political* decision about how to proceed further' (2010; my emphasis).

55

We are thus back to the very question that was time and again declared obsolete: 'Who is ultimately in charge of Europe?' Following Schmitt, this question could also be formulated as: 'Who decides on the exception?' Was it Draghi, who is said to have rescued the project in July 2012 by saying the ECB would do 'whatever it takes' to safeguard the currency? Was it Angela Merkel, who—however reluctantly—authorised numerous bailout packages and tolerated the ECB's usurpation of power? Or was it Macron, who convinced his German counterpart to take even bolder measures in the summer of 2020? If we accept Neil MacCormick's understanding of the EU as 'a genuinely polycentric system' of governance 'without a single power centre that has ultimate authority for all purposes', our difficulties in answering such questions are a sign of progress (2010: 151). Celebrating this constitutional ambiguity, MacCormick compared the pooling of sovereignty with the loss of virginity: 'something is lost without anyone else gaining it' (cited in Kalmo and Skinner 2010: 21). What proved far more difficult to lose was the sovereign debt, much to the annoyance of people in Greece, Cyprus, Italy, Spain, Portugal and Ireland—nations that experienced various forms of the EU's 'economic governance', which they perceived as austerity regimes.

For Quentin Skinner, the very possibility of a sovereign debt serves to illustrate the complex meaning of the term and its enduring importance. The idea of a sovereign state remains indispensable, Skinner argues, so that we can 'make sense of the claim that some government actions have the effect of binding not merely the body of the people but their remote posterity' (2010: 46). When a government decides to incur a public debt, Skinner asks,

> Who becomes the debtor? We can hardly answer … that the debt must be owed by the sovereign body of the people. If the debt is sufficiently large, the people will lack the means to pay it. But nor does it make any better sense to suggest in commonsensical terms that the debt must be owed by the government that incurred it. If the government changes or falls, this will have no effect in cancelling the debt. (2010: 46)

The only coherent solution to this puzzle, Skinner suggests, is to posit the idea of the state as a *persona ficta*—the artificial and eternal 'person of the state', who is 'able to incur obligations that no government and no single generation of citizens could ever hope to discharge' (ibid.). This concept is also of great importance in times of emergency, which inevitably test the legitimacy of government actions. 'If there is a genuine national crisis', Skinner argues, 'there must be a strong case for saying that the person whose life most urgently needs to be saved is the person of the state' (ibid.). In his reasoning, Skinner, like Schmitt before him, is following Thomas Hobbes, whose insights the EU was meant to have defied. For Hobbes, of course, sovereignty was meant to be indivisible. There is a sad irony to be found in the fact that the only aspect of the EU's member states' sovereignty that remains obdurately indivisible is their public debt.

'Yes, We Can'—or Can We? Refugee Crisis in Germany and Europe

It may have been partly in response to Germany's tarnished reputation as a champion of austerity that Merkel's government showed its generosity in mid-2015. Hundreds of thousands of migrants, mainly civilians escaping the protracted civil war in Syria, were fleeing from the Middle East to Europe. For once, German people had the opportunity to turn 'the spirit of brotherhood and harmony' (Merkel 2020) into concrete actions that had the potential to transform both the lives of refugees and the very character of Germany as a nation. This was not, then, merely a humanitarian gesture, it was an attempt to make Germany even more worldly, a place that welcomes strangers. The question of belonging in Germany, and by extension in Europe, would thus be more about sharing common values, such as liberal democracy, than about ethnicity. Though in line with the values that underpin the European project, this bold step marked a fundamental turnaround in both European and German migration policy. Merkel's decision to effectively open Germany's borders to refugees took the notion of the 'unbundling of territoriality' (Ruggie 1993: 171) to a new level. Up to then, it was a given that the very existence of a Europe without borders was predicated on the fact that the EU's external borders were to be protected. Reflecting this logic, the Schengen agreement that formalised freedom of movement in 1995 (ten years after the treaty was signed) was followed by the creation of Frontex, an EU agency tasked with border control, albeit with a significant delay (it launched in 2005) and with limited budget and capabilities. In fact from the start there was a disconnect between the perceived need for an EU-wide coordination of asylum and immigration policies and a shared commitment to protecting the EU's external borders on the one hand, and a commitment to the freedom of movement on the other. This flaw was largely ignored as the Schengen agreement was celebrated 'as a flagship political symbol of European unification'—the most visible and popular expression of an 'ever-closer union' (Betts and Collier 2017: 62–3).

The European refugee crisis was a long time coming. It can be traced back to the Arab Spring—the spontaneous wave of pro-democracy movements that engulfed the Middle East and North Africa in the early 2010s. What initially seemed to be a series of non-violent uprisings, which in their aims and methods echoed Central Europe's 'Velvet Revolutions' of 1989, soon turned into violent conflicts. While the Jasmine Revolution in Tunisia in 2011 was relatively successful, the Syrian uprising that followed similar developments in Egypt, Yemen and Libya quickly descended into the region's most violent conflict. Europeans were largely taken by surprise by these upheavals, and their responses were either non-existent or half-hearted. For a while, the only formidable foreign power threatening a military intervention in the Syrian conflict was the United States. In the summer of 2012, President Barack Obama threatened the Syrian dictator, President Bashar al-Assad, with 'enormous consequences' if his military was to use chemical weapons. This was the infamous 'red line', which was not enforced. Despite such setbacks, owing to the determination of the rebels and the wide popular support they enjoyed, by the summer of 2015 Assad's military was on the brink of collapse. With Western intervention out of the equation, Russia intervened on the side of the regime, tipping the balance of power to Assad's advantage and further increasing the intensity of the conflict. The cost in human lives and destroyed livelihoods was staggering. Between 2011 and 2015, some 10 million people—half of Syria's population—had fled their homes in the wake of the violence (Betts and Collier 2017:

73). By 2014, some 4 million of those internally displaced people had fled Syria. Hundreds of thousands of them headed for Europe.

What Syrians faced in Europe was a dysfunctional system of refugee protection, which did not effectively serve either the member states or the people in search of protection. In the absence of an effective common EU external border control, the member states representing the points of first entry were incentivised to protect their borders by the so-called 'Dublin Regulations'. These obliged refugees to seek asylum in the first country of their arrival, and threatened to return them to that country if they attempted to move elsewhere. The arrangement was unbalanced and unfair, with a country like Germany having no external borders, while Greece and Italy were forced by virtue of being 'frontline states' to bear a disproportionate burden. For years, tens of thousands of refugees reached Europe via the Mediterranean Sea. While few countries properly enforced the Dublin Regulations—Italian and Greek authorities, for example, found it easier to let many refugees go further without any registration—it was only in the summer of 2015 that the German government openly and publicly suspended these rules.

This policy reversal did not just represent a radical turnaround for the EU. It was in fact a complete reorientation of the stance Angela Merkel and her ruling party had taken towards migration for more than a decade prior to 2015. For example, after Germany had accepted hundreds of thousands of refugees from the former Yugoslavia in the 1990s, the Christian Democratic Union's federal election manifesto in 2002 stated that

> Germany must reduce migration and gain stronger control over it. Migration cannot be viewed as a solution to Germany's demographic challenges. We clearly reject any extension of migration from third countries, as it would overtax the ability of our society to integrate the newcomers. Higher levels of migration would endanger societal peace and strengthen the popularity of extremist parties [*Leistung und Sicherheit*].

In a similar vein, in October 2010 Angela Merkel was reported to have 'courted growing anti-immigrant opinion in Germany by claiming the country's attempts to create a multicultural society [had] "utterly failed"' (Weaver 2010). And even as recently as July 2015, in a televised debate with a group of high school children, the German Chancellor told a sobbing Palestinian teenager whose family was threatened by deportation that 'Germany "just can't manage" to take every refugee' (cited in Connolly 2015). The discussion caused a significant backlash against Merkel that was indicative of the changing mood in Germany and, to some extent, in Europe at large. As the media reported extensively on the hundreds of refugee drowning deaths in the Mediterranean Sea each month, people began to pressure the government to relax the rules. A photograph of a drowned three-year-old Syrian boy named Alan Kurdi became emblematic of the human cost of the refugee crisis. Merkel's change of heart was as swift as it was radical.

Germany's position in the summer of 2015 was confused and confusing. While the government continued to assure its European partners that the Dublin Regulations would be followed, the director of Germany's Federal Office for Migration and Refugees tweeted on 25 August that Syrian refugees who made it to Germany would no longer be sent back to their first country of arrival. In the meantime, tens of thousands of refugees were stranded in Budapest as Hungary became an unlikely epicentre of the crisis. This was an accident of geography, as very few of them had the intention of staying in Hungary; it just so happened that Hungary was the first country within the Schengen system that attempted to enforce the rules (Greek authorities having largely ignored that obligation). As a result of the suspension of the Dublin requirements, Syrians were unwilling to register, and instead initiated a march to Germany that forced the hand of the German government. Having criticised the Hungarian authorities for their inhumane treatment in their zeal to protect their borders, Germany appeared to have no other option but to welcome the refugees. What was meant to be an exceptional measure became Europe's new normal, with thousands of refugees arriving in Germany every day, totalling a million in less than a year.

The initial response of most Germans was overwhelmingly positive. Riding the wave of popular support, Merkel captured the can-do attitude of ordinary citizens by proclaiming at a 31 August press conference that yes, 'Wir schaffen das' ('We will manage it'), arguing that a country as rich and populous as Germany could accommodate the sudden influx of thousands of refugees. To reinforce her new position, Merkel stressed that there was no upper limit on the right for asylum in the German constitution.[16] This memorable call to action was heard (and heeded) not merely across Germany, but all the way to the Middle East, including by the hundreds of thousands of Syrian refugees who were struggling to support themselves in Jordan, Lebanon and Turkey. Similarly, even internally displaced Syrians—including the Alawite population that fought on the side of the Assad regime—were attracted by the prospect of reaching Europe, which became less elusive virtually overnight. As noble as this change of policy might have seemed, it raised a number of difficult questions about the ethics of migration that the EU and Germany's leaders had to face in the months and years that followed. In fact, it was clear from the outset that stricter border controls would have to be reimposed eventually. But this was not what the German Chancellor was willing to openly contemplate at the height of the crisis.

Instead, Merkel was adamant that enforcing borders was neither feasible nor desirable. Europeans cherish and benefit from an intensely interconnected world, the argument went, and enforcing borders would undermine this. And border enforcement would be morally indefensible in any case, as all Europeans had a shared responsibility towards those in need of protection. Both these claims are problematic. First, as numerous responses to the more recent Covid-19 pandemic have demonstrated, it is possible to enforce border controls provided there is enough political will to do so. Second, while there can be little doubt that citizens in rich, Western countries have moral obligations towards refugees, there is no easy answer about how to best discharge this obligation. Devoting all attention to the refugees who managed to reach Europe might give short shrift to the even more vulnerable displaced people back in the Middle East. The contrast between the levels of Western support given to those refugees who reached their countries and those who did not is jarring. For every US$1 spent on refugees in the developing world, US$135 is spent on their counterparts in Europe (Betts and Collier 2017: 3). Following Max Weber, what this intractable situation requires is a political leader who is 'equal to the challenge of the world as it really is', one who is able to combine 'passion and a sense of proportion' (Weber 2004: 93). In contrast, as a recent study has suggested, 'the European policies that have shaped the Syrian refugee disaster have lurched between the headless heart and the heartless head' (Betts and Collier 2017: 92). Germany's 'headless heart' generated a number of problems, the consequences of which will continue to shape politics in Europe for a long time to come.

Merkel's policies divided public opinion in Germany and the rest of Europe. The Chancellor reached the decision in an ad hoc manner, consulting neither a major coalition partner in her own government nor her European partners. Horst Seehofer, the then Interior Minister and head of the Christian Social Union (CSU) in Bavaria, only learned about Merkel's decision after the event. At the European level, one of the unintended consequences of the policy was the strengthening of the argument in favour of Brexit, as the UK referendum debate unfolded against the background of a Europe that appeared to be losing control over migration. As we will see, the policy also exacerbated the pre-existing East-West divisions, with the populations in the new member states being particularly anxious about the protection of their national identities, and thus more hostile towards the prospect of large-scale migratory movements (notwithstanding the fact that very few refugees aimed to settle there). Domestically, the controversial policy significantly boosted support for the extreme right party, Alternative für Deutschland (AfD, Alternative for Germany), which emerged initially in response to the eurozone crisis (mis-)management. It had been particularly popular in the former East Germany, but its support was diminishing by 2015. What helped to strengthen the AfD's popularity was the rhetoric deployed in defence of this new migration policy; the language of 'there is no alternative' (TINA) other than to open borders echoed the arguments about there being no alternative to bailouts and austerity deployed in defence of the eurozone. 'You cannot really close borders', argued Merkel, turning the old dictum of 'politics as the art of the possible' into 'the art of the only thing possible' (Alexander 2017: 111). Not surprisingly, such rhetoric alienated electorates across Eastern *and* Western Europe, turning the crisis into a major contributing factor to the success of nationalist parties (Marks et al. 2021).

Furthermore, it is questionable whether this bold policy change advanced the aims of justice in migration. There are at least two problems worth considering. First, publicising a '*Willkommenskultur*' (a culture that welcomes newcomers) through the slogan of 'Wir schaffen das' made sense in relation to the domestic audience, as strong public support for immigrants was necessary to make the policy work. The fact that Germany managed to absorb up to a million migrants within a year was a remarkable achievement in its own right. However, this welcome had the unintended consequence of enticing more migrants to make the dangerous journey to Europe. With the increasing number of refugees, the number of those drowned and missing in the Mediterranean also increased, reaching a peak of 5,136 in 2016.[17] This is one of the reasons why migration experts such as Paul Collier have argued in favour of increasing material and logistical help to refugees closer to their homelands (Collier 2013; Betts and Collier 2017) rather than encouraging their transit to Western Europe. Second, maintaining public support for a generous refugee policy requires a shared understanding that the government retains effective control of migratory movements. The backlash which followed the 'open border' policy did not merely undermine the authority of the national governments and EU institutions which supported the new approach; it also threatened to erode public support for migrants and for development assistance in general. Sweden is a good example of this phenomenon. The country, which 'prides itself on generosity to strangers' (Traub 2016), received more refugees per capita at the height of the crisis than any other, including Germany. Yet, as the Swedish government struggled to meet their financial needs, it decided to reduce its aid budget by half, effectively subsidising the relatively few refugees who reached Sweden at the expense of the many more who did not.

Well before a public backlash materialised, Donald Tusk, in his role as President of the European Council, said what many people thought. If Europe's unity was to be preserved, the EU's external borders had to be protected more effectively. 'The greatest tide of refugees and migrants is yet to come', Tusk warned his colleagues at an EU summit on 23 September 2015, arguing that 'the policy of open borders and windows' had to be corrected (Middelaar 2019: 103). Here was a former Polish Prime Minister, with impeccable European credentials, advancing an argument that was the centrepiece of Orbán's migration policy. In fact, even Merkel came to accept that Hungary's strict border protection measures saved Germany and Europe, but she did so only obliquely and with a significant delay. While Austria followed Orbán's lead in early 2016 by coordinating the closure of the Balkan route, together with Slovenia, Croatia, Serbia and Macedonia, Merkel only acknowledged the importance of stricter border controls about a year after the outbreak of the crisis.

Notwithstanding the pro-open border rhetoric, the German Chancellor also attempted to modify her migration policies shortly after the turning point was reached in late August 2015. Her strategy was two-pronged. First, the emphasis on *Willkommenskultur* was quietly abandoned. Instead, Merkel initiated EU-led negotiations with Turkey to 'outsource' the protection of EU's external borders. Second, the German government sought to reduce the burden on Germany by attempting to distribute refugees across Europe. This redistribution followed an agreed formula that would take into consideration the absorption capacity of individual member states— for example, population size and economic performance. This was a departure from the Dublin Agreement, which de facto constrained transnational solidarity towards refugees. As we have seen, people wishing to claim asylum were meant to register their claims and be processed in the EU member state in which they first arrived, a provision which left Mediterranean states such as Greece, Italy, Malta and Spain to shoulder most of the responsibility for dealing with recently arrived asylum seekers. It was in this context that, in September 2015, the Council of the European Union adopted a decision on a Commission proposal to relocate 120,000 asylum seekers from Italy and Greece and redistribute them among EU member states according to a quota. Controversially, this decision was taken by qualified majority voting (QMV), despite the vocal opposition of some Central and Eastern European member states.

Ultimately, the Czech Republic, Hungary, Romania and Slovakia voted against the measure. Finland abstained. Poland voted in favour of the decision after having initially opposed it (only to oppose it again a few months later, after the change of government). The decision to use QMV on an issue that was so contentious and so close to the core sovereign prerogatives of member states was both surprising and controversial. There were immediate indications from at least some of the governments that had opposed the relocation plan that they would not implement it, despite its legally binding nature.[18] The refugee relocation scheme proved unrealisable and undermined the credibility of both the European Commission that had designed it, and the German government which had pioneered the idea in the first place and worked hard towards its realisation. Describing compulsory asylum quotas as 'a fiasco', a participant observer neatly summarised the reasons for their failure: 'the Brussels machinery, encouraged by Berlin and facilitated by Luxembourg, tried to control an unprecedentedly dramatic event using the old prescriptions of the politics of rules' (Middelaar 2019: 100). An emergency measure was quickly turned into a question of law compliance. This was a classic example of the EU's hubris and technocratic overreach. 'The Commission, as was its habit, relied on its panacea of depoliticisation but came up against political emotions that ascended to unparalleled heights, touching on citizenship, identity, sovereignty and even religion' (ibid. 100–1). The scheme was also clearly at odds with the very logic of borderless Europe created by Schengen. Paradoxically, it 'created a Schengen legal structure which stripped nationality of significance for citizens of member states, while defining the rights of Syrian refugees by an assigned pseudo-nationality' (Betts and Collier 2017: 87).

Concluding Remarks

By any standard, the EU's refugee policies have failed. Two years later, even Donald Tusk conceded that the redistribution policies were 'divisive and ineffective' (Rankin 2017). Just as the euro became a currency in search of a state, the refugee crisis necessitated a search for a sovereign who could decide on the exception. In the absence of one, a technical solution was sought in response to a number of highly political questions: What was the appropriate response to the mass influx of refugees from the Middle East and North Africa? Who determines the boundaries of a political community and how? The indeterminate result of Europe's refugee crisis was neatly summed up by Alexander Betts and Paul Collier: 'The Schengen Area was de facto dismantled. Europe's border controls were outsourced, on humiliating terms, to a non-European state with an authoritarian leader' (2017: 93). It was not merely President Recep Tayyip Erdoğan's Turkey that benefited from this European malaise. The incoherence of EU refugee policy made Europe vulnerable to blackmail by authoritarian leaders in its neighbourhood as well—a weakness exploited with brutal efficiency in late 2021 by Belarusian President Alexander Lukashenko. In response to EU sanctions imposed on Belarus' autocratic regime, Lukashenko created a refugee crisis on the borders between Belarus and Poland, Lithuania and Latvia, by bringing in migrants from the Middle East. And indeed, more than anything, it was Europe's unity that suffered as a result of refugee crises, as populist leaders in Central and Eastern Europe were able to posture as the defenders of a different kind of Europe, one that rejects Germany's 'moral imperialism' and seeks to protect primarily the interests of EU citizens.

Only ordered societies can provide the security that refugees seek. Through the very act of crossing borders, refugees validate the importance of borders. They are voting with their feet in favour of a traditional political order based around popular sovereignty. In a truly cosmopolitan world without borders, any talk about human rights would be pointless, because there would be no viable states left to protect them. Drawing on Arendt, Margaret Canovan argued that 'without bounded nations or quasi-national republics, no one would enjoy human rights. This is so because powerful political structures able to mobilise the consent of their citizens are necessary not only to guarantee rights inside their own borders, but also to try to protect human rights across the world' (1999: 148). Stable and viable political communities are bounded. The eurozone and refugee crises reminded Europeans of this fact. The Covid-19 pandemic did so as well, with much more urgency.

3

A SOVEREIGN EUROPE?

FRANCE, EUROZONE, SECURITY, BREXIT

Before becoming incarnate in Humanity, the Hegelian Weltgeist, which has abandoned the Nations, lives in the Empires.

Alexandre Kojève,
Esquisse d'une doctrine de la politique française[1]

Europe, what is it for? It must be used to avoid domination by either the Americans or the Soviets. At six [countries], we should be able to do as well as each of the two superpowers. And if France manages to become the first among the Six, which is within our grasp, she will be able to use this Archimedean lever. She will be able to lead the others. Europe is the means for France to become again what it stopped being after Waterloo: the first in the world.

Charles de Gaulle, cited in Alain Peyrefitte,
C'était de Gaulle (Gallimard, 2002), 158–9[2]

As we have seen, a post-sovereign Europe that largely evades the question of power and authority has given rise to a dysfunctional political regime that alternates between technocracy and the rule of emergency. Technocracy is the flipside of the EU's failed attempt

67

at becoming a truly political project. It is the result of opting for more *governance* instead of *government*. When power is dispersed, we struggle to identify the agency: who did what, for whom and how? But that means we also lose the ability to hold those in power accountable. This is why Europeans cannot escape questions about the nature of 'the political' and the location of sovereignty, whether it be at national or supranational level.

Studies calling for 'a sovereign Europe' remain few and far between (Morgan 2009; Heine 2019; Guérot 2020). All the while, political debates amongst key actors have been changing. Instigated largely by French President Emmanuel Macron, Europe is at last learning to speak the language of power, and yes, even sovereignty. This is consistent with French political traditions and a number of the Republic's post-Second World War leaders, spanning Charles de Gaulle, François Mitterrand and Jacques Chirac, who were not afraid of defending French sovereignty. What is fairly new is the amalgamation of concern for the French national sovereignty with an explicit endorsement of a 'European sovereignty'. This is at the heart of Macron's La Republique en Marche! (The Republic Forward!)—a political movement that promises to revolutionise both the French Republic and the European Union. Rather than Europe sliding 'into a new dark age' (Nougayrède 2017), Macron's victory in 2017 against Marine Le Pen's Rassemblement National (National Rally) party was hailed as the emergence of 'a stronger Europe' (Kirkegaard 2017).[3] Macron was explicit about the connection between democracy, popular sovereignty and nationhood:

> Yesterday's world is gone. Today, people everywhere want to choose their destiny. Sovereignty has become the great cause of our time. [...] The French people did not emancipate themselves from absolute monarchy in 1789 with the declaration that 'the principle of any sovereignty lies primarily in the nation'. True emancipation arrived in 1792, when citizens across France rose up to defend the revolution against foreign kings. It is when a people makes its own choices that it becomes sovereign. It is time for Europeans to become sovereign. (Macron 2017a)

'Keep sovereignty sovereign!' (Bach 2007) may seem like a tautological demand, but it remains a rather iconoclastic position amongst scholars of European integration. Exceptional in this respect is Glyn Morgan's study *The Idea of a European Superstate* (2009). Morgan is prescient in describing the EU's current predicament and its place in the world. Major powers are asserting their sovereignty with a vengeance. The US had acted as a superpower, prioritising its own interests, long before Donald Trump declared 'America first' to be the US official foreign policy doctrine. China has not been shying away from asserting its own interests, and neither has Russia. The hopes and expectations that Europe would be an example for the rest of the world to follow have not been fulfilled. 'Soft power' Europe is not 'running the 21st century' (Leonard 2005), and neither is it likely to do so at any time soon (see also Chapter 4). Morgan's answer to this series of challenges amounts to a comprehensive defence of European integration with the ultimate aim of a 'European Superstate'. In a similar vein, Ulrike Guérot seeks to build on Walter Hallstein's federalist ideals, according to which the ultimate goal of European integration is the sublimation of the nation state into something bigger and better. This, Guérot argues, cannot be achieved by nation states and their political representatives. What Europe needs instead is a new beginning, a European republic created by and for a truly European citizenry (Guérot 2016).

A precursor to thinking about Europe as a state uniting like-minded nations and citizens can be found in Alexandre Kojève's blueprint for a 'Latin Empire', which prefigured some of the enduring French and European preoccupations. As we shall see, conceptualising Europe as a state helps to clarify the main challenges that the European project continues to face, particularly with respect to democratic accountability and legitimacy. The key promise of a sovereign Europe is that it should provide its citizens with effective protection against threats from both within and without. Yet, the realisation of this ambition remains elusive.

One of the aims of this chapter is to interrogate the contradictory impulses that have shaped French conceptions of European unity. De Gaulle's vision of a Europe of nations continues to be present as much as his commitment to France as *La Grande Nation*. Alongside this, however, there is a growing understanding that Europe, this 'profoundly French venture' (Macron 2017b: 201), can only succeed if it gains enough support amongst a significant majority of *all* EU citizens. Revealing in this respect was the appointment of the current European Commission President, Ursula von der Leyen, who got her position in December 2019 thanks largely to the strong backing of the French government (ironically *against* some opposition from Germany). A former German defence minister and a self-declared Francophile, von der Leyen promised to work towards a sovereign Europe that would speak with one voice led by a 'geopolitical Commission'. Controversially, she also created a new position of a 'vice president for protecting our European way of life'—an aim that was viewed as a concession to Europe's 'counter-revolution' (Zielonka 2018), mainly located in Central and Eastern Europe. Thus the EU would stand up for the interests of both European peoples and citizens at home and abroad.

Conversely, the sovereign Europe that many French people want is the one that voters in the UK rejected (albeit by a narrow margin). Another focus of this chapter is thus the UK's ambiguous relationship with the European project. To put it bluntly, France and the UK can be seen as mirror images of each other in the sense that while sovereignty very much remains an important part of both countries' political vocabulary, France aims to regain it *through* Europe, while the UK now seeks to reclaim it outside of, or even *against* Europe. As we shall see, Britain's preoccupation with protecting its interests as a sovereign nation has also resulted in Europe asserting its own interests in the name of EU sovereignty. Echoing the structural problems with the single European currency, Brexit too in its final stage became a process in search of an EU state. Who was the one with enough authority to make the last-minute adjustments to the EU's negotiating strategy to facilitate the deal? In other words, who was the one to decide on the exception? While the British Prime Minister, with a secure majority in the House of Commons, had significant space for manoeuvre, the President of the European Commission had no comparable powers.[4]

Like France, the UK too has always been engaged in European affairs, but it has done so willingly only insofar as such entanglements did not undermine its key constitutional principle, that of parliamentary sovereignty. In contrast to France and Germany, a remarkable feature of British political history is its sense of continuity, which made the prospect of sharing national sovereignty distinctly less attractive. It was in fact only through its entry into the European Economic Community (EEC) in 1973 that the UK's constitutional order was significantly altered. In other words, succeeding in 'taking back control' does not necessarily lead to splendid isolation, but might instead bring the country closer to being 'with Europe, but not of it', to quote Winston Churchill's iconic dictum.

Furthermore, it is worth noting that the democratic impetus in the Brexit promise to reclaim self-government at the national level has supporters in France too, even if few of these would openly advocate a 'Frexit'. Noticeable in this respect is a motley group of intellectuals gathered around the quarterly magazine *Front Populaire*, launched in the summer of 2020, with the first issue dedicated to 'Souverainisme!', a notion that stands in clear opposition to the idea that France would 'recover full sovereignty' through the creation of 'a sovereign Europe' (Macron 2017b: 209). The shifting mood was reflected in changing political priorities. Many candidates for the April 2022 presidential elections sought to challenge Macron by promising to further constrain EU powers. Not surprisingly, anti-EU rhetoric has characterised the electoral campaigns of populists like Marine Le Pen and Éric Zemmour. However, less extreme candidates and parties did not shy away from similar arguments. For example, all five front runners for the leadership of Les Républicains, the mainstream conservative party, vowed to reclaim control over migration. Michel Barnier, as one of the centre-right candidates, sought to strengthen his presidential prospects by promising 'changes to the constitution to reassert French legal sovereignty over European courts' in order to make that aim possible (Hall 2021).[5]

While Europe is central to both the French and German political imaginations, the aspirations, needs and expectations of both nations have differed. Yet they've often been complementary, leading to what became known as a 'Franco-German engine'. For France, Europe was the vehicle through which it might restore its greatness and fulfil its civilisational mission, while (West) Germany sought to restore its

71

credibility by joining a club of Western democracies after the nation disgraced itself with Nazism. Up until 1989, the European project appeared to have served as an effective tool to 'tame' Germany's power, notwithstanding her growing economic might. As the prospect of German unity looked to bring about an even bigger, wealthier and more powerful central power, or *Macht in der Mitte* (Münkler 2015), the 'German question' re-emerged. In response, as we have seen, French President Mitterrand convinced German Chancellor Helmut Kohl about the urgency of the single European currency. This paradoxically resulted in an enhanced German influence over Europe—an outcome nobody seems to have intended. As French power continued to wane, President Macron sought to compensate by proposing to strengthen French *and* European sovereignty. By suggesting that 'France must make it possible for Europe to take a leading role in the free world' (Brinkbäumer, Heyer and Sandberg 2017), Macron was keen to reclaim the country's dominant position within the European family of nations.

A Protective Sovereign?

Macron often refers to French and European sovereignty interchangeably, reflecting 'the peculiar nature of French nationalism, which sees itself as universalism' (Streeck 2018: 182). Following this logic, in late 2020 Macron sought to launch 'what you could call "Paris Consensus", but which will be a worldwide consensus' (Macron 2020).[6] Clearly, French, European and worldwide consensus are simply different spheres for the realisation of Macron's political ambition. As Streeck puts it, 'from a French perspective, there is no conflict between a "sovereign France" and a "sovereign Europe," as long as Europe is properly constituted on universal, i.e., French principles and governed out of Paris, as an extension of French sovereignty' (2018. 182). Advancing a series of bold proposals, Macron first outlined his vision for 'Europe's transformation' in his programmatic 'Sorbonne speech' in September 2017.[7] The French President offered a vision for 'a fair, protective and ambitious Europe', because only such a Europe would have 'rediscovered the meaning of this fraternity that we placed at its heart'. Yet Macron has had only limited success in delivering on these promises to French citizens, let alone to Europeans at large. Far from acting as a sovereign, the EU has struggled to find an adequate response to a number of recent challenges. The eurozone crisis continues to exacerbate Europe's divisions between North and South; the refugee crisis divides Europeans within each member state as well as between East and West; and the crisis in the EU-Russia relationship shows the European Union's weakness as a geopolitical actor. There is no need to side with the controversial French intellectual Michel Onfray (2018), who attributes all the problems France faces to the 'l'empire maastrichien' ('the Maastricht empire'), to acknowledge that the institutional innovations introduced by the Maastricht Treaty significantly reduced the ability of member states to respond to an emergency. Porous borders, for example, have made it more difficult to safeguard basic security. If any reminder of this were needed, the public health crisis in the autumn of 2020 was exacerbated by a series of terrorist attacks, which in turn could be partly attributed to the unresolved refugee crisis. Just as people in France were getting ready for a major lockdown in response to the second wave of the Covid-19 pandemic, a number of spectacularly violent incidents threatened societal peace.

On 16 October 2020, Samuel Paty, a 47-year-old history teacher at a secondary school in Conflans-Sainte-Honorine, on the outskirts of Paris, was beheaded by an Islamic fundamentalist, an 18-year-old Chechen-born refugee. The teacher had become the subject of an online-based hate campaign, orchestrated by the father of one of his pupils, after showing his class controversial cartoons of the Prophet Muhammad as a way of instructing students about freedom of speech. This was neither the first nor the most devastating attack of its kind, either in France or in the rest of Europe. In fact, the controversy over the depiction of the Prophet started in January 2015, when the editorial offices of the satirical magazine *Charlie Hebdo* were attacked by Islamist extremists, who killed twelve people in response to the publication of these cartoons. What was especially significant about the murder of the teacher was its target. The attack on Paty was an attack on *laïcité*, the ideal of strict separation between church and state that underpins the

French educational system. It was thus perceived as an attack on the French Republic and its self-understanding. In response, President Macron promised to enhance security so that Islamists would 'not be able to sleep easy in our country' and fear would 'change sides' (Mallet 2020a). Yet less than two weeks after Paty was beheaded, another three people were murdered in the Notre Dame church in Nice by a 29-year-old Tunisian refugee, who had arrived in France just a few days before via the Italian island of Lampedusa. In the meantime, the French President was criticised abroad for alleged 'Islamophobia' and ridiculed by the Turkish President Erdoğan, who claimed that 'Macron needed mental treatment' (Haddad 2020). The French state appeared weak, both domestically and internationally. Since 2012, 'more than 260 people of all backgrounds have died in terrorist attacks', including in a Jewish school, a concert hall and in the streets of Nice (Haddad 2020). This is the context in which the French response to Germany's flirtation with open borders in September 2015 should be understood. It goes some way towards explaining the lack of enthusiasm shown by the French leader for the refugee redistribution scheme adopted by the EU to reduce pressure on Germany.

While a number of prominent commentators attributed the crimes in part to 'France's dangerous religion of secularism' (Khosrokhavar 2020)[8] and Macron's 'rousing rhetoric', which was said to have been aimed at out-manoeuvring his far-right rival Marine Le Pen (see Mishra 2020), to consider the French commitment to *laïcité* as its actual cause is far-fetched. The primary problem was radical Islam. As Pascal Bruckner (2020) put it pithily, 'France is hated not because it oppresses Muslims, but because it liberates them.' Just a few days after the French attacks, a rampage in Vienna's old city centre, in which a twenty-year-old Islamic fundamentalist with Austrian and Macedonian passports killed four people with a machine gun, showed once again that France was not the only target. In response, Austrian Chancellor Sebastian Kurz, echoing Macron, stressed that his government would punish those responsible and warned against a misguided tolerance towards 'the ideology of political Islam', urging the EU to 'finally realise how dangerous [it is] for our freedom and the European way of life' (*Euractiv* 2020). Undoubtedly, the incidents underlined the importance of EU-wide cross-border cooperation to reduce the vulnerabilities generated by EU-wide mobility. This was easier said than done. Even as committed a European as Macron felt obliged to stress the importance of border controls at a *national* level and promised to double the number of gendarmes and troops to 4,800, 'to fight against clandestine immigration'. In addition, he proposed a 'profound' reform of the Schengen system to deliver on his promise to 'take back control' of immigration policy (Mallet 2020b). Unwittingly, Macron's rhetoric was not far removed from that of the Brexit campaign, which also promised to 'take back control of the borders', but applied to EU level, rather than to individual member states.

Dealing with the challenges of internal security (or, in EU parlance, the 'area of freedom, security, and justice'—ASFJ) is particularly difficult. The willingness to cooperate is hindered by the reluctance of member states to relinquish controls that impinge on core areas of state sovereignty. It was in fact following the *Charlie Hebdo* attacks in Paris that a number of initiatives were started at EU level in order to increase cooperation on internal security and counterterrorism.[9] Whether these are sufficient is another matter.

Of course, security is not everything. But it is not much of an overstatement to say that without security everything is nothing. This basic insight only becomes apparent when security can no longer be taken for granted, when we experience a (partial) breakdown of social order and authority. Similarly, the questions of identity and belonging do not seem all that important in a democracy until they do. As nineteenth-century liberals like John Stuart Mill and Alexis de Tocqueville understood well, these questions go to the heart of the democratic project, which is primarily about self-governance. Who is the self that is to govern itself? Here again we face the EU's 'sovereignty paradox', with nation states having lost control to the supranational level unable to act effectively on their own, while at the same time, they keep enough power to obstruct common solutions. This strengthens the rationale for transferring sovereignty to the EU level, as advocates for a Europe as a fully-fledged state have argued. Such visions have a longer history, of course, which come with their own revealing contradictions.

From a 'Latin Empire' to Maastricht and Beyond

Post-Second World War leaders from de Gaulle to Macron have believed that France is destined to lead as *primus inter pares*, maintaining its preeminent position in Europe and the world, particularly vis-à-vis Germany. One root of this enduring preoccupation is a curious proposal for a 'Latin Empire'. Long before Fukuyama popularised Kojève's interpretation of Hegel by proclaiming the 'End of History', Kojève wrote about 'the political unreality of nations', arguing that the age of nation states was finished by the defeat of Nazi Germany: 'Germany lost this war because she wanted to win it as a *nation*-State' (Kojève [1945] 2004: 6). Oddly—especially since he was writing towards the end of the Second World War—Kojève seemed more concerned about nationalism than the twin totalitarian movements that shaped the twentieth century, Nazism and communism. He contrasted 'Stalin's political genius', which showed its pragmatism by abandoning the 'Trotskyist utopia of *humanitarian* internationalist socialism' with his slogan of 'socialism in one country', against 'the Hitlerian anachronism of "*national*-socialism," founded on the politically antiquated reality of the Nation' (ibid. 8). As humanity was too large and nations too small, what France and Europe needed in the interim, Kojève argued, was to build 'a post-national empire' (ibid. 38). Foreshadowing contemporary debates about the 'EU's strategic autonomy', Kojève thought of this project in statist terms, warning that 'a State no longer driven by an absolute will to autonomy lowers itself to the level of a simple administration' (ibid. 21). To be in control of its destiny, that is to say to be '*politically* viable', Kojève wrote, 'the modern State must rest on a "vast 'imperial' union of affiliated Nations"', proclaiming apodictically that 'the modern State is only truly a State if it is an Empire' (ibid. 4).

In line with this, Kojève advanced the idea of a 'Latin Empire'. This would be a collaborative arrangement of fellow Catholic, Romance language-speaking Mediterranean nations, whose support would make France more powerful. Under French leadership, this Latin Empire would also reach reconciliation with the predominantly Muslim countries in North Africa and counterbalance the influence of the Anglo-American world of free market capitalism in the West, and the Soviet Union in the East. This is the only way in which a France that is 'politically dead for once and for all qua nation-*State*' could be resurrected:

> For the Nation can and must go beyond itself in and through an international union of affiliated nations, where it must and can reaffirm its cultural, social, and political specificity by submitting it, in a peaceful, friendly, egalitarian, and free competition, to the largest group to whose creation it contributes by eliminating itself as an exclusive and isolated Nation. (ibid. 14)

In this way and only in this way—dying as a nation 'only to engender the Empire'—can France redeem itself (ibid. 14). Without using the term, Kojève fears France will be reduced to the status of a vassal state. As a nation, you either become part of a bigger whole of your choosing, or you become part of a bigger whole of someone else's choosing. Yet Kojève's advocacy of 'peaceful, friendly, egalitarian, and free competition' (ibid. 14) has its limits. When it comes to the countries of North Africa, for example, Kojève envisages France, Italy and Spain pooling 'the resources of their colonial holdings' to 'establish a unique plan for colonial exploitation' (ibid. 19). This unashamedly imperialist perspective seems at odds with Kojève's optimistic assertion that 'there is no reason to believe that, within a true *Empire*, this synthesis of opposites [Arab Islam and Latin Catholicism] could not be freed of its internal contradictions, which are really irreducible only with respect to purely *national* interests' (ibid. 19).

Yet the true aim of Kojève's plan was not the synthesis of Islam and Catholicism, but rather to act as a counterweight to Germany, whose influence in such a world would be negligible. In its determination to keep Germany down, Kojève's proposal was reminiscent of the Morgenthau plan, designed by the US Secretary of the Treasury in 1944, which foresaw the transformation of Germany into an agrarian nation. In its opposition to the Anglo-American West, the proposal was reminiscent of Schmitt's *Grossraum*, which anticipated the division of the world into great spaces.[10] As it happened, France ended up pursuing its ambitions *with* Germany, not against it. We have to work towards a 'Europe united and self-confident', one 'that has clarity about its aims and is resolute in attaining the means needed to reach these aims', wrote de Gaulle to his German counterpart, Chancellor Konrad Adenauer in 1965 (cited in Lepenies 2016: 46). A similar letter could have been written by Valéry Giscard d'Estaing to Helmut Schmidt in the 1970s, by Mitterrand to Kohl in the 1980s, or by Macron to Merkel in the last few years.

In fact, the process of Franco-German reconciliation has been instrumental for the success of the European project. It also showed that 'integration through crisis' can actually work. Somewhat schematically, the European Union can be seen as the result of a series of responses to the major crises that shaped the twentieth century, starting with 'the primal catastrophe' (George F. Kennan) of the 'Great War' of 1914–18, which instead of ending all wars gave rise to the even more devastating Second World War. Such a mistake was never to be repeated. The foundational moment of the Union was thus the creation of the European Coal and Steel Community, spearheaded by the Schuman Declaration of 9 May 1950, which set out a plan to overcome the historic rivalry between France and Germany by making war between them 'not merely unthinkable, but materially impossible' (Fontaine 2000: 36). By subjecting these two industry sectors, coal and steel, to the control of a supranational authority, no member state would be able to wage a war. France and Germany were joined by Italy and the Benelux countries, bringing together the founding six members of the Union. Europeans were never again going to 'sleepwalk' into yet another major military conflagration (Clark 2013). While the initial political impetus focused on Europe as a peace project, the tool deployed was economic integration, which became yet more important in the 1970s. The economic instability caused by the collapse of the gold standard and the Bretton Woods system led to the Single European Act of 1986, which aimed to complete the agenda set out in the Treaty of Rome to create a truly common market and ensure that the four freedoms of movement—for goods, services, capital and people—became a lived reality for all European citizens. As we have seen, this was further cemented by the Maastricht Treaty, which gave rise to the European Union as we now know it, including by creating provisions for a single European currency and for EU citizenship.

This is the quasi-automatic logic of functional integration. According to Ulrike Guérot, 'Each time that Europeans experienced a crisis, which made the lack of mutual solidarity palpable, what followed was a deeper integration of relevant areas' (2020: 5). However, nothing of similar magnitude has occurred over the last twenty years or so, with a Europe that turned fifty at the turn of the millennium apparently stuck in a protracted 'midlife crisis' (ibid.).

Following this historical pattern, a number of observers and practitioners sympathetic to the project believe that the most recent and severe culmination of crises—in particular Brexit and the Covid-19 pandemic—ought to once again push Europe towards more unity. Rather than undermining its cohesion by showcasing the possibility of exit, so the thinking went, the UK's departure revealed the EU polity 'as valued and valuable to its remaining member states'. It is 'how the EU27 came to be' (Laffan 2019: 13). The heightened awareness of 'its own mortality' (Middelaar 2019: 123) made the EU all the more determined to live up to its full potential. 'The reaction to Brexit', Brigid Laffan argued, 'reveals the DNA of the EU as a maturing polity exemplified by the Union's determination to use its full capacity when faced with an existential threat' (2019: 1). Building on Macron's idea, Guérot (2020) went even further, urging EU citizens, business elites and politicians to make the final leap and turn Europe into a state. However passionate these and similar pleas are, they tend to downplay the negative effects of the 'ever-closer union' doctrine. Time and again, a push towards more unity brought about the opposite result—strengthening the forces of fragmentation.

Here again, the Franco-German partnership provides a useful lens through which to consider this challenge. While the commitment to this relationship has remained a constant, driving the European project forward, the further integration has advanced the more potential there has been for conflict. This became particularly visible at the height of the eurozone crisis, leading to a revival of interest in a 'Mediterranean Union', which—echoing Kojève's 'Latin Empire'— would comprise countries surrounding *mare nostrum*,[11] constituting a counterbalance to what many observers feared was becoming a 'German Europe' (see, e.g., Beck 2012). The project, initiated by

French President Nicolas Sarkozy in 2007, was largely stillborn, as it failed to garner sufficient support from either European partners or North Africa. But it reveals the enduring anxiety the French have had about Germany's preponderance, which appeared more acute still when the prospect of a eurozone collapse threatened the very survival of the European project. This is when Italian philosopher Giorgio Agamben came up with a provocative proposal that explicitly built on Kojève's blueprint, which he praised as remarkably prescient:

> According to Kojève, Protestant Germany, which would soon become the richest and most powerful European nation (which it did, in fact, become) would inevitably be swayed by its extra-European tendencies and turn towards the Anglo-Saxon Empire—a configuration in which France and the Latin nations would remain a more or less foreign body, obviously reduced to the peripheral role of a satellite. (Agamben 2013)

What particularly appealed to Agamben was Kojève's emphasis on the importance of shared culture, which is something that in his view the European Union had ignored at its own peril. Agamben saw Kojève's predictions vindicated. Integration focused merely on economics, Agamben argued, disregarding 'all true affinities between lifestyles, culture and religion'. In Agamben's view, this approach had run its course:

> Not only is there no sense in asking a Greek or an Italian to live like a German but even if this were possible, it would lead to the destruction of a cultural heritage that exists as a way of life. A political unit that prefers to ignore lifestyles is not only condemned not to last, but, as Europe has eloquently shown, it cannot even establish itself as such. (ibid.)

In other words, culture and identity matter.[12] Agamben thus echoes Schmitt's basic insight in his *Constitutional Theory*, which emphasised that a certain degree of commonality was required for a political community to work (as discussed in Chapter 2). It is worth restating that neither Schmitt nor Agamben wrote about ethnic (let alone racial) purity. What they are concerned about is the awareness of shared affinity and the problem that a polity faces when social and socio-economic differences are reinforced by differing national and ethnic belongings. This has practical consequences. As Europe advanced towards both an ever deeper and ever wider union, starting with the initial six members and reaching twenty-eight in 2013, its population became not only bigger but also far more heterogeneous both in terms of its ethnic and linguistic diversity, as well as its vastly different levels of economic prosperity. This is a formidable challenge for a welfare state, which relies on a shared sense of solidarity (see, e.g., Miller 1995). As Claus Offe warned more than two decades ago, deterritorialisation may well lead to *desolidarisation* (*Entgrenzung als Selbstentpflichtung*), whereby people feel so overwhelmed by the demands of their vast political community—and alienated from it—that they resist fulfilling their mutual obligations (Offe [1998] 2019: 275). In other words, as the boundaries become more porous, or non-existent, the sense of shared responsibility for the common good dissipates. What is more, the problem is not limited to the construction and maintenance of the welfare state. It is about the viability of democracy, in which the questions relating to appropriate size of both population and territory are of great importance (Jörke 2019; Streeck 2019). A strong argument against the EU as a reincarnation of *Grossraum* can thus be made with the help of its original architect. It was Schmitt, after all, who famously postulated that 'the concept of the state presupposes the concept of the political' (Schmitt [1928] 2007: 19), which in turn is predicated on the existence of the people. We are thus back to the 'no demos' thesis, with which the German Constitutional Court sought to stop Europe's transformation into a fully-fledged federal state.

Who is the Sovereign?

Considering all these developments, many opponents of European integration may feel vindicated in their suspicion of the very idea of 'sovereignty shared'. Conversely, even those who openly speak in favour of a sovereign Europe seldom spell out who the ultimate bearer of sovereignty is. To be sure, there are many who see themselves as speaking *for* the people of Europe. A number of EU presidents are obvious candidates for this role, whether it be Ursula von der Leyen leading the European Commission, Charles Michel leading the European Council, or Roberta Metsola presiding over the European Parliament—the only European institution that is elected directly by the peoples of Europe. Curiously, even the European Central Bank, a technocratic institution par excellence, claims to 'serve the people of Europe' (Lokdam 2020). However, can we meaningfully speak of 'the people of Europe' in the singular? The question is important, for there can be no such thing as a sovereign Europe so long as there is no European sovereign. The European Parliament, for example, does not represent *a* European people, but European *peoples*. In fact, if the key principle of democratic representation is one person, one vote, then the European Parliament is actually not all that democratic, because voters from smaller member states are significantly over-represented. As Richard Rose has argued, because the EU is a union of states which are extremely unequal in population, it is 'impossible to give European citizens the equality of representation that they enjoy in their national parliament' (2020: 45). There is no easy way out of this problem and the challenge is not merely theoretical. A certain degree of societal cohesion generated by a 'we, the people' feeling is necessary for a community to work as a polity.

Echoing Schmitt, but unlike him writing decisively in defence of liberal democracy, Böckenförde is convinced that a state-like constitutional order must be underpinned by political unity that the state itself struggles to maintain. As he outlines,

> [The state] is not in place as an entity that is fixed once and for all, and it is not independent of individuals and their willingness to integrate into and commit to the state. As a unifying actor, the state requires continuous affirmation and reproduction in and through the actions of the humans who constitute it. (Böckenförde 2017: 45)

The emphasis on flexibility is something that could support the argument in favour of the EU *becoming* a state, along the lines advocated by Robert Schuman, who envisaged that Europe would 'be built through concrete achievements, which first create a de facto solidarity' (Fontaine 2000: 36). However, what Europe in its seven decades since the Schuman Declaration has demonstrated is just how difficult it is to create and maintain such 'continuous affirmation'. In fact, the contemporary crisis of actually existing democracies across the world is to a large extent caused by the difficulties that modern societies have in sustaining this 'we-feeling'. This became known as Böckenförde's dilemma, which is worth quoting at length:

> The liberal, secularised state draws its life from presuppositions it cannot itself guarantee. This is the great risk it has made for the sake of liberty. On the one hand, as a liberal state it can only survive if the freedom it grants to its citizens is regulated from within, out of the moral substance of the individual and the homogeneity of society. On the other hand, it cannot seek to guarantee these inner regulatory forces by its own efforts—that is to say, with the instruments of legal coercion and authoritative command— without abandoning its liberalness. (Böckenförde 2017: 45)

This challenge is greatly magnified for a quasi-federal state in the making, which the EU increasingly resembles. Denying this state-like quality does not help the argument. As we have seen in a growing number of areas, the EU's effectiveness demands that it takes on state-like roles, including by resorting to 'the instruments of legal coercion and authoritative command'. Yet, if it is hard to force individuals to be liberal,[13] it is all the more challenging to force member states to be *ordoliberal* (or even just liberal, considering the populist anti-EU rebellions in Hungary and Poland). As discussed in Chapter 2, this was the painful experience in the early stages of the eurozone crisis, when nations like Greece, Portugal, Ireland and Cyprus had to accept restrictive conditions for bailout packages, which seriously undermined the EU's democratic legitimacy. Was Europe 'restoring dignity to the Greeks, by cancelling their votes?', Perry Anderson (2020) asked polemically, decrying 'the humiliation of commissioners from Brussels dictating laws, policies, regulations in Athens'. This strategy appeared to be both illegitimate and ineffectual. 'The Troika's regime inflicted misery on the poor, the elderly and the young', Anderson continues, while 'Greek public debt today stands higher than when Papandreou was forced by Berlin and Paris to call off one referendum, or Tsipras capitulated after another.' In this context, Christian Kreuder-Sonnen warned against the 'autocratic self-empowerment' of EU institutions, arguing that 'the distinct European emergency politics that characterized the euro crisis have introduced traits of authoritarian rule in the EU's supranational governance' (2018: 456, 452). To make matters worse, not all member states were affected in equal measure. 'The ascendancy of neoliberal ideology since Maastricht', Costas Lapavitsas argued, 'has coincided with the hegemonic ascendancy of Germany in the institutions of the EU, matched by a growing divergence among member states' (2019: 21). As a result, Europe's 'authoritarian turn' (Kreuder-Sonnen 2018) also undermined the EU's credibility when confronting authoritarian tendencies *within* individual member states.

The ongoing struggle over the single European currency exemplifies the conflicting pressures that the European project continues to be exposed to. The eurozone crisis reinforced functional pressures to turn the EU into a state, all the while making that aim less palatable for a significant proportion of EU citizens. In mid-2020, the economic slowdown caused by the pandemic led to a bold new initiative spearheaded by France and Germany. The EU Council agreed to a novel budgetary instrument, 'New Generation EU', which partly relied on the Union taking on debt. While some critics considered the size of the package insufficient relative to the task ahead, many others, including the then German Finance Minister Olaf Scholz, praised it as a 'Hamiltonian moment' (interviewed by Dausend and Schieritz 2020), alluding to a crucial moment in American history which propelled the United States towards a true Union via the mutualisation of public debt in 1790. The New Generation EU initiative represented a significant break with Germany's previous opposition to any attempts to mutualise public debt. However, mixed responses to the scheme in Germany were a foretaste of a possible backlash in the future.[14] Furthermore, the EU's increased fiscal firepower was unlikely to diminish suspicion of Germany amongst the rest of the EU 27.

Undoubtedly, the very possibility of incurring sovereign debt makes the EU look more like a sovereign state. It is worth recalling that Quentin Skinner uses that very example (see Chapter 2) to illustrate how indispensable the Hobbesian concept of sovereignty as a '*persona ficta*' still is today. And it is precisely for this reason that the measures were criticised as inappropriate, or even illegal, under EU law (see, e.g., Sinn 2020: 17). The 'Hamiltonian moment' was accompanied by a great many acrimonious negotiations between the 'frugal four' (Austria, Denmark, the Netherlands and Sweden)— who were opposed to debt mutualisation—and the rest of the EU 27. It is worth noting that this was well before the modalities were agreed on by which the debt would be repaid, particularly considering the length of the loan with the final repayment planned for 2058. The potential for future conflicts was thus built into the new scheme. Moreover, the impact of the pandemic differed significantly amongst EU member states. The fact that Germany had handled it better than the rest was bound to reinforce the discrepancy in their economic performance, exacerbating the eurozone's structural imbalances. Similarly, the protracted dispute over the rule of law crisis, which was meant to be addressed via the conditionality requirements for the new fund, was likely to worsen the tension between some countries in Central Europe (Hungary, Poland and Slovenia) and the rest (see also Chapter 5). While the defenders of the new policy praised it as an effective mechanism against further democratic backsliding, its opponents—particularly in Poland and Hungary—rejected it as a foreign dictate from Brussels (Gutschker 2020b: 6). The resulting compromise was criticised for weakening the EU's commitment to Europe's fundamental values. On the other side of the equation, Hungarian and Polish governments celebrated their 'victories'. Though they did not go as far as the advocates of Brexit who sought to 'take back control' from Brussels, the likes of Viktor Orbán, resisting new instruments that would further empower the European Commission, also used the promise to (re-) claim control over their nations' destiny as an effective rhetorical tool that resonated with a significant proportion of their electorates.

Glorious Brexit?

British Conservative Eurosceptics were prescient in 'predicting that the European Economic Community would evolve into some form of political union' (Morgan 2009: 59). Intriguingly though, one of their most influential leaders, Margaret Thatcher, was an enthusiastic supporter of the UK's membership in the Community in the first referendum of 1975. Later, she was instrumental in relaunching European integration towards an 'ever-closer union' through the Single European Act of 1986, and was praised for it as a 'founding mother of the new Europe' (Gillingham 2003: 136). Yet Thatcher became better known for her principled opposition to the Maastricht Treaty, which she saw as a federalist project, aiming at the creation of a United States of Europe. In fact, this opposition could already be detected in her stance towards the Single European Act, which she supported in its aims—pushing towards the completion of the single market—but not in its formalised approach. As Luuk van Middelaar vividly described, Thatcher was 'astonished and furious' in response to the idea of a new Treaty, which was only accepted through a qualified majority voting (QMV) in the European Council—a move that was then so controversial that it was likened to a coup (Middelaar 2013: 104). Despite her astonishment and fury, Thatcher underestimated the extent of political integration, which she then unwittingly authorised. By breaking with the convention of the Luxembourg Compromise of 1966, which gave every member state the power to veto an initiative negotiated at the European Council, the Italian Prime Minister Bettino Craxi, who chaired the meeting of the European Council of Heads of State or Government in 1985, recast Europe's constitutional order. Prior to this, as Middelaar noted, 'the most powerful European *pouvoir constitué* had remained concealed within the *pouvoir constituant* of the states' (2013: 107). Craxi's clever move basically pushed the European Economic Community closer towards a political union, to which Thatcher vehemently objected. As she explained in a speech to the House of Commons on 30 October 1990, 'Mr. Delors ... wanted the European Parliament to be the democratic body of the Community, he wanted the Commission to be the Executive and he wanted the Council of Ministers to be the Senate.' Thatcher's memorable response to this was 'No, no, no.' Turning the EU into a quasi-federal state and increasing its powers 'at the expense of the House' was unacceptable.

Thatcher's counteroffensive failed spectacularly both in Europe and in Britain. The rest is history. Thatcher was sidelined in the

Conservative Party and lost the premiership to John Major, who would sign the Maastricht Treaty in 1992. Major's reasoning, echoed later by his successors, whether from the Labour Party (Tony Blair, Gordon Brown) or the Conservative Party (David Cameron), was that it was better for the UK to remain part of the project, ensuring that it had a seat at the table where decisions were being taken. Nevertheless, it was Thatcher's opposition to a supranational European quasi-state in the making, rather than Major's acquiescence to it, that better reflected the UK's political culture, based as it was on a strong appreciation of sovereignty. As the doyen of British constitutionalism, Vernon Bogdanor, explained:

> The concept of parliamentary sovereignty is not like that of national sovereignty a tradeable asset. It is not like baldness a mere matter of degree. It is, rather, absolute, like virginity; just as one cannot be a qualified virgin, so also one cannot be a qualified sovereign. A parliament is either sovereign or it is not. (2019: 29)

Yet, as discussed in earlier chapters, the entire project of European integration was predicated on the idea that such either/or options were obsolete.[15] Unlike Britain, as Bogdanor acknowledges, the EU has 'no single sovereign institution' (2019: 43). In contrast, prior to the UK's entry into the European Economic Community in 1973, 'the British constitution could have been characterized in just eight words: "Whatever the Queen in parliament enacts is law"' (ibid. 30). Considering that parliamentary sovereignty is a cardinal feature of the UK political system, the way in which Brexit was decided is distinctly odd. For the means of popular referendum undermined the very principle of parliamentary sovereignty that it sought to restore. Furthermore, there is no denying that a referendum is a very crude instrument for reaching a decision on such a complex and consequential issue.[16] At any rate, even British constitutional monarchy could not disregard the will of the people, however fraught the process of determining that will might have been. In particular, there were significant differences between the results of the referendum in Scotland and Northern Ireland,[17] where most voters opposed Brexit, in contrast to England and Wales, where the leave campaign prevailed. And yet, the UK government largely succeeded in presenting its promise to 'take back control' as reflecting the democratic will of the sovereign people.

Seen in this light, Brexit could be construed as rectifying the 'mistake' of Maastricht. Thirty years after Thatcher's demise, Prime Minister Boris Johnson, despite being one of the key supporters of a 'No' vote in the June 2016 Brexit referendum, was ebullient, celebrating Brexit on 3 February 2020 as 'our glorious revolution'.[18] His critics did not like it. Opponents of Brexit did not think of it as glorious, or a revolution for that matter. They viewed it as a retrograde step that would diminish Britain's position in the world and undermine the freedoms of UK citizens, for whom departure from the EU meant they would no longer enjoy the rights of EU citizens. They had lost the freedoms and privileges that came with it, including the freedom of movement, for example, which enabled UK citizens to live and work in any of the twenty-seven member states, access their welfare systems, and vote in local and European elections. The popular English writer Ian McEwan (2020) spoke for many when he declared Brexit 'the most pointless, masochistic ambition ever dreamed of in the history of these islands'. Still, Johnson's reference to 1688 was not all that outlandish. As noted above, it is a remarkable feature of the UK's political history that we have to go back so far to find a major constitutional change. The Glorious Revolution of 1688 gave birth to a constitutional monarchy and established the principle of parliamentary sovereignty that has endured to this day.[19] It means that parliament ought to have the final say, with no other institution standing above it. In relation to Europe, this has often presented a serious problem. Regardless of which political party was in the government, the UK tended to be a reluctant member of the European Union.

By accomplishing Brexit, Johnson argued, British people 'have settled a long-running question of sovereign authority', ending 'a debate that has run for three and a half years—some would say 47 years' (Johnson 2020). The debate can be traced back further still. As Beatrice Heuser recently demonstrated in *Brexit in History*, concerns about 'the loss of sovereign control' and 'rejection of any higher authority than that of the government of Britain—have a long pedigree of precedents' (2019: 2). However, the same study also shows that to think of the referendum result as preordained is mistaken. Despite their geographic location, the history of the people inhabiting the British Isles has always been intertwined with continental Europe. Perhaps the best-known artistic representation of this predicament is a seventeenth-century poem that pleaded for an English intervention on the Protestant side in the Thirty Years' War in Europe, John Donne's 'No Man is an Island'. Adapted to our context, the poem can be read as 'no country is an island': not even a country that is actually an island, as a matter of geography.[20] To sum up, the result of the Brexit referendum was not predetermined. But it is equally misguided to think of it as a peculiarly British problem.

In particular there were two major aspects of EU politics preceding the referendum that shaped the outcome. They both exposed major weaknesses of the EU system of governance, which in the perception of many in Britain was moving inexorably towards that of a supranational state. First, the result of the referendum was impacted by the eurozone crisis, despite the fact that by 2016 the situation appeared to have stabilised somewhat. Even more immediately, the referendum campaign unfolded in the shadow of the refugee crisis in continental Europe, which, rightly or wrongly, was presented by the pro-Brexit camp as representing an imminent threat to Britain and its way of life. Ironically, the UK was neither in the eurozone nor in the Schengen Agreement, so none of these developments should have had any direct bearing on the British people. But both crises impacted the referendum in a way that also exposed the limits of what became known as 'differentiated integration'—the fact that a number of countries were participating in certain EU fields, but not others. The Eurogroup became very important owing to the eurozone crisis, yet it was making decisions that had significant impacts on *all* EU members. For example, the UK was spared a major economic slowdown comparable to what happened in Cyprus, Greece, Portugal, Spain, Italy and Ireland— to name some of the countries that were particularly badly hit by the global financial crisis, with very high levels of unemployment, particularly in the early 2010s. The fact that the British economy began to recover earlier than in the countries of the eurozone became a liability of sorts. As Helen Thompson observed, 'the Single Market turned the United Kingdom into an employer of last resort for a monetary union to which it did not belong' (2021: 24). Former Prime Minister David Cameron could do very little to change this constellation under the existing EU rules, and he spectacularly failed to deliver on his promise to negotiate a better arrangement for the UK prior to the referendum. This was largely the result of the EU's internal power dynamic and its institutional architecture. As Thompson remarks,

> On the one hand, eurozone matters had to have priority for eurozone member states and no other non-eurozone member state was experiencing the same problem. On the other hand, any significant change to freedom of movement that could have been contemplated would have required revisions to the EU treaties. That the EU-27 could not move after Cameron formally asked that they did, served to demonstrate to British voters that the Single Market is a protected constitutional order, unresponsive to national democratic politics. (2021: 24)

To make matters worse, the refugee crisis that peaked in mid- to late 2015 was perceived as Europe's loss of control. While developments in continental Europe were unlikely to have much direct impact on conditions in the UK, people worried that their concerns over EU policies were not being heard. Brexit thus once again brought to the foreground the problem of the EU's 'over-constitutionalisation' (Grimm 2016: 18), which constrains the possibilities for democratic contestation within member states. This is not to deny that the referendum campaign relied at times on misleading claims: Nigel Farage and his Brexit Party, for example, sought to frighten the British electorate by the prospect of Turkish accession to the Union, which is unlikely to happen for decades to come. Nevertheless, Farage's claim had traction with the electorate, partly because the EU itself reaffirmed its commitment to Turkish membership, promising President Erdoğan that accession talks would be expedited in exchange for Turkey taking on the ungrateful task of protecting the EU's external borders. This was part of an agreement that Merkel negotiated with the autocratic Turkish leader 'after the

Commission blundered with bureaucratic overreach in trying to set quotas for the reception of refugees' (Anderson 2020; see also Chapter 5 below).

Less Glorious: UK-EU Future Relations

The referendum result came as a shock, and not only to the British political establishment that had overwhelmingly supported the remain option: EU leaders too were taken by surprise. Chancellor Merkel spoke of a 'watershed for Europe' (Delcker 2016). Later, Donald Tusk, then President of the European Council, was to warn that it would be a mistake to assume that Brexit was just about British Euroscepticism—'a symptom of political aberration or merely a cynical game of populists exploiting social frustrations' (Tusk 2016). The concerns that had led British voters to vote against EU membership were widely shared across the continent. 'Questions about the guarantees of security of the citizens and their territory, questions about the protection of their interests, cultural heritage and way of life', Tusk warned, had to be urgently addressed, 'even if the UK had voted to remain' (2016).[21] Like many opponents of Brexit in the UK, Tusk was also convinced that the decision could and should be reversed. The vote itself, many observers believed, was the result of miscalculation. As a Brussels insider reported, the British were seen from the outset as 'apostates, lamentable victims of a false doctrine'; a view that led to the assumption that 'they would backtrack once they saw the error of their ways' (Middelaar 2019: 128). Even as it became obvious that there was no credible political force in the UK that could engineer a reversal of the decision, with the main advocate of Brexit, Boris Johnson, securing an overwhelming majority in the December 2019 parliamentary elections, many EU leaders continued to view the British position as untenable. Essentially, Brexit was a lie, they believed. In the interconnected world we live in, the promise of national sovereignty was a dangerous fantasy. The UK's ability to control its own destiny would be severely diminished, rather than enhanced. Moreover, the country would suffer severe economic disruption followed by decline. What sensible voter could want that?

Claus Offe captured this sense of disbelief when he wrote of 'the temptation to exclaim, with the words of the great Austrian poet Ernst Jandl, "What an error!"' (2017: 26).[22] Yet the pithy statement unwittingly revealed a deeply apolitical understanding of politics, foreshadowing many of the practical consequences of the Brexit vote which followed. As it happened, the conflicting understandings that the UK and EU leaders had about the 'meaning of Brexit' shaped their expectations about the future relationship, leading to arduous negotiations that resulted in a deal that appeared rather suboptimal for both sides.

From the EU perspective, the key aims of the Brexit negotiations were clear early on. First, there was a widespread acceptance of the premise that the Union had to preserve the integrity of the single market. In other words, if the UK chose to become a 'third country' that no longer had a desire to fulfil the obligations of membership, its access to the single market would be constrained. This provision became known as the concern for a 'level playing field', which would ensure that British businesses would be prevented from undercutting their EU competitors by operating under less stringent rules. Second, honouring the principle of solidarity meant that the EU would vigorously support one of its smaller member states which was going to be most seriously affected by the UK's departure, the Republic of Ireland. In particular, the EU accepted the Irish demands that special attention be paid to the preservation of peace in Northern Ireland, which had resulted from the Good Friday Agreement. The Northern Ireland peace process had greatly benefited from the fact that both countries, as EU members, were able to reconcile their differences, which in turn helped to heal sectarian divisions there. The status of Northern Ireland was thus to be preserved, including the permeability of borders between the Republic of Ireland and the North.

On the face of it, there was a compelling logic to these EU positions which the EU's chief negotiator, Michel Barnier, represented with admirable tenacity. EU membership had to matter (Laffan 2019). It was thus imperative that an outsider should not be allowed to cherry-pick benefits without paying any political costs. Whether it liked it or not, the UK would have to become a rule taker. Alongside countries like Switzerland and Norway, it would become a part of the EU's regulatory orbit and thus had no other choice but to accept its influence. As the opponents of Brexit never stopped reminding people in Britain, the EU was a significantly stronger actor in these negotiations, with a population of about 450 million and a combined output amounting to a multiple of the UK's GDP. To sum up, most observers were adamant that the UK needed the EU more than the other way round, and thus that it had no choice but to accept most of the EU's demands. This was the harsh 'truth of Brexit', as Irish Foreign Minister Simon Coveney put it towards the end of the negotiations—the 'truth' that successive UK governments, and at times even the opposition, had attempted to conceal from the British people (Reuters, 30 November 2020). 'Brexit is a national tragedy build on a chimera', wrote a British commentator in a similar spirit, and that chimera was called sovereignty (Stephens 2020). As a result, the UK was 'about to discover that it has traded the real power to shape its destiny for an illusion drenched in nostalgia' (ibid.).

Brexiters' views could not have been more different. From the outset, their leaders like Boris Johnson were adamant that the UK—once freed from the regulatory shackles of EU membership—would thrive like never before. Yet, the EU's two key aims clearly represented a formidable obstacle to those of the UK. First, complying with the level playing field's provisions would force the UK to adhere to EU rules and regulations without having any say in their creation. The country would thus lose its ability to shape the decisions that would impact on its businesses and citizens. Rather than recovering its sovereignty, the UK would become a 'vassal state'. Second, honouring the key provisions of the Good Friday Agreement while leaving the single market would result in undermining the UK's territorial integrity. As the Good Friday Agreement does not permit any physical infrastructure to be erected to police the borders between the Republic and Northern Ireland, some border controls became necessary between Northern Ireland and the rest of the UK. Thus, it is far from clear how much Brexiters could deliver on their promise to reclaim self-government by regaining full control of the UK's borders, money and law.

'Who Killed Soft Brexit?'[23]

And yet, while there are numerous studies outlining the shortcomings of the UK's ever changing negotiating position, the EU's track record in facing up to the challenge of Brexit is also mixed. Both sides share a degree of responsibility for a deal that damages their respective interests and has the potential to undermine their relationship for years to come. In a manner not dissimilar to its dealings with the eurozone and refugee crises, the EU showed itself at times to be rigid and overly legalistic while at other times it bypassed its own regulations and laws in the name of emergency. Two examples will suffice to illustrate this.

First, consider the dispute over the freedom of movement. As we have seen, the issue had been of great salience to both sides even prior to the Brexit referendum, so much so that it is plausible to argue that if EU negotiators had conceded to David Cameron's demands to gain more control on intra-European migration, the 'remain' side might have won the referendum (particularly considering that the 'leave' side won by a very narrow margin of 52 per cent). Even after the referendum, the UK might have accepted a close relationship with the EU—a 'soft Brexit'—if it 'had been offered the capacity to invoke an emergency brake on free movement even while staying part of the single market' (Nicolaidis 2020: 480).[24] In a revealing tit-for-tat, the then British foreign secretary, Boris Johnson, described the link between access to the single market and free movement as 'complete baloney', to which the German Finance Minister, Wolfgang Schäuble, responded with an offer to 'gladly send her majesty's foreign minister a copy of the Lisbon treaty' (*The Guardian*, 23 September 2016). What is striking is the purely legalistic interpretation of the conflicting positions—all the more so considering that the purpose of Brexit was precisely to free the UK from the legal obligations underpinning the European Union. Clearly, the EU's commitment to uphold 'the indivisibility of the four freedoms', nay, to declare them sacrosanct, was in itself a political decision. The legal doctrine is in fact not explicitly spelt out in EU treaties. Yet it was presented in such a dogmatic way, that a mischievous observer might have been reminded of the medieval Christian disputes over 'the indivisibility of the Holy Spirit' (Nicolaidis 2020: 480).

Second, the thorny issue of the position of Northern Ireland in a post-Brexit Europe bedevilled the negotiations of both the withdrawal treaty and the future relationship between the UK and the EU. A fairly open-ended formulation of Article 50, which regulates how the modalities of exit and the future relationship should be negotiated, was interpreted in a way that weakened the UK's negotiating position from the outset. While the Article simply stipulates that once a member state has notified the European Council about its intention to withdraw, 'the Union shall negotiate and conclude an agreement with that State, setting out the arrangements for its withdrawal, taking account of the framework for its future relationship with the Union' (cited in Dixon 2018: 903), the EU side established early on that negotiations had to be sequenced with the withdrawal agreement negotiated first and the future relationship arrangements to follow. As one legal scholar concluded, 'there is nothing in Article 50 that compels this interpretation' (Dixon 2018: 905). The rigid 'requirements as to the sequence of negotiations have been read in' somewhat arbitrarily (ibid. 940), as they were deemed advantageous for bolstering the EU's negotiating position. All the same, the EU representatives repeated time and again that they were not merely relying on 'superior bargaining power, but [were] acting according to the legal requirements of Article 50' (ibid. 940). What is more, the EU did not feel bound by this restriction on sequencing. Accepting the demands of the Irish government to safeguard the existing arrangements in Northern Ireland, the EU was willing to bend its own rules in the name of emergency. To protect peace in Northern Ireland, Prime Minister Theresa May accepted the so-called Northern Ireland 'backstop'—doing exactly what Article 50 was meant to have prevented both sides in the negotiations from doing: regulating their future relationship as a part of the withdrawal agreement.[25] We thus see a similar pattern repeated across a number of crises scenarios discussed here—a decision taken in response to a (perceived) emergency is later justified as simply necessitated by the EU's commitment to adhering to rules.

This legalistic approach masks the ideological commitment to an ideal of an ever-closer union that is not to be challenged. Dissenters are to be punished to prevent future attempts at non-compliance. This has serious implications for the EU. On the face of it, the suboptimal outcome of the Brexit negotiations appears in line with Macron's aspiration for the EU 'to become more sovereign, more democratic and closer to its citizens' (Braun 2020). If we accept the assumption that a deal that was too generous to the UK might incentivise free-riding, undermining the EU polity as a result, making the prospect of exit unpalatable strengthens Europe's unity. Yet the one-sided transformation of Article 50 from a provision that was understood as an explicit 'confirmation of a unilateral right of a Member State to withdraw' into a clause that created 'a hostile rather than friendly environment for withdrawal', calls into doubt 'the pooled-sovereignty model of the European Union' (Dixon 2018: 902, 901). Just as the very existence of Article 50 is a legal expression of member state sovereignty, its reinterpretation eroded the core principle on which the Union was meant to be based—that is, that it is constituted by a *voluntary* association of member states.

Yet very few proponents of the European project were willing to see Brexit in this light. Instead, many observers were ready to side with Macron's claim that 'the Brexit campaign was made up of lies, exaggerations and simplifications' and that the result of the referendum thus amounted to a collective error of judgment. To recall the phrase of the Irish Foreign Minister Coveney, 'the truth of Brexit' is that it was a mistake. The problem with this viewpoint, however, is that it is potentially inimical to the very democratic ideal that it seems to defend. Democratic contestation cannot be settled once and for all through establishing 'correct answers', which are to be found by the process of rational deliberation. Democratic politics is shaped by emotions, not just reason; political tradition might be more important than instrumental rationality, and primordial attachments more relevant than material interests. In fact, the Brexit vote could be seen as a protest vote against 'a world of There Is No Alternative governance' (Roussinos 2020).

Concluding Remarks

The focus of this chapter has been on sovereign Europe, which is seen as a precondition for genuine democratic self-governance by some, while it is rejected for strikingly similar reasons by others. France and the United Kingdom have been discussed as exemplifying these conflicting positions, but divisions are to be found as much within these countries as between them. Just as there are significant political forces in France opposing the mantra of an 'ever-closer union', a sizeable proportion of the British electorate opposed the UK's departure from the European Union and felt disenfranchised by a referendum that was seen as too crude an instrument to determine the 'will of the people'. Similar divisions can be identified within all member states and are particularly pronounced in Central and Eastern Europe (see Chapter 5). Brexit should thus be seen as an indication of a broader European malaise and an expression of the growing disillusionment with a project that is perceived as removed from the very people it is meant to serve—European citizens. It raises fundamental questions about the optimal size for a political community to work in a way that is compatible with the ideal of democratic self-government. In pondering these problems, we are well advised to show epistemological modesty. We are yet to see what the true impact of Brexit is going to be both in the UK and the European Union. Though the project of European integration successfully transformed nation states into member states (Bickerton 2012), whether and how the process can be reversed is far from certain. Rather than reclaiming control over its destiny, will a country that chooses to be outside end up becoming a 'vassal state' (Morgan 2021)?

'Brexit can be told as a great new beginning', argues Kalypso Nicolaidis (2019: 117), suggesting that it could serve as 'a political wake-up call for the rest of Europe' (ibid. 152), and reminding us of the experimental nature of the European project. In ongoing public debates about Brexit, which were at times more heated than the actual negotiations, Nicolaidis sounded a note of caution, hoping that 'perhaps all sides one day will come to question their original assumptions, revisit their hypothesis, revise their inferences' (ibid.

126). If this position sounds ambiguous, it is because it is. Grappling with the meaning of Brexit, Nicolaidis praised ambivalence, citing an American political scientist in whose view 'democracy is a political system for people who are not sure that they are right' (Elmer Eric Schattschneider, in Nicolaidis 2020: 465). It was thus a fitting choice for the President of the European Commission, Ursula von der Leyen (2020), to quote T. S. Eliot's 'Little Gidding' when making an announcement about the deal on the future EU-UK relationship: 'What we call the beginning is often the end/ And to make an end is to make a beginning.'

If we are serious about our commitment to democracy, we must remain open to the idea that there is not one correct answer to the question of an appropriate location of sovereignty, or whether sovereignty as a term is relevant in the first place. Democrats should be wary of believers in absolute truth. Hans Kelsen used a counterintuitive image to illustrate the matter. Recalling the biblical story of Pilate who was to decide on Jesus' fate against the allegations that he falsely claimed to be the son of God and the king of the Jews, Kelsen praised the governor of Judaea for *not* taking sides. Pilate, a sceptical Roman, wondered, 'What is truth?' and handed over the decision to the people, giving them the opportunity to pardon Jesus. Yet the people decided that Barabbas, a robber, should be freed rather than Jesus. Pilate, who is commonly seen as a relativist, void of moral principles, who seeks to avoid responsibility by allowing the Jews to decide the fate of their religious compatriot, is presented by Kelsen as a principled democrat who accepts that his is not to be the final word. The famous episode in the Gospel of John thus becomes a 'tragic symbol of relativism—and democracy' (Kelsen [1929] 2019: 134).

Though the UK's departure from the European Union has been accomplished, with Prime Minister Johnson delivering on his promise to 'get Brexit done', arguments over Britain's relationship with Europe will continue. At their basis, as we have seen, are conflicting understandings of sovereignty. For many proponents of Brexit, the very idea that sovereignty can be shared is a misnomer. In their view, it is based on a fundamental misunderstanding of what sovereignty is all about. A nation that agrees to pool its sovereignty ceases to have it, they assert, for 'sovereignty that cannot be exercised is sovereignty lost' (Tombs 2021). This is not just relevant to Brexit. Sovereignty remains a point of reference for the countries of Central and Eastern Europe, where many political leaders claim to defend their (national) interests against Brussels overreach. And conversely, Europe is forced to consider its own vital interests in relation to a growing number of challengers from within and without. Thus, pace Kelsen, even democracies cannot evade the question of fundamental values and whether, when and how to defend them—a question that has proved particularly challenging for the EU's experimental polity, as I will discuss in Chapter 4 in relation to the EU's ambition to be a global player, and in Chapter 5 in relation to the EU's internal challenges to democracy and the rule of law.

4

THE RETURN OF GEOPOLITICS
THE EUROPEAN UNION IN A WORLD OF
SOVEREIGN STATES

Ukraine chose the European way, which implies the rule of law, democracy and change of power. Ukraine's success on this way is a direct threat to Putin's power because he chose the opposite course—a lifetime in power, filled with arbitrariness and corruption.

Boris Nemtsov, *Kyiv Post*, 1 September 2014

When everybody was still a mindless advocate of globalization making noise about a flat world without borders, Moscow clearly reminded [everybody] that sovereignty and national interests all have meaning.

Vladislav Surkov, *Nezavisimaya Gazeta*, 2 November 2019[1]

Echoing Hobbes, Andrey Zvyagintsev's compelling 2014 film *Leviathan* depicts life in Putin's Russia as truly 'poor, nasty, brutish, and short'. *Leviathan* also shows some of the reasons behind this misery: vodka, and the absence of the rule of law. As the fictional local tyrant Vadim Sergeyich drunkenly tells the main character Nikolai 'Kolya' Sergeiev: 'Remember this: you've never had any

101

rights, and you'll never have any rights.' It's no mystery as to who prevails in this unequal contest. The film begins with a depiction of Kolya, his wife Lilya, and his old friend and lawyer Dima, 'united as the powerless against the powerful'. They fight together against the expropriation of Kolya's home by the town's authorities, which represent the eponymous *Leviathan* and thus the Russian state. There is no happy ending to the story, with Dima barely surviving the confrontation with state power, Lilya dead and Kolya imprisoned (Wengle et al., 2018: 998).

This bleak cinematic depiction of Russian society is an unfortunate reflection of reality. Vladimir Putin may be no fan of vodka, but neither is he a fan of the rule of law. This used to be mainly a problem for ordinary Russians. However, with Putin's Russia demonstrating equal contempt for international law, it has become a serious problem for its neighbours, such as Ukraine, and for Europe at large.

Putin's Russia poses a formidable challenge to Europe. How should a post-sovereign polity respond to challenges created by an increasingly hostile world of sovereign states? This predicament was further intensified by a shift in US policy with the rise of Donald Trump, whose disregard for a rule-based international order showed the limits of the EU's reliance on the transatlantic alliance. Trump's defeat in November 2020, and the ensuing presidency of Joe Biden, marked the US's return to multilateralism, but Europe is unlikely to be a major strategic priority for any US administration. The rise of China too has had profound implications for a rule-based international order. Though China's geopolitical ambitions appear to be focused on the South China Sea, and on Hong Kong and Taiwan, China's growing assertiveness in the world creates problems for the Western alliance, which the European Union ignores at its own peril. Moreover, Russia and China share the fear of what they term 'colour revolutions'—democratic movements which these authoritarian regimes mislabel as foreign influence operations. Both countries deploy sovereignty as a shield against Western interference, denying their domestic opponents any independent agency.

If any reminder of the EU's weakness as a global actor were needed, Belarus delivered it in May 2021, when President Alexander Lukashenko authorised the hijacking of a commercial plane chartered from Athens to Vilnius to arrest a Belarusian journalist in exile, Raman Pratasevich. The fact that the autocratic ruler of one of Europe's poorest countries was so unconcerned with upsetting the EU reveals much about the EU's international standing. Though there have been significant efforts to turn the EU into a major global actor, which can be traced back to the Maastricht Treaty's Common Foreign and Security Policy (CFSP), Europe still often behaves like 'an economic giant, a political dwarf and a military worm' (Manners 2010: 75).[2] There has been no shortage of initiatives (and confusing acronyms) to overcome this. Alongside CFSP, there is the Common Security and Defence Policy (CSDP), which was made possible by the 2009 Treaty of Lisbon. Building on this, in late 2017, twenty-five EU member states signed up to PESCO, which stands for Permanent Structured Cooperation, aimed at deepening defence cooperation between EU member states. This initiative came about partly in response to the EU's inability to deal with the protracted civil war in Syria and the Russian annexation of Crimea in March 2014. More recently still, under the German EU presidency in the second half of 2020, the 'Strategic Compass' was called into life, with the aim of pointing 'the way for the EU's actions in the area of security and defence'. As Angela Merkel proclaimed in May 2021, 'Europe must act together; the concept of national states acting alone has no future' (cited in German Federal Ministry of Defence 2021). Yet, the reality is that neither nation states nor Europe seem capable of decisive actions. Most attempts to give Europe a military dimension continue to be constrained by the unanswered question of European sovereignty—a problem that Europe first encountered with the stillborn attempt at the European Defence Community, proposed by the French Prime Minister René Pleven in 1950 and rejected by the French Assemblée nationale in 1954. Then and now, there can be no effective European army without a European sovereign. Like the single European currency, security and defence are thus policies in search of a state.

To be sure, Lukashenko's and Putin's transgressions did not go unpunished. Following the takeover of Crimea, the EU imposed a series of sanctions on Russia, including targeting high-ranking officials with asset freezes and travel bans. Similarly, the Belarusian regime, which had already been subject to sanctions in 2004 following the disappearance of two opposition politicians, was sanctioned again in the second half of 2020 in response to the 'brutality of the Belarusian authorities and in support of the democratic rights of the Belarusian people' (European Council, 17 December 2020). The brutality against which the EU protested in 2020 was Lukashenko's response to the peaceful demonstrations triggered by his electoral fraud during the presidential elections on 9 August, which denied victory to the opposition candidate Sviatlana Tsikhanouskaya. Finally, in response to the forced landing of the civilian plane, the EU imposed a ban on Belarusian airlines flying over EU territory and urged EU-based airlines to avoid Belarusian airspace. None of these actions appeared to have much impact on Lukashenko's or Putin's behaviour at home or abroad. If anything, they brought the two authoritarian leaders closer together, which was hardly in the interest of domestic pro-democratic opposition movements, or indeed of Europe at large. The EU's half-hearted actions were strong enough to force Putin and Lukashenko to overcome their differences, but not strong enough to undermine their hold on power. If anything, Lukashenko's regime was sufficiently emboldened to cause major disturbances to Poland and the European Union again in late 2021. Thousands of asylum seekers from the Middle East were flown to Minsk by the state-owned airline, Belavia, to be escorted by Belarusian security forces to the Polish borders, which they were then encouraged to cross. With these actions, Lukashenko sought to exploit yet another weakness of the European construct: owing to numerous divisions within and between member states, the EU appears to be at a loss to find an adequate response to migratory pressures. Once again, the simple fact that an illegitimate leader of one of the smallest and poorest countries of Europe was able to trigger a major crisis on the EU's Eastern borders speaks volumes about the limitations of Europe's Common Foreign and Security Policy.

Carl Schmitt in the Kremlin (and in Brussels)

What the state of EU-Russia and EU-Belarus relations shows is Europe's self-imposed impotence. It is not clear whether the EU can effectively set, let alone achieve, its foreign policy goals. All too often it is not even clear what these goals are. So much for Macron's call for 'Europeans to become sovereign', Ursula von der Leyen's promise to lead a geopolitical Commission, or Merkel's vision of a 'Europe capable of great things'. What is striking is the disconnect between the EU's ambition and the reality of its limited power. Europe's international role continues to be characterised by 'the capability-expectations gap', which in Christopher Hill's prescient observation, presents Europe 'with difficult choices and experiences that are the more painful for not being fully comprehended' (1993: 306). The challenge partly stems from the very nature of the EU's experimental polity—'a semi-supranational entity working alongside sovereign states' (ibid. 308). The problem that the Union has had in dealing with both the eurozone and migration crises applies equally to its dealings with the outside world. As Fritz Scharpf has argued, there is just no government either at the European or at the national level with sufficient 'capacity to provide effective solutions for manifest common problems and common aspirations' (2017: 315–16).

The present chapter seeks to explain how this situation came about and to suggest some remedies, all the while acknowledging that many of the challenges the EU faces as a global actor are intractable. However unwillingly, Germany has played an important role in EU foreign policies. Once again, as suggested in Chapter 1, Europe's challenges can be illuminated through some of Carl Schmitt's basic concepts, which are enjoying growing popularity in Russia. In response to an increasingly revanchist and, in many ways, 'Schmittian' Russia, both Germany and the European Union would do well to draw their own lessons from Schmitt's critique of liberalism and 'the age of neutralizations and depoliticizations' (Schmitt [1928] 2007: 80).

As a recent comprehensive study of Russia's 'New Authoritarianism' has documented, the dominant political discourse there 'increasingly reflect[s] many of Schmitt's ideas, such as the centrality of sovereignty, the defining moment of the exception, illiberal forms of democracy, the identification of enemies, and a highly spatialised theory of geopolitics' (Lewis 2020: 46). Channelling Schmitt, an influential Russian intellectual emphasised in 2002 that politics is not primarily about the mundane business of the government. Rather, 'politics lives in the cracks, the breaks, the intervals of the institutional routineness of management' (cited in Lewis 2020:43). In the EU context, Middelaar writes in similar terms when praising 'events-politics', in which leaders face the challenge of coming to terms with unforeseen events: 'This form of political action is not played out within a specific framework; it occurs when that framework itself is put to the test, in the most extreme case by a war or disaster' (2019: 11). Or in Schmitt's own words, 'the exception is more interesting than the rule. The rule proves nothing; the exception proves everything' (1985a: 15). Thus 'the political' is that special realm of human activity which is characterised by conflict between foes and friends. Of particular relevance here is Schmitt's idea of *Grossraum*, discussed in previous chapters, which continues to inform the thinking of many Russian and Chinese thinkers, as well as some (West) European commentators and policy-makers.

Schmitt himself sought to disown some of the more troublesome aspects of his *Grossraum* thinking with the publication of his postwar magnum opus, *The Nomos of the Earth* (1950). Schmitt's writings about *Land and Sea* ([1942] 2008b), prefiguring the key arguments of the *Nomos* in the early 1940s, tended to be anti-American, anti-British and anti-liberal: 'the people of the land' were presented as somewhat superior to 'the people of the sea'. In contrast, after the defeat of Nazism Schmitt started to view the relationship between these two conflicting civilisational impulses as a more symbiotic one. England, in this view, was seen as the possessor of a 'universal, maritime sphere', fulfilling a positive role as 'the protector of the other side of the jus publicum Europaeum, the master of the equilibrium of land and sea' (cited in Derman 2011: 188). However, the First World War, Schmitt said, had destroyed this order. After the Second World War, he declared, 'That is the new *Nomos* of the earth; no more *Nomos*' (16 July 1948; in Schmitt 1991: 179).

Presently, the established European order—*jus publicum Europaeum*—is once again being challenged. We could say that Schmitt is back as both an actor and an observer. This is not merely about the growing attraction of Schmitt's political thinking among Russia's intellectuals, including the likes of Alexander Dugin, Alexander

Filippov and Mikhail Remizov, who in turn have influenced the country's political establishment. It is also about Schmitt as a theorist of Germany's Weimar Republic and a compelling polemicist against liberalism. In fact, what is advanced here is *not* a causal argument about Schmittian ideas giving rise to Russia's autocracy. Dugin's influence, for example, was less pronounced than he made others believe (including the US administration, which sanctioned him alongside fourteen other Russian figures considered responsible for the 2014 conflict in Ukraine). Just as Schmitt did not quite become the uncontested 'crown jurist of Nazi Germany', owing to his insufficient commitment to the party and his lack of anti-Semitic zeal, Dugin tried and failed 'to attach himself to Putin's pet project, the Eurasian Union, by boldly proclaiming that he could become its de-facto theoretician' (Laruelle 2015). That said, ignoring the influence of these controversial thinkers is as unhelpful as overstating their input. 'Do they read Carl Schmitt in the Kremlin?' Filippov asked rhetorically, only to say that the issue is not about 'who reads Schmitt, why and to what extent' (2008: 51). Instead what matters are the common tendencies between Schmitt's arguments and the salient characteristics of the contemporary Russian state. These are plentiful.

'Look back at Weimar and start to worry about Russia', wrote Niall Ferguson (2005) more than fifteen years ago. The spectre of the failed German experiment with democracy was also invoked by a number of Russian politicians and observers. These figures ranged from Westernisers such as Yegor Gaidar, who referred to it back in the 1990s, to proponents of 'managed democracy' such as Sergey Markov (a Duma member of the United Russia party), to Valery Zorkin (head of the Russian Constitutional Court), who did so more recently to defend Putin's increasingly authoritarian regime (Herpen 2013: 17–18). Like all historical comparisons, the Weimar metaphor has its limitations, but the analogy is important as 'it became a central trope in the intellectual discourse of post-Soviet Russia' (Lewis 2020: 12). For our purposes, it suffices to highlight some geographical and socio-psychological aspects of Russian society that are reminiscent of interwar Germany, such as the 'post-imperial pain' caused by the loss of territory and prestige (Herpen

2013: 20). Stephen Hanson and Jeffrey Kopstein have argued that 'As in the case of Weimar, the Russian Republic was born as the result of imperial collapse' (1997: 264). Echoing this, David Lewis has posited that 'almost every Russian intellectual agreed with Putin that "the question of finding and strengthening national identity is of a fundamental nature for Russia"' (cited in Lewis 2020: 12). And just as the elites in the Weimar Republic cultivated the myth of the 'stab in the back' that had robbed Germany of victory in the First World War, Russian post-Soviet elites believed they had seen their country 'sold out' to the West by the likes of Mikhail Gorbachev, Boris Yeltsin and Yegor Gaidar. Adding insult to injury, they claimed, the West had then proceeded to 'encircle Russia' with the rapid expansion of its alliances. With the enlargements of NATO in 1999 and the EU in 2004, West European political and military structures took over significant areas of territory formerly under Soviet control. The (failed) attempts by Ukrainians to join these structures via the 'Orange Revolution' of 2004, and again in 2013, were perceived by many Russians as provocations, bringing old-fashioned geopolitics firmly back onto the agenda.

This is what makes Schmitt's philosophy useful when reflecting on the possibility of a more robust European stance towards Russia. Moving away from 'a post-traditional conception of sovereignty' that reduces it to 'a speech act' (Avbelj 2020: 300) should enable us to be more open and honest about the EU's limitations. The claim that a sovereign European Union—in the European Commission's words, one that 'protects, empowers and defends'—need not necessarily take the form of a state, as Matej Avbelj suggested recently (2020: 301), appears less convincing when assessing the EU's standing as a global actor. Not only is a united Europe *not* standing up against Russia, but individual member states that could and should have a stronger foreign policy are able to hide behind the EU's weakness and disunity.

Germany is the paradigmatic example of such a member state. It was once a truism that France needed the EU to conceal its weakness, while Germany needed it to hide its strength. However, when it comes to foreign policy, one could argue that Germany uses the EU's weakness to justify its own inaction. To be sure, the

German relationship with power remains 'unusually complicated' (Maull 2018: 461), despite its partial normalisation. This complexity is reflected in the myriad of descriptors attached to it by scholars, ranging from 'autistic' to 'reflective', 'shaping', 'civilian', 'geo-economic' and 'semi-hegemonic'. Nevertheless, while history helps to explain the German aversion to the open projection of power, it does not excuse the unwillingness of German policy-makers to clearly grasp, let alone respond to, the threat that countries like Russia pose. Yet, by deferring to the EU's non-existent foreign policy, German leaders are able to make a virtue of their abdication of responsibility. This has significant costs for both Germany and Europe.

Ukraine as 'the Borderland' between the EU and Russia

What is Ukraine? Its very existence as an independent nation has been largely ignored by most Europeans, with many regarding it as 'a nation on the borderland'. This attitude reflects the literal meaning of the word Ukraine as 'borderland'[3] and its position 'as a province and backyard of far larger entities—Russia and, earlier, the Soviet Union' (Schlögel 2018: 7).[4] This has changed more recently owing to the Orange Revolution of 2004–5, and even more so with the 'Revolution of Dignity' that erupted in 2014. In both cases the EU played an important part both as a normative power and a geopolitical competitor to Russia. It did so, however, without sufficient awareness of its power. The EU's apolitical approach backfired, triggering bloody conflict and unwittingly encouraging Russia's neo-imperial ambitions. In 2014, the EU's soft power proved sufficient to trigger another revolution in Ukraine, but it was impotent when it came to protecting Ukraine's territorial integrity vis-à-vis Russia. The confrontation between the EU's 'neo-medieval empire', which prides itself on having blurred boundaries (Zielonka 2006), and a revisionist Russia which muscularly asserts its sovereignty claims, occurred to the detriment of the Ukrainian people, whose ambitions to 'return to Europe' proved elusive.

Observers of the EU's half-hearted attempt to bring Ukraine within its orbit have bemoaned its failure to engage fully with the political and geopolitical dimensions of this project. Elena

Korosteleva has argued that 'much of the EU politics in the neighbourhood to date has been essentially depoliticised' (2017: 323; compare Browning 2018). Similarly, Kataryna Wolczuk described the European Neighbourhood Policy (ENP) as 'a technocratic exercise which provided a "bureaucratic answer" to the question as to where the geopolitical and cultural boundaries of Europe lie' (2016: 61). The Eastern Partnership (EaP) which augmented the ENP in 2009, avoided the issue of EU membership, instead offering a number of post-Soviet states, including Ukraine, the prospect of an Association Agreement. What was on offer was not quite enough for Ukraine, but too much for Russia. The result of this confused and indeterminate policy was 'ineffectiveness and overreach' (MacFarlane and Menon 2014: 100). Fashioning itself as 'a post-modern security actor', the EU sought to attain 'mutually beneficial' outcomes (Youngs 2017: 216, 17) rather than pursuing its interests at the expense of other states.

But what if there are no 'mutually beneficial' outcomes, or none that are perceived as such? Schmitt's dictum about politics leading to conflict is relevant here. The EU's modus operandi of seeking 'peace through conversation' (Jones 2005) emboldened Putin's Russia to take over Crimea. The EU's non-traditional polity found in Russia not a partner for peace (as the ENP envisaged) but an actor willing to engage in non-traditional war. Ukraine's conundrum was that 'the EU does not care about Ukraine's European choice while Russia cares too much' (Wolczuk 2016: 69). Putin's Russia demonstrated with brutal efficiency that enmity cannot be eradicated from politics. As Schmitt cautioned:

> It would be a mistake to believe that a nation could eliminate the distinction of friend and enemy by declaring its friendship for the entire world or by voluntarily disarming itself. The world will not thereby become depoliticized, and will not be transplanted into a condition of pure morality, pure justice, or pure economics. If a people is afraid of the trials and risks implied by existing in the sphere of politics, then another people will appear which will assume these trials by protecting it against foreign enemies and thereby taking over political rule. ([1928] 2007: 51–2)

Of course, Europe has not (yet) voluntarily disarmed itself, but it came close to it in its dealings with Russia in early 2014, when Angela Merkel, alongside a number of other Western leaders, publicly declared that there could be no military solution to the crisis in Ukraine (Youngs 2017: 88). Rather than defusing the conflict, the friendly gesture was taken as a sign of weakness, unwittingly encouraging the Russian President to continue with his own intervention. Europe has not yet given up on the 'trials and risks implied by existing in the sphere of politics' either, but it came close to de facto abandoning eastern Ukraine, leaving it to Russia to decide 'who the enemy is by virtue of the eternal relation of protection and obedience' (Schmitt [1928] 2007: 51–2). The tendency, particularly pronounced in Germany, to believe that military forces are somewhat superfluous, does not enhance but rather weakens the EU's diplomatic position (Lau and Topçu 2021).

The EU 'sleepwalked into the crisis' by underestimating both its influence and Russia's belligerence (Kuzio 2017: 116). To be sure, the EU, led by Germany, eventually responded to Russia's aggression via the imposition of sanctions. Concurrently, Germany and France have made numerous attempts at negotiating a peace settlement, culminating in the two Minsk Agreements in September 2014 and February 2015, which may well have defused the conflict somewhat, but at the expense of solidifying Russian gains. The so-called 'Normandy format' (Germany, France, Russia and Ukraine) unwittingly privileges Russia, as Germany and France are not credible actors in the conflict, while Ukraine is a poor match for Russia's military capabilities. Just as the initial inaction of the EU enabled Russia's hybrid war in eastern Ukraine and the military takeover of Crimea, the subsequent lack of resolve on the EU's part proved conducive to Russia's 'hybrid annexation' (Kuzio 2017: 114) of the Donbas region (the so-called Donetsk and Luhansk People's Republics). In a similar way, the EU's symbolic gestures in favour of the Belarusian democratic opposition, including an ambitious package of economic sanctions, were no match for Putin's support for Lukashenko. Ironically, while the Minsk Agreement utilised Belarus' capital as a somewhat neutral ground, the deterioration of the EU-Belarus conflict in mid-2021 brought about renewed efforts at the creation of the Union State of Russia and Belarus. With respect to Belarus then, it was once again Putin's Russia, rather than the EU, that was unafraid of taking bold actions in support of their preferred regime.

Russia's Sovereign Democracy

The conflict between Russia and Ukraine was not totally unexpected. In fact, Andreas Umland (2021) argues that the surprising thing is that Ukraine was able to enjoy relative peace in the Russian neighbourhood for so many years after the demise of the Soviet Union in 1991. This was only true of countries which, like Poland and the Baltic states, were firmly included in the Western alliance via their membership in NATO and the EU; or those countries that accepted Russia's tutelage (however unwillingly), such as Armenia, Belarus and Kazakhstan.[5] Ukraine, Umland posits, was somewhat protected against an open invasion by the high degree of economic interdependence between the two countries. This interdependence was the legacy of the Soviet Union, which constructed a pipeline enabling Russia to export gas to Western Europe, but only via Ukrainian territory. With the construction of an alternative route—Nord Stream 1, which started operating in 2011—the perceived costs of Russia's interference were greatly reduced. These would diminish further still with the completion of Nord Stream 2, the construction of which was launched with German support by Gazprom in 2015, just one year after the annexation of Crimea. Yet a focus on geo-economics would be incomplete without taking into account the role of the ideas and contingencies that facilitated Putin's intervention.

From the outset, Putin and his numerous supporters have seen Russia's role as one of standing up to a world led by the US and ruled by Western norms and institutions. To defy it was to reclaim Schmittian sovereignty 'as freedom to make decisions unconstrained by norms or law' (Lewis 2020: 53), the kind of freedom Russia believed the US took in relation to the outside world, imperilling peace and stability. As Putin stated in his Munich speech of 2007 (echoing Schmitt's *Grossraum* argument in favour of subdividing the world into large spaces),

[W]hat is a unipolar world? However you dress it up, in the end it means in practice only one thing: one centre of power, one centre of force, one centre of decision-making. It is a world of one master, one sovereign. And in the end this is disastrous not only for everyone inside this system, but also for the sovereign itself, because it destroys it from within. (Putin cited in Lewis 2020: 53)

It is in this context that a series of non-violent revolutions has to be understood, which Putin's Russia viewed as endangering its own existence. The 'Spectre of Velvet Revolution' (Horvath 2013) reinforced Russia's anxiety about the West. Of particular concern was the series of uprisings in Russia's neighbourhood. These included a 'Rose' revolution in Georgia in 2003, an 'Orange' revolution in Ukraine in 2004, and a 'Tulip' revolution in Kyrgyzstan in 2005. As Vladislav Surkov, one of the leading ideologues of 'sovereign democracy' in Russia, said ahead of the 2008 presidential elections: 'we will either preserve our sovereignty or be ruled externally' (cited in Lewis 2020: 49). Surkov and others succeeded in associating coloured revolutions with chaos, capitalising on the prevalent sentiment in Russia which framed politics as an ongoing contest between chaos and order. In fact, Russia's role in the world was to be realised by becoming 'a moral, tragic bulwark against the chaos and destabilisation wrought by the West' (Lewis 2020: xii). 'An overdose of freedom is lethal to a state', mused Surkov in his defence of Russia's authoritarian regime, praising the model he helped to create as 'a good compromise between chaos and order' (Surkov 2021). Staged elections in which fake 'opposition' parties ensure Putin's victory are as much a part of that 'good compromise' as the ruthless repression of any dissent (including the attempted murder and subsequent imprisonment of leading opposition figure Alexei Navalny).[6] Exemplary of this method was the 2008 victory of Putin's favourite candidate for the presidency, Dmitry Medvedev, by means of which Putin was able to successfully bypass constitutional restrictions by becoming Prime Minister. Continuing to dominate Russian politics, he embarked on a number of policies which ultimately paved the way for Russia's intervention in Ukraine, as well as enacting constitutional and legal amendments that will enable him to rule until 2036. Of particular importance were Russia's invasion of Georgia in 2008, and its successful veto of Ukraine's aspiration to NATO membership. And finally, 2008 brought about the global financial crisis, another coincidence that was to weaken the West in its dealings with Russia, particularly as it morphed into a European sovereign debt crisis in 2009–10. These developments led the likes of Russian foreign policy expert Igor Panarin to predict the emergence of a powerful 'Eurasian Union' led by a truly sovereign leader, *gosudar* Putin.[7]

It is clear that the numerous advocates of Eurasia must have felt vindicated by Russia's annexation of Crimea and its capacity and determination to continue destabilising eastern Ukraine. Dugin, for example, predicted as early as 2008 that Russian troops would eventually occupy 'perhaps even Ukraine and the Crimean Peninsula'. In fact, Putin's major speech of March 2014 celebrating the takeover of Crimea centred on the concept of Eurasia and extended an invitation to Germany to support Russian ambitions in Ukraine. Drawing parallels with German unification, Putin felt that 'the citizens of Germany will also support the aspiration of the Russians, of historical Russia, to restore unity'. He also argued, citing Kosovo as a precedent, that Russia's land grab was perfectly legal:

> Pursuant to Article 2, Chapter 1 of the United Nations Charter, the UN International Court agreed with this approach and made the following comment in its ruling of July 22, 2010, and I quote: 'No general prohibition may be inferred from the practice of the Security Council with regard to declarations of independence,' and 'General international law contains no prohibition on declarations of independence.' Crystal clear, as they say. (Putin 2014)

Here, Putin clearly delighted in making 'decisions unconstrained by norms or law', all the while paying lip service to international law.[8] There were two ways in which he acted as a Schmittian sovereign would. First, by deciding what constitutes the exception; second, by determining what course of action is to be taken to deal with that exception. After all, it was Putin and his supporters who succeeded in construing the situation in Crimea as exceptional—claiming that the Russian-speakers there faced an imminent threat from the illegal (and, in their view, also illegitimate) government in Kiev. And it was Putin and his military leaders who were able to take the quick initiative, exploiting a power vacuum in Ukraine.

Putin's boldness paid off. As Schmitt understood well (drawing on Hobbes' *Leviathan*), internal political conflict in a community can be neutralised by a political conflict directed towards the outside world. Filippov, reflecting on the challenges that Putin faced after being appointed Prime Minister in 2008, echoed Schmitt: 'Inside the polity there is political neutrality—in fact the absence of politics as such ... Radical opponents are quickly identified as enemies, and not just enemies from within the state, but also as the agents of hostile states' (Filippov 2008: 51–2). The result is that domestic politics in Russia has been reduced to technocracy, in which 'nobody raises any questions about obedience (which the state requires) and protection (which the state promises)'. One of the astounding consequences of Putin's adventure in Crimea was his approval rating, which soared to 83 per cent in May 2014 (Ray and Esipova 2014).

'Soft Power Europe' and its Limitations

By contrast, Europe's response was slow and ineffectual. Here too, ideas and contingencies mattered, shaping the policies. Since 2010, the European Union has been preoccupied with the eurozone crisis. Led by Germany's reluctant hegemony, the EU has become increasingly inward-looking and unprepared to face external challenges. The amount of time, political capital and money that European leaders had up to then devoted to Greece, for example, dwarfed all efforts directed towards Ukraine.[9] The migration crisis too, particularly in the second half of 2015, appeared to be of greater urgency for the EU.

But the problem that Europe faced in its relationship with Russia was also conceptual. Partly because geopolitics became 'the theme that dare not speak its name' (Behnke 2012), international relations were to be shaped by the EU's power of attraction, that is, merely by its normative power. This is not to say that geopolitical considerations

115

did not play a role in the past: far from it. In fact, the European project was initially meant to serve some fairly traditional imperial ambitions, though directed towards Africa rather than Europe's East. As Peo Hansen and Stefan Jonsson (2014) have demonstrated, European integration and colonialism are intertwined to an extent that few proponents of the EU are willing to acknowledge. In 1961, an Italian geopolitical theorist described the European Economic Community and its association of African countries as the realisation of 'Eurafrica', a first step towards creating 'the largest ensemble, the largest space, the largest mass in material, human and economic terms, which will become the greatest economic power in the world' (cited in Hansen and Jonsson 2014: 239). Somewhat contradictorily, 'Eurafrica was perceived both as the end of colonialism and as authorizing its continuation; or, if you like, as anti-independence yet non-colonial' (ibid. 251). This is what Kojève defended as 'giving colonialism' ([1957] 2001: 123–7). In the early stages of the project, European political elites convinced themselves about the possibility of 'non-colonial' colonialism. Similarly, contemporary elites are certain that Europe has entered a post-historical age, in which lethal conflicts are largely a thing of the past.

The revolutions of 1989 gave a significant boost to this optimistic narrative. Exactly 200 years before, the French Revolution had left a pernicious legacy—the Jacobin exaltation of revolutionary violence. But the events of 1989 left that legacy behind. Its revolutionaries were proud of *not* being revolutionary; that is to say, they were non-violent. Thus, it is not far-fetched to say that 1989 dramatically changed the very meaning of revolution (Auer 2004b). Building on this, the 'coloured revolutions' which emulated the 1989 example sought to transform societies by strikingly moderate means. From Slovakia's 'Second Velvet Revolution' in 1998 to Kyrgyzstan's 'Tulip Revolution' in 2005, they all followed a similar script: an authoritarian leader was challenged by public protests triggered by civil society organisations, social media, students and others. In appearance, these events often resembled rock concerts or carnivals (Kenney 2002); in their aims they were about democratisation and the rule of law, rather than any radically new ideological projects.

However appealing these methods might have been, they had their limitations. To start with, they could only work against rulers who themselves refrained from violence. Thus we must question whether the more recent revolutionary upheavals in the Middle East—Libya, Egypt, Syria—should be in the same category. Even the Ukrainian revolution in 2013–14 was far more violent than its predecessor and, sadly, the violence is not over yet, particularly in parts of eastern Ukraine. In Belarus too, Lukashenko's determination to hold onto power through the police and security apparatus, as well as Russia's support, also points at the limits of non-violent power.

How does the EU fit into these developments? To start with, we can simply say that the EU loves non-violent revolutions; it sees its own beauty reflected in them, because the EU defines itself as a non-violent power. This is why many West European intellectuals were quick to assimilate the 1989 collapse of communism into the narrative of European integration. For Habermas (1990), these were merely 'catching up revolutions'. According to the late Ulrich Beck, 'the Soviet Empire made a peaceful exit from the Stage of world history' (2006: 175), making Beck's 'cosmopolitan vision' realistic, not utopian:

> In what sense is the EU an empire? The European states have definitively ended five hundred years of war, culminating in two world wars which devastated Europe, in order to form a new union which shares a currency and the aspiration to promote internal democratization and find broad commonalities in their foreign and security policies. Viewed historically, this undertaking among states with different cultures can only be described as revolutionary. For the first time in history states have learnt that their power is not diminished but increased by renouncing national sovereignty. (ibid. 175)

An American journalist was even bolder in his conclusion: 'By 1990 [sic], the Soviet Union was history, the Warsaw Pact states free. What did it? Fundamentally, the EU did it' (Pfaff 2007). Such accounts ignore the fact that the EU's role in the collapse of communism was rather marginal. As for 'renouncing national sovereignty', the nations of Central Europe reclaimed it, liberating themselves from

117

Soviet tutelage. As discussed in Chapter 2, theirs was a liberal nationalism, which combined a commitment to Europe with a strong sense of belonging to a national community (see also Auer 2004a). Even someone as passionately pro-European and leftist as Aleksander Kwaśniewski, for example, thought of Poland's place in Europe as a proudly sovereign nation. Speaking as President on 30 April 2004, on the eve of Poland joining the European Union, he stressed that 'We [the Poles] have earned this historic moment. Let us congratulate ourselves on the independence and sovereignty of the Republic of Poland that has been restored with our own hands: paving our way to Europe' (2004).

To be sure, the West influenced the East through the power of attraction, but the East played an important role too. The 1989 revolutions in Central Europe reminded West Europeans of the key values that underpinned the project of European integration: democracy and liberty under the rule of law. At any rate, post-communist democratisation in Central and Eastern Europe seemed to have vindicated Europe as a 'soft power'. 'In contrast to the United States', Andrew Moravcsik has asserted repeatedly, Europe is 'a "quiet" superpower' (2002; 2010: 93). Instead of resorting to military means, in this view, Europe cleverly employs tools such as 'European Union enlargement, neighbourhood policy, trade, foreign aid, support for multilateral institutions and international law, and European values' (Moravcsik 2010: 91). Yet post-1989 developments in Central and Eastern Europe reflect the EU's potential strength as much as they expose its weakness: strength, in that the 2004 enlargement has, on the whole, been fairly successful; weakness, in that the EU's Neighbourhood Policy was largely a failure.

What is soft power and how does it work? Soft power is the ability of an actor to make you want what it wants you to want, without you even noticing. But for this power to work, you need to want it a bit from the outset. In other words, the EU has had an influence in Central Europe because the people there wanted to be influenced by it. They desired a return to Europe, as one of the main slogans of the 1989 revolutions put it. It is not much of an overstatement to say that enlargement was the EU's 'most effective foreign policy tool' (Vachudova 2014: 122), and it is still being used in the Balkans. Undoubtedly, when a country aspires to EU membership and the EU has a credible strategy towards it, the Union's power is substantial. The problem occurs when full membership is not on the table, either because the country does not desire it (as with Russia), or because the prospect of it raises difficulties that the existing members do not want to contemplate (size, economic and political backwardness, or a combination of both, as with Ukraine). For these countries, the EU came up with the Neighbourhood Policy, which has proved inadequate.

Why did the Neighbourhood Policy fail? To put it bluntly, it failed because not all the EU's neighbours have behaved as decent neighbours should. While Western Europe grew accustomed to living in a post-modern, post-national polity, in which conflicts are settled by committees and negotiations, Russia embarked on an old-fashioned imperialist project, in which conflicts lead to violent confrontation.

One senior British diplomat praised Europe for the creation of 'a post-modern order where state sovereignty is no longer seen as an absolute'. Among the key characteristics of this system were 'the rejection of force for resolving disputes' and 'the growing irrelevance of borders' (Cooper 1996: 21–2). Moravcsik maintains that Europe's soft power trumps not only that of the US, but of all other major global competitors, asserting that 'Nowhere is Europe's ability to confound the skeptics clearer than in foreign policy' (2020: 48). He cites the challenges of Russia's attack on Ukraine, the 2015 migration crisis and Trump's disruptions towards NATO and the transatlantic alliance: 'In each case, newspapers published lurid reportage and think tanks issued dire predictions of Europe's imminent collapse', writes Moravcsik, 'but in each case Europeans quietly prevailed' (ibid. 48). How the silent acceptance of Russia's takeover of Crimea amounts to Europe's victory is unexplored, as is the danger of the EU's dependence on Erdoğan's Turkey for its 'solution' of the migration crisis. In fact, the deal with Turkey might have inspired Lukashenko's attempt in late 2021 to exploit the EU's vulnerability with respect to migration—he too wanted to be 'bribed' by the EU to end a crisis of his own making, whether by having the sanctions imposed on Belarus lifted, or even by securing EU financial assistance.

Moravcsik's optimistic assessments echo the liberal internationalist dream of Fukuyama's 'end of history'. As discussed in Chapter 1, the very existence of the European Union is meant to have vindicated such liberal assumptions, refuting geopolitics as a useful theoretical lens through which to view power relations in Europe. According to Stefano Guzzini,

> the EU has staked its reputation on being an anti-geopolitical unit. In the memorable phrase of Ole Wæver, 'Europe's other is Europe's past', the EU being a peace organization, a 'civilian' or 'normative' power, aimed precisely at overcoming the militarism and nationalism, historically associated with classical geopolitical thought that had plagued Europe's early twentieth century. (2012: 62)

In this vein, proponents of critical geopolitics praised a novel 'civilizational project of European construction', which gave rise to 'a new nomos'. Building on Schmitt, J. Peter Burgess described this nomos as one

> characterized by a dialectical mix of 'limited' universality and local particularity, espousing a multi-cultural flux of values, which have a systematically blurry connection to territory, which function in the global economy and which are, moreover, protected by a security agenda that reaches beyond the 'traditional' international space of Europe. (2007: 187)

However, many of Burgess' claims about the 'flux of values' and 'local particularity', and his upbeat assessment of the EU's ability as a global actor, are predicated on the assumption that the EU has developed a robust constitutional order (despite the 2005 defeat of its Constitutional Treaty). Yet, European constitutionalism has been in crisis for the last two decades (Scicluna 2015), and there are no signs of a new constitutional settlement.

In contrast to Europe, Putin's Russia is both more old-fashioned and more post-modern. Russia's stance towards Ukraine is traditional, following Schmittian, or even Machiavellian, prescriptions about power politics. The takeover of Crimea was an excellent example of Schmittian *Landnahme* (taking of land), imposing order on a territory that was indeed in flux (if only for a while). Yet this occupation was also remarkably post-modern, if we understand this term to include the decentring of traditional concepts of the subject as an autonomous source of action. Applying the idea of an autonomous subject to states, it makes sense that wars are usually conducted by uniformed soldiers who embody the state's power and authority. Not so with Putin's twenty-first-century (continuing) invasion of Ukraine. There, Russia has practised its own version of 'a systematically blurry connection to territory' by invading its neighbouring country with soldiers who are not what they seem. Their uniforms have no insignia, and though they look and speak like Russians from Russia, they are presented to the outside world as Ukrainian Russians. The arguments used by the Russian leadership in its defence are at times comical—take, for example, claims that any Russian soldiers in Ukraine must simply be on holiday.

What has occurred in Russia's interaction with Ukraine is a new kind of warfare, which appears to fuse two distinct driving forces of politics identified by Schmitt through the metaphor of *Land and Sea*: order is associated with the *Landnahme*, and the chaotic freedom of a pirate is associated with the boundless sea. Russian military tactics employ the logic of pirates, who pretend to follow the international rule of law. The conflicting principles of *Land and Sea* are thus merged into one.

This is not to deny the EU any influence over its eastern neighbourhood. Clearly, the Ukrainian crisis illustrates Europe's power of attraction too. The 2013 Maidan protests in Kiev were triggered by President Yanukovych's abandonment of the association agreement negotiated with the EU. Later, in February 2014, the foreign ministers of Germany, Poland and France negotiated a compromise solution that exposed Yanukovich's weakness, precipitating his hasty escape. This provided one of the decisive moments of the crisis. Whether and when the actor was the EU rather than Europe was always ambiguous, as was the usage of EU symbols.[10] The flipside of this story is that the EU appears ineffective in constraining Russian efforts to destabilise Ukraine. As discussed above, the current 'Normandy format' consisting of Germany, France, Russia and Ukraine has its limitations, particularly given that public opinion in Germany and France shows a great reluctance to deploy force. The reports about Ukrainian President Volodymyr Zelenskiy agreeing in 2019 with President Trump that neither France nor Germany had done enough for his country further eroded mutual trust. Yet by stating this, Zelenskiy echoed the assessment of many observers who considered the Minsk Agreements ineffectual, leading at best to a 'managed defeat' (Youngs 2017: 142).

Putin's Preventive Counter-Revolution

It is Putin's Russia, rather than the EU, that has perfected the confluence of soft and hard power. To be sure, the entire process was triggered by the public mobilisation of Ukrainian citizens, which in itself was an example of soft power. But even Putin's empire-building has had—at least in its appearance—some 'velvet' elements. This is the peculiar story of 'Putin's preventive counter-revolution' (Horvath 2013). While the Ukrainian revolution of 2004 lost its way, it attracted unlikely followers. In response to the threat of democratic ideals infecting Russia, Putin and his ideologues engineered a veritable 'velvet counter-revolution'. The spectre of a Moscow Maidan was to be kept at bay by state-sponsored public mobilisation, which gave rise to a nationalist project with distinctly imperial dimensions.

Putin adopted a dual strategy. One aspect was rather old-fashioned: a crack-down on opposition movements, increased control of the media, restrictions on civil society organisations and the like. The other aspect was fairly novel. The public space was crowded out by state-sponsored 'spontaneous' support, engineered by the political technologists surrounding Putin. Among the most famous and consequential was perhaps the Nashi youth movement, which prided itself on having staged an alternative 'Moscow Maidan', pre-empting the coloured revolution in Russia (Horvath 2013: 208). It was through mimicking the methods of the Velvet Revolutions of 1989 and the Ukrainian Orange Revolution that Putin and his followers succeeded in solidifying their autocratic regime of 'sovereign democracy'. This has been a distinctly nationalist project, 'reinforcing national borders against Western soft power, and nurturing the patriotic sensibility of a new generation of youth' (ibid. 208). Echoing this logic, I would argue that a 'preventive counter-revolution' culminated in the 'velvet occupation' of Crimea in 2014. Domestic counter-revolution was thus exported into Russia's neighbourhood, posing a significant challenge to the existing international order.

Ironically, as Lilia Shevtsova notes, 'the Kremlin's efforts to keep things the same at home—to prop up the personalized system of power and the domestic status quo—have turned Russia into a revisionist power abroad' (2015: 173). Just as the Russian preventive counter-revolution employed tools strikingly similar to those used by the 'velvet' revolutionaries of 1989 and the 'coloured revolutions' which followed, the Russian invasion of Crimea mimicked, or even 'satirized' the West and its past justifications of various humanitarian interventions, particularly the NATO-led invasion of Kosovo (Dunn and Bobick 2014: 405).

Putin's strategy has not been without success. It is revealing in this context that the leaders of the 2014 'Umbrella movement' in Hong Kong, which displayed striking similarities to non-violent revolutionary movements elsewhere, including in Ukraine, felt obliged to distance themselves from the legacy of the coloured revolutions. In an open letter to President Xi Jinping, the student leaders stressed that their movement 'is definitely not a colour revolution or its alike [sic], but rather a movement for democracy' (*South China Morning Post*, 11 October 2014). This marks a partial propaganda victory for the enemies of democratisation in Moscow and Beijing. The Russian critique of coloured revolutions has found keen followers amongst Chinese communist ideologists (Chuanjia et al.: 2012; compare Gore 2014: 217), who claimed that the Umbrella movement as well as the 2019 mass protests were simply instruments of foreign domination, particularly by the United States. As the official Chinese Communist Party newspaper, the *People's Daily*, commented:

> The results of America's 'Color Revolutions' have hardly been a success. The 'Arab spring' turned to be an 'Arab winter' and

Ukraine's 'street politics' have resulted in secession and conflict. There is little evidence of any real democracy in these countries, but the US turns a blind eye. (Yiwen 2014)

Seven years later—*after* Hong Kong's democratic movement had been largely defeated—*Global Times* continued to warn against 'West-backed color revolution', which was viewed as 'a "top threat" to China's national, political security' (Sheng and Qingqing: 2021). The article cites an expert from the Chinese Academy of Social Sciences, who proposed that China and Russia cooperate in their fight against the colour revolutions, 'not just [to] protect themselves but also safeguard regional peace and stability' (ibid.). Russian Foreign Minister Lavrov, for his part, appealed to those 'clearheaded politicians in Europe and America' who realise that they must be pragmatic in dealing with China and Russia, 'recognising that the world has more than just one civilisation' (Lavrov 2021). Without spelling it out, what Chinese and Russian leaders advocate and desire is a world of Schmittian *Grossräume*, dominated by major powers like themselves.

Not surprisingly, this is also the world that the nations of Central Europe seek to avoid, concerned as they are about having their legitimate fears ignored. Poles in particular are reminded of the infamous Hitler-Stalin Pact of 1939, which facilitated both Nazi and Soviet imperial projects. This non-aggression agreement included a secret protocol which envisaged the division of Central and Eastern Europe (including the Baltic states) between German and Soviet spheres of influence. It is well known that the Second World War in Europe started on 1 September 1939 with Germany's invasion of Poland. A lesser-known aspect of that story is the fact that on 17 September 1939, Poland was also invaded from the East by Soviet troops. The pact paved the way also for the annexation of the Baltic republics of Latvia, Lithuania and Estonia in 1940. To be sure, the conservative Polish government led by the Law and Justice Party (PiS, Prawo i Sprawiedliwość) instrumentalised these historic traumas when it repeatedly criticised Germany for its conciliatory approach to Russia. Yet, the Polish government's argument that Nord Stream was a trap through which Putin aimed to co-opt Germany must have resonated across the EU's new member states and their Eastern neighbours. In response to a Franco-German initiative in June 2021 to reopen EU-Russia consultations, Polish Foreign Minister Zbigniew Rau warned that 'along with Nord Stream gas, Germany is expected to import Russia's idea of the Concert of Powers and its kleptocratic model of development, based on an interdependence between the worlds of politics, business and crime'.

By contrast, in an unusual speech at the height of the eurozone crisis in 2011, the then Polish Foreign Minister Radek Sikorski suggested that he was more fearful of Germany's refusal to lead Europe than of its dominance. Yet, if Sikorski was right to criticise Germany's inaction, no less problematic has been the more recent tendency of the German government to present its actions as apolitical. Facing criticism for the Nord Stream 2 project from the US, as well as a number of EU countries including France, Poland and the Baltic states, the then German Chancellor Merkel, speaking at the Munich Security Conference in February 2019, defended the project by stating the obvious: 'a Russian gas molecule is a Russian gas molecule, whether it comes via Ukraine or via the Baltic Sea' (Merkel 2019). It is against this background that Zbigniew Rau wrote that unlike his liberal predecessor Sikorski, he was 'more afraid of Germany's lack of responsibility' for its actions than its inaction.

In a rather bizarre twist, it was up to the former German Chancellor-turned-lobbyist, Gerhard Schröder, to speak the language of geopolitics. Schröder was invited by a parliamentary committee of the German Bundestag in July 2020 to testify as one of the 'expert witnesses' in response to sanctions imposed on Nord Stream 2 by the Trump-led US administration. The parliamentary hearing under the heading, 'Securing the German and European Sovereignty in Energy Policy (Nord Stream 2)', enabled Schröder to allege that the US was merely pursuing its own economic interests as it sought to boost sales of liquefied natural gas to Europe. All the while, he ignored his own obvious conflict of interest: Schröder is well known to be close to Putin, and cannot be an impartial witness considering his role as chairman of the board of Nord Stream and the Russian energy giant Rosneft. Repeated calls for Schröder to resign all his posts in Russia, which intensified after Navalny's poisoning in August 2020, remained unheeded.

While the German government found it harder in the wake of the Navalny affair to maintain the fiction that Nord Stream 2 merely represented a 'commercial project' (Shagina 2021: 4), its efforts to keep politics out of energy policy proved remarkably successful. This was echoed by the EU Commission's strategy, praised as being 'conducive to the depoliticisation of the EU-Russian energy relations' (Siddi 2018: 1568), though even EU-sympathetic observers acknowledged it largely failed in pursuit of its geopolitical interests. This is not to deny that economic sanctions have their own limitations in relation to both allies and adversaries. In particular, the US effort to stop the completion of the pipeline by putting its West European allies under economic pressure has proved counterproductive in the past. Towards the end of the Cold War, a young US analyst argued this point in an examination of the German-Soviet partnership that led to the construction of the Druzhba oil pipeline in the 1960s (Blinken 1987; Shagina 2021). When this analyst, Antony Blinken, author of *Ally versus Ally: America, Europe, and the Siberian Pipeline Crisis*, became Secretary of State in a Biden administration keen to improve its relationship with both Germany and the EU, the US largely abandoned its opposition to Nord Stream 2. Nevertheless, this did little to ease the tension over the pipeline within the EU.

EU's Machiavellian Moments or the Rise and Fall of Merkiavelli

The aim of this chapter has been to assess the EU's ability to act as a global actor, and to question whether it is living up to its own rhetoric about strategic autonomy and European sovereignty. Focusing on the challenges posed by a more assertive Russia and its relationship with Ukraine and Belarus, we have seen that the EU's rhetoric was seldom matched by its action. Like its reluctant hegemon, Germany, Europe too was partly paralysed by its own reticence to think in terms of geopolitics and power. The EU wanted to 'be a force of normative attraction for its neighbours while at the same time denying that it thereby projects power' (Middelaar 2016: 499), an act of self-denial that has become increasingly untenable. To be sure, this basic insight is ever more widely acknowledged, including by key EU actors. Josep Borrell, the EU's High Representative for Foreign Affairs and Security Policy, has stressed time and again that 'Europe must learn quickly to speak the language of power, and not only rely on soft power' (Weiler 2020). What is less clear is how credible that language can ever be without the means of projecting power (Lau and Topçu 2021). Without a European demos there can be no European army, and without the possibility of a credible threat of military force, there is little the EU can do when confronting actors like Putin's Russia, which do not hesitate to resort to violence in pursuit of their aims.

On numerous occasions—the collapse of communism, the global financial crisis, the refugee crisis, the crisis of the EU-Russia relationship and, more recently, the rise of Trump and Brexit in 2016—an acute sense of vulnerability was meant to have woken Europe 'from its geopolitical slumber' (Middelaar 2013: 183). According to Middelaar, these were 'Machiavellian moments'—that is, turning points—when 'a people becomes conscious of a state's mortality and takes hold of its fate by turning to face the future' (ibid. 86). Middelaar was far from denying the existence of the *peoples* of Europe (rather than *a* people) and their ever more fraught relationship with the Union, but he assumed that adversity would force EU leaders at both the national and supranational level to embrace 'the politics of events', which would ultimately turn the EU into a truly *political* community. This has failed to materialise. Instead, one could say that an acute sense of vulnerability drove the actions of a national leader, who was fearful for her own political survival. This takes us back to the peculiar leadership style of Angela Merkel, whom the late German sociologist Ulrich Beck ridiculed as 'Merkiavelli'. While the German Chancellor was 'widely regarded as the uncrowned queen of Europe' (Beck 2012: 47), Merkel's political decisions were, as discussed in previous chapters, rather erratic and driven more often than not by her desire to follow the ever changing mood of the German electorate (Alexander 2017) rather than by wider strategic considerations. Yet, once again, this is not just about Merkel, however impactful her chancellorship has been both on Germany and Europe. Merkel's approach both reflected and reinforced the EU's preference for depoliticisation, leading to suboptimal policy decisions which were justified alternately by the rhetoric of necessity and the politics of the exception. Evaluating her legacy, Wolfgang Münchau (2021) was unsparing, writing that what she bequeathed to posterity was 'a recognition that "Europe" as a political entity—the idea of European strategic autonomy—has been tried and that it failed'.

The European Union was meant to become more than just the sum of its member states. Yet, in a number of important areas it is less than some of its individual members might have been. Paradoxically, Europe at times appears to weaken both the capacity and resoluteness of its members states, while it remains unable to reconstitute that power at the European level. What Europe needs is a more hard-nosed realist approach, which recognises that Russian expansionist ambitions can only be constrained by its own readiness and willingness to deploy power both politically and, if it is necessary, even militarily. In the absence of the EU's supranational capacity to perform such tasks, individual member states, including Germany and France, could and should do more.

Concluding Remarks

This seems a fitting description of contemporary Russia:

> Europe 'lives under the gaze of the more radical brother ...' The Russians are the new 'ascetics' who are willing to forgo the 'comfort' of the present for control of the future. They will dominate their own nature for the sake of dominating external nature in others. If European intellectuals continue to indulge their passively aesthetic enrapture with the status quo, they abdicate their duty and privilege to lead, and they invite domination by their more radical brother. (McCormick 2003: 137)

Though economic sanctions have had a serious impact on Russia's economy, this is not reflected in any decline in the popularity of its political leaders. If anything, people appear to have rallied around Putin in defiance of Western pressure. Conversely, not just European intellectuals but political leaders too have failed to pay enough attention to the most serious challenge to Europe's peace since the end of the Cold War. Yet the passage above is John P. McCormick's summary of Schmitt's application of his *Grossraum* theory to 'Central Europe as Anti-Russia', not his musings about contemporary Europe. Consistent with previous chapters, I am not arguing in favour of the EU becoming a Schmittian *Grossraum*. This would simply reverse the argumentative strategy of the Russian proponents of Eurasia, feeding into Dugin's ideal of continental Europe being divided into German and Russian spheres of influence. In fact, this is one of the reasons why any talk about Russia being 'promised' by Germany (and the West in general) that NATO would not expand eastwards must be questioned. As Mark Kramer demonstrated, the claims made about such an undertaking are based on conflicting accounts of negotiations leading up to German unification in 1990, at a time when 'NATO expansion was simply not even an issue' (2009: 47). But even if such an agreement had been made (as a number of more recent studies have indeed argued, e.g., Trachtenberg 2021), the idea that Germany and Russia would agree on what sovereign nations in Central and Eastern Europe are to do for decades to come in terms of their choice of alliances is misguided. Such an undertaking would have been illegitimate.[11]

Going back to Ukraine's position between Europe and Russia: it seems at times that the few people in the West, particularly in Germany, who think in geopolitical terms are those who defend Putin and his aspiration to imperial greatness. Gerhard Schröder exemplifies this attitude, but there have also been a number of journalists and academics outside Germany echoing Russian propaganda claims. Tariq Ali decried 'the recent demonisation of Putin' (2015), claiming that 'the hatred of Russia now [...] is related to the fact that the Russian government has taken back its sovereignty' (2021); John Mearsheimer (2014) deplored 'the liberal delusions that provoked Putin'; and Richard Sakwa argued that the conflict in Ukraine 'rests on the consciences of the current generation of Atlantic and Eastern European leaders', which by 'demonizing' and 'encircling Russia' caused 'a mimetic cold war' (2015: 248, 6, 4, 5). These and similar accounts deny agency not just to the Ukrainian people who were at the heart of the Maidan movement, but also to the political leaders in Moscow.

What I advocate here is a more muscular liberalism that can stand up to Putin's Russia. Generations of European intellectuals, from Jean-Jacques Rousseau to Jürgen Habermas, conjured the possibility of a world in which all conflicts might be solved by communicative rationality. The EU is meant to have embodied these ideas. But we do not live in such a world. This is why Europeans, too, need to think of their values and interests in a more traditional way. In response to Russia's geopolitical ambitions, Europe needs more than the mere rhetoric of the EU's 'geopolitical' Commission; it needs its own geopolitics, as is increasingly recognised even by its Foreign Policy chief, Borrell (cited in Weiler 2020). To start with, however, EU leaders need a realistic assessment of their combined ability to project power, both soft *and* hard.

There is a fundamental difference between Putin's Eurasian Union and the European Union, that is worth restating. While the former aims to subjugate other nations, the latter is meant to enable them to pursue self-government. That is the Europe for which the Ukrainian demonstrators fought, the Europe to which the velvet revolutionaries of 1989 aspired. Europe needs to live up to the challenge of Putinism if its project is to survive. Which brings us to one important aspect of Schmitt's *Grossraum* concept that is worth pondering: the idea that no political project is sustainable without a set of underlying values and convictions. As I will discuss in the next chapter, the EU has struggled to live up to its values even within its own borders, and a number of new member states are now flirting with Putin's authoritarian methods domestically. The absence of the rule of law in Russia underlines the importance of the ongoing struggle against the erosion of the rule of law in Europe, both at national and European levels. This brings us back to Hungary and the new member states in Central and Eastern Europe, where populist rebellions were sustained by a strange complementarity between the EU bureaucracy and aspiring autocrats at the national level, like Viktor Orbán.

A SOVEREIGNIST EUROPE?

REBELLIONS FROM WITHIN AND WITHOUT

*I stand here now and defend my homeland, because to Hungarians
freedom, democracy, independence and Europe are matters of
honour. ... Hungary's decisions are made by the voters in
parliamentary elections. What you are claiming is no less than
saying that the Hungarian people are not sufficiently capable
of being trusted to judge what is in their own interests. You think
that you know the needs of the Hungarian people better than the
Hungarian people themselves.*

Viktor Orbán, The European Parliament,
11 September 2018

Why do Germans think they can teach Poles what democracy is?

Wolfgang Schäuble, *Politico*, 24 June 2021

The birth of a new European order started with a burial. The date 16
June 1989 was a turning point in Hungarian, Central European and
even broader European history. Thirty-one years after his execution,
Imre Nagy, the leader of the 1956 Hungarian Uprising, was put to
rest in a solemn ceremony. Nagy was executed in 1958 in the name

of the communist ideology he served. But by 1989, communism was being buried both as an ideology and a political regime in the name of the liberal democratic ideals that had defined the nineteenth-century 'Springtime of Nations'. At Heroes' Square in Budapest, a largely unknown student leader addressed a gathering of 100,000 people. He called upon the best aspects of 1848 to imagine a better future:

> Since the beginning of the Russian occupation and the communist dictatorship 40 years ago, Hungarian people once had an opportunity, once had adequate courage and strength to attempt to reach the objectives articulated in 1848: national independence and political freedom. To this day our goals have not changed, today we still have not relented on '48, just as we have not relented on '56 either. (Orbán [1989] 2013)

'I could see a dictatorship blowing up in front of my eyes', said Adam Michnik, a Polish dissident journalist who was there that day, commenting three decades later (Hopkins 2019). The student leader of the Alliance of Young Democrats (Fidesz) was, of course, none other than Viktor Orbán, whose personal transformation over the following decades has shaped and reflected the changing nature of Hungarian politics and society. The uprising of 1956 was led by an old communist, Nagy, who morphed into a liberal of sorts. By contrast, 1989 was (partly) led by Orbán, a charismatic young liberal who, within a few decades, would become synonymous with Central European illiberal rebellions. What many observers who are surprised by Orbán's transformation tend to overlook is the fact that most Hungarians, just like their counterparts in Poland and the former Czechoslovakia, saw their fight against communism also as national liberation. Ideologically, Michnik and Orbán were as far apart from each other in 2019 as Orbán was from Hungary's communist leaders in 1989. Yet, while Michnik's liberal political creed struggles to garner enough electoral support in Poland, Orbán remains one of the most popular and longest-lasting politicians in Hungary. Orbán's political transformation thus also reflects changes in European societies more generally.

With only some exaggeration, we could say we are all Central Europeans now. And not in a good way. In the midst of the eurozone crisis that affected the countries on Europe's periphery particularly badly, a historian of post-1989 Europe asked a pertinent question: 'Are the southern countries of the European Union taking the place of the East?' (Ther 2017: 237). The populist parties gaining ground in Italy and other parts of Southern Europe over the last decade or so appear to follow similar agendas to those pioneered by Fidesz before them. And just as the eurozone crisis proved a catalyst for anti-establishment parties in the West, so the global financial crisis of 2008–9 paved the way for Orbán to solidify his rule with his provocative programme of 'illiberal democracy'. As discussed in the previous chapter, Surkov boasted that Putinism was the ideology of the future, pointing at the rise of Donald Trump in the US and the Brexit vote in the UK. This was Russia—a country outside of the EU, and to some extent even positioning itself as being in opposition to Europe. More disturbingly, Orbán has become 'the poster child of conservative illiberalism' (Rone 2021: 4) from within Europe. As Ivan Krastev and Stephen Holmes (2019: 44–45) noted, Orbán used to be seen as Europe's past, yet increasingly he seems to be pointing towards Europe's future.

Revealing in this respect is the appeal Orbán's confrontational style has outside of Hungary. In Bulgaria, for example, parties across the political spectrum seek to outdo each other in their rhetorical support for Orbán's policies, all the while attempting to maintain the appearance of being 'good Europeans' in Brussels. The former Slovak Prime Minister Róbert Fico (2006–10 and 2012–18) too had positioned himself as a moderate, pro-European Social Democrat when in Brussels, while often resorting to more extreme nationalist rhetoric at home. Not surprisingly then, Fico did not hesitate to embrace Orbán's agendas when he judged them beneficial to his own popular appeal, as happened, for example, in the midst of the 2015 migration crisis. It was also in 2015 that the Deputy Prime Minister of the Czech Republic, Andrej Babiš (he became Prime Minister in December 2017) supported Orbán's position on migration, in contrast to his normally agreeable position towards Brussels. Conversely, in Poland the leader of the Law and Justice Party, Jarosław Kaczyński, has been defending Orbán so consistently that he vowed to wage a 'cultural counter-revolution' with his Hungarian ally to transform the EU (Foy and Buckley 2016). This is a field in which neither the EU nor the Hungarian-Polish coalition is likely to prevail. However, the conflict is bound to benefit the conservative leaders in Central Europe, rather than enhancing Europe's unity and its progressive ideals. Their carefully staged defiance of the EU's alleged power grab enables them to downplay their own power ambitions. Populists remain popular not despite being under constant attack, but because of it. Across Europe, populist leaders on the right and the left have positioned themselves as the true defenders of national interests against faceless bureaucrats in Brussels, technocrats at the European Central Bank in Frankfurt, or judges in Luxembourg. Yet, not so long ago, defending one's nation was a liberal cause.

From the Habsburg Empire to the EU Empire and Beyond

'Truly, if there had not long been an Austrian state, we should need to act swiftly, in the interest of Europe, indeed of humanity itself, to create it' (cited in Evans 2020: 288). In April 1848, the Czech historian and nationalist leader František Palacký, writing in German, praised an Austrian state that was to perish seven decades later. Franz Palacký (as he was addressed by his German counterparts) wrote in response to an invitation issued to him by liberals preparing a constituent assembly in Frankfurt that was to give rise to a viable political programme for a modern 'Greater German' state, of which Czechs would be a respected minority. Instead, Palacký's 'Letter to Frankfurt' provided the Czech national movement with an alternative political programme, which remained a source of inspiration even for the founding father of the First Czechoslovak Republic, Tomáš Garrigue Masaryk.

Both the German and the Czech liberal revolutions of the mid-nineteenth century failed, but the lessons drawn from these failures were strikingly different, foreshadowing divisions that have shaped European politics to this day. The failure of a liberal revolution in Germany greatly diminished the credibility of a *liberal* nationalism in Germany—a trend that was further reinforced through the rise of Nazism and from which Germany's political culture arguably never fully recovered.[1] By contrast, in the case of Czechoslovakia,

1848 foreshadowed the possibility of Czech (and Slovak) liberal nationalism(s).

The Habsburg Empire fell apart as a result of the upheavals of the First World War, but its end was a long time coming owing to numerous challenges from within. Once the multi-ethnic Austrian state was perceived by its many peoples as a 'prison of nations', its demise seemed preordained. Yet, it could have been otherwise. In fact, more than a century later, the causes of the fall of the Habsburg Monarchy remain open to contestation. At the heart of this is 'an apparent paradox: that the rule of the Habsburgs was destroyed by its chief beneficiaries' (Evans 2020: 271). Can the European Union succeed where Austria failed? On one view, yes it can: not by being more ambitious than the Habsburg rulers once were, but by embracing its incomplete, imperfect, in-between state:

> If there is one thing Europeans can learn from the Habsburg empire, it is probably that they should accept the EU more as it is. … Federalists are constantly disappointed that the EU is not powerful enough. Nationalists, by contrast, portray it as a superstate that is too powerful. Both camps are permanently disappointed and impossible to please. Instead of dreaming of an EU they will never get, Europeans should learn to accept that *fortwursteln* ('muddling through') is in the European DNA. (De Gruyter 2021)

'*Fortwursteln*' will not do. As we have seen in previous chapters, the EU as a halfway house has served Europeans fairly well in good times, but far less so in times of crisis. Does it follow that the European Union must become an empire in order to protect its core values from enemies without *and* within? If Jan Zielonka (2006) imagined Europe as a kind of post-modern 'neo-medieval empire' with fuzzy borders and a great degree of heterogeneity, the French Finance Minister Bruno Le Maire's recent call for Europe's 'New Empire' is decisively more ambitious, modern and thus also homogenising: 'Europe must be a political project with values and a culture. It must have borders, ambitions, strength and the capacity to defend its interests' (Le Maire cited in Ellison 2019). While Zielonka praised the EU's polycentric system of governance, Le Maire calls for the abolition of the requirement for unanimity, demanding, in other words, that the EU becomes more like a federation. Echoing this, Glyn Morgan is refreshingly honest in defending a mild version of imperialism. He argues in favour of 'imperialism in the fifth degree', which shuns the idea of the periphery being dominated by the more powerful centre against its will, but embraces an EU in which 'the Centre forces the abolition of all cultural practices incompatible with freedom and equality *as the Centre understands those terms*' (Morgan 2020: 1428; my emphasis).

This approach is misguided both normatively and practically. Far from serving as 'a reminder of the EU's liberal character and its inability to accommodate illiberal nationalism' (Morgan 2020: 1432), it undermines its democratic credentials and erodes the basis for liberal nationalism in Europe. For the question that remains unresolved is this: what legitimacy does 'the Centre' have to decide how those basic values—freedom and equality—are to be understood? And who is to be 'the Centre' anyway, France and/or Germany? Or, moving away from nations, should it fall to the European Commission and European Courts to define what constitute the basic values underpinning a 'European Superstate' (Morgan 2009)? This would be deeply problematic. The very idea of a European superstate has unwittingly advanced the political agenda of anti-liberal forces across Europe, rather than weakening them. As we shall see, the EU's recent attempts at disciplining member states have proved self-defeating. One problem with these attempts is that they are easily rebutted as acts of neocolonisation. In the eyes of their many supporters, the populist rebels against 'the Centre' were redolent of the nineteenth-century resistance to a 'greater German state', or the more general threat of a 'universal monarchy'.

Central Europe between 1848 and 1989

Palacký viewed Austria as a natural protector of Europe's small peoples against the threat of an autocratic Russia, which appeared destined to become a 'universal monarchy' (Connelly 2020: 172). This is an important aspect of Habsburg rule, which is being rediscovered by those historians and commentators who view the surprisingly progressive features of the Empire at the turn of the twentieth century as prefiguring a viable alternative to the world of nation states. While it might be a stretch to think of what was by then the dual monarchy of Austria-Hungary as a predecessor of the EU, its track record tended to be far better than many nationalist histories written after its collapse were willing to acknowledge:

> Stretching from today's western Ukraine to Switzerland and from the Czech Republic's northern border with Germany down Croatia's Adriatic coast, the Austro-Hungarian monarchy had no internal borders, one currency, two parliaments (in Vienna and Budapest), 11 officially recognized peoples/languages and almost as many religions, including Yiddish-speaking Jews, Bosnian Muslims and a variety of Orthodox Christians and Protestants to complement its Catholic majority. (Miller-Melamed and Morelon 2019)

Indeed, the turbulent history that followed the fall of the Habsburg Empire vindicated Palacký's fears. However messy—and at times violent—the history of Europe's 'most lovable' (Kumar 2017: 145) empire was, the destruction caused by the twentieth-century expansions of first the Nazi and then the Soviet empires was far worse. There are two interconnected ways in which Palacký's diagnosis proved prescient.

First, the Wilsonian ideal of national self-determination that aimed to create a Europe of self-governing nations proved ill-suited for a region in which the very question of who constituted a nation was unresolved and appeared unresolvable. Even US President Woodrow Wilson himself would come to admit the challenge (and his own ignorance), once exclaiming, 'Why, Masaryk never told me that!' when informed about the large number of minorities to be included in the future Czechoslovak state (MacMillan 2002: 237). Yet Wilson's concept of self-determination must be seen alongside his other vision, the League of Nations, which he hoped would provide the framework within which international politics, including the adjudication of disputes over self-determination, would be conducted. In combination, these two elements helped form a watershed moment for the emerging international order and its central tenet—sovereignty. In fact, the Paris Peace Conference of 1919 that was to turn Wilson's democratic ideal into a political reality led not merely to a transformation of Europe, but altered also the very term sovereignty. Sovereignty was not 'a solved historical problem' offering solutions for the riddles created by the collapse of the old order, argues Leonard V. Smith (2018: 3). Rather, the sovereigns in Paris in 1919 were 'those who decided upon not just the answers but also the questions of the international order' (ibid. 8). Chief amongst these questions was that of sovereign statehood in relation to the principle of *national* self-determination: who decides on whose rules rule over whom?

The creation of the First Czechoslovak Republic is a case in point. Masaryk himself served briefly as a member of the Austrian Reichsrat, and initially merely advocated a greater degree of autonomy for Czechs and other Slavic nations *within* Austria-Hungary, but later felt compelled to fight for Czech and Slovak independence. With significant US support, Czechoslovakia was established in October 1918 as a quasi-nation state, all the while inheriting a mind-bogglingly complex ethnic composition that replicated the problems of the empire from whose collapse it emerged. To achieve a clear numerical majority of Czechs (particularly against Germans, the second largest nationality) the fiction of a Czechoslovak nation was pursued, in which Czechs and Slovaks were declared two brotherly tribes of one state-founding nation. The promise of minority rights for Germans, Hungarians and other smaller ethnic groups, which were to be monitored and supervised by the League of Nations, did not prevent grievances, which would in turn greatly contribute to the destruction of the First Republic by Nazi Germany two decades later.

Hungary, by contrast, achieved a far greater degree of ethnic homogeneity, but at the expense of losing two thirds of its territory and almost the same proportion of its population (even if not all of them would have considered themselves Hungarians). This stoked resentments for a long time to come. Though claims about the contemporary resurgence of Hungarian irredentism tend to be overstated, as there is no significant political force in Hungary aiming to change the present borders, a century after the Treaty of Trianon Orbán continues to capitalise on lingering resentment against the post-First World War settlement that made Hungary, alongside Germany, a major loser. For Poland, on the other hand, the end of the First World War brought about the restoration of the Republic, bringing to an end the partition of the country between Austria, Prussia and Russia which had lasted for more than a century. Yet even Poland, like Czechoslovakia, struggled to find an adequate accommodation for its ethnically diverse people, as reflected in competing conceptions of the Polish nation—ethnocentric and chauvinist on the one hand, versus open-ended and inclusive on the other.[2]

Second, the newly created small nations of Central Europe proved easy prey to imperial ambitions on both their Eastern and Western borders, located as they were between Prussia and Russia in Palacký's time, and between Nazi Germany and the Soviet Union before and during the Second World War. If the League of Nations had originally been intended as a way to prevent future war, the American failure to join quickly rendered it irrelevant to the security needs of the new Central European states. Instead, as Palacký once feared, it was the region's unenviable location between its powerful neighbours, East and West, which determined its fate. This is what the Czech writer and intellectual Milan Kundera later described as the 'Tragedy of Central Europe' (1984), in an essay that was to frame discussions about the region for decades to come. In Kundera's view, the nations of Central Europe had been 'kidnapped' by imperialist Russia—a tragic accident of history which had removed them from the West. Kundera cited Palacký's warning about 'a Russian universal monarchy [which] would be an immense and indescribable disaster' (1984: 33) and presented it as directly applicable to the menace of Soviet domination. What was particularly disturbing for the Czech writer was the fact that few people in Western Europe seemed to care much about it. The West forgot about its 'kidnapped' part in the middle of the continent, Kundera argued, because the West had lost itself, forgetting its true identity. This identity was based on a commitment to democracy and the diversity displayed in Europe as 'the greatest variety within the smallest space'. This was in stark contrast to 'a Russia founded on the opposite principle: the smallest variety within the greatest space' (ibid. 33). Soviet-style communism, on this reading, was something utterly alien to the nations of Central Europe, all the while corresponding perfectly well with the logic of Russian history.

If Kundera was concerned about the West 'forgetting' the nations of Central Europe, more recently these nations appear to be at the centre of everybody's attention, albeit mostly as targets of criticism for betraying the very European values that they claimed as their own during the 1989 Velvet Revolutions. To be sure, Kundera's was an idealised vision of Central Europe, and it was not free of anti-Russian sentiments which went beyond its core anti-colonial argument. Yet, some of the key points which Kundera made then have gained relevance since 1989. First, Kundera astutely identified the existential anxiety common to all small nations 'whose very existence may be put in question at any moment' (1984: 35). This is the reason that people in Central Europe are particularly sensitive to the prospect of foreign domination. Even Poland, though numerically fairly large by European standards, can be viewed as a small nation in this way. As Kundera put it, 'a small nation can disappear and it knows it' (ibid.). Second, and related to the first point, people in Central Europe do not see a major contradiction between the fight for liberty and the nation. Kundera's dramatic opening of his seminal essay offers an excellent illustration of this. In it he recalls the Soviet invasion of Hungary in November 1956, in response to which the director of the Hungarian News Agency sent out what was to become his last message: 'We are going to die for Hungary and for Europe.' What did this statement mean, Kundera asked, 'In what sense was Europe in danger?' Clearly, there was no imminent danger of a Soviet invasion of Western Europe. What the director meant, Kundera wrote, was that 'the Russians, in attacking Hungary, were attacking Europe itself. He was ready to die so that Hungary might remain Hungary and European' (ibid. 33). Perhaps even more so than the Springtime of Nations in 1848, this was a liberal revolution for Hungary *and* Europe.[3] And while it failed in 1956, its aims appeared to have been vindicated in 1989.

Liberal Nationalism in Central Europe and its Limitations

The problem to which neither the Habsburg rulers nor their liberal democratic opponents found an adequate solution was how to accommodate ethnic diversity (Connelly 2020: 172). In this crucial respect, Hungarian and Czech liberals were hardly any better than their German counterparts in the mid-nineteenth century. For example, some of the key leaders of the Hungarian Uprising of 1848 showed little sympathy towards the calls for national emancipation of the Slavic nations of the empire, expecting instead that their full assimilation would benefit them and Hungary. 'A great Hungary', Lajos Kossuth believed, 'would benefit all the inhabitants of the lands of the Crown of St. Stephen and contribute to peace, progress, and liberty in Europe' (Deák 1976: 48). This was not convincing to many Slovaks and other smaller nationalities who faced forced assimilation, and they still recall that part of their history very differently from Hungarians. Yet, the experience the nations of Central Europe had in 1989 was rather different. By then, perhaps even more so than in the nineteenth century, their fight for liberty was also a fight for the nation, and thus nationalism no longer appeared to be inimical to liberalism. This is why far fewer people there are attracted to an ideology of 'Europeanism' advocating a 'postnational Europe', which for many intellectuals remains 'the last remaining utopia' (Speck 2006: 243). If Europe as a political project is to resonate outside of Germany, it needs to be conceptualised as one derived from—and being conducive to—liberal nationalism.

Kundera's description of the Hungarian News Agency director's willingness to sacrifice himself for a Hungary that 'might remain Hungary *and* European' can be seen as a concise articulation of the basic premise of liberal nationalism. Europe, in this formulation, stands for freedom from foreign domination. Thus, far from hindering the aims of European integration, such a sentiment would make it viable. In a similar way, in the Czech (and Czechoslovak) context, the first post-communist president, Václav Havel, stressed time and again Masaryk's famous dictum that '*věc česká je věc lidská*', that is, that the Czech concern must be a universal human concern. This was accompanied by Havel's insistence that communism was ultimately defeated in the realm of ideas. 'Truth prevailed' in 1989, Havel believed, vindicating the motto of the First Czechoslovak Republic adopted by Masaryk, which the Czech Republic maintains as one of the symbols of statehood to this day. Havel popularised the notion at the time of the Velvet Revolution with his campaign slogan, 'Love and truth conquer lies and hatred' (Holy 1996: 40). Masaryk's legacy resonated particularly in the early stages of the Velvet Revolution, including in the fluid way the founder of the First Republic conceptualised, or even embodied, Czechoslovak identity.[4]

In his attempt to restore 'voices to historical actors who have hitherto been denied the power to speak', James Krapfl marshalled rich historical evidence demonstrating that the *demos* in the Czechoslovak democratic revolution of 1989 conceived of itself in a fairly inclusive and open-ended manner (2013: 2). As an activist in a small town in Western Slovakia wrote in a local bulletin in December 1989:

> In unity is strength. We shall be victorious, because we have succeeded in uniting ourselves. It is something magnificent, this feeling of belonging to the nation. Nation? I'm not thinking now just of Czechs and Slovaks, but also of Hungarians, Germans, Ukrainians, Russians, of everyone who has proven capable of coming together for this noble goal: that we might breathe freely in a free and democratic country. (cited in Krapfl 2013: 111)

As grassroots movements from the regions were eclipsed by newly emerging political structures in Prague and Bratislava, which positioned themselves respectively as Czech(-oslovak) and Slovak capitals, the democratic impetus itself was constrained. This unwittingly gave rise to ethnocentric nationalist mobilisation, which first brought about the demise of Czechoslovak unity and later strengthened anti-liberal forces in both republics. Ironically, these new political structures followed the imperial logic of empire, rather than responding to democratic demands.[5] Because of this, they contributed to a general sense of disillusionment that shaped politics for decades to come. As Krapfl observed, 'history has not unfolded the way most citizens of Czechoslovakia expected it would in 1989' (2013: xi). The experience Krapfl describes in his nuanced study of the Czechoslovak 'Revolution with a Human Face' vindicates the warning that the late Polish intellectual Marcin Król directed towards his fellow intellectuals and political leaders over a decade earlier:

> whoever represents a dualistic vision of the world which is dominated either by liberalism, or nationalism is not only wrong about political realities, but causes irreparable damage, because the chances of implementing the liberal democratic project are decreased in direct proportion to the height of the wall which was created between liberalism and nationalism. (Król 1999: 38)

This is not to deny that liberalism and nationalism can be and often *were* opposed to each other. Though nationalist mobilisation was instrumental in the defeat of Nazi Germany, nationalist excesses in the immediate aftermath of the Second World War meant that 'horrific experiences of genocide, ethnic cleansing, and territorial reapportionment' were not yet over (Roshwald 2006: 264). Apart from being morally reprehensible, the forced expulsion of the Germans from Czechoslovakia, for example, seriously undermined attempts at rebuilding democracy there, strengthening the position of the Czechoslovak Communist Party, which supported the principle of collective guilt. Yet, four decades later the situation was rather different. 'It is a sad irony', Aviel Roshwald observes, 'that the successful establishment of liberal democracy in many East European states following the end of the Cold War was to some extent an indirect consequence of these devastating mid-century events, which left many of these countries far more linguistically and culturally homogeneous than before' (2006: 264). Roshwald is right to note that 'pluralistic values, it seems, are much easier to embrace in the absence of diversity' (ibid.). Apart from sizeable Hungarian and Roma populations, there were not many minority nationalities left in Czechoslovakia, while Poland and Hungary were even more ethnically homogeneous. At any rate, the most promising turning point for contemporary political developments in the countries of the former Eastern bloc—with the notable exception of Yugoslavia—were neither the failed liberal revolutions of the long nineteenth century, nor the post-Second World War developments, but the Velvet Revolutions of 1989. They were pursued in the name of a return to Europe. And they appeared to demonstrate the success of non-violent power.

Yet now we need to ask: are these revolutions about to fail too? Were liberals misguided in believing in their success? Is the illiberal backlash irreversible? If not, is it in the power of the European Union to rectify these failures?

Globalists and Nationalists

Reflecting on the legacy of 1989 in Poland a quarter of a century later, Król (2015a) was unsparing: 'We were stupid.' One of Poland's leading political thinkers wondered whether liberals put too much faith in *economic* liberalism, assuming free market capitalism would eventually benefit the many, not just the few. Dissident intellectuals like himself, Król argued, were removed from the vast majority of Polish citizens, and tended to believe that once the main goal— that is, freeing the country from communism—was achieved, the rest would sort itself out. 'At the time, we all thought that it would be great, if Poland were to simply become a Western democracy' (Król 2015b). The liberal intelligentsia in Poland also failed its people by underestimating nationalism's positive potential. 'Fearful of nationalism', Król wrote, 'no attempt was made at that time to rebuild Polish patriotism and the sense of national community' (2015a). What is worse, Król observed, 'patriotism and the national community in today's Poland simply no longer exist. All attempts to restore these forms of social ties have failed. And the new nationalists, at times dangerous and extremely brutal, have not been successful either' (ibid.). Król's diagnosis remains relevant not just to contemporary Poland, but to wherever there is a growing division between the 'Somewheres' and the 'Anywheres' (Goodhart 2017).

Czechoslovak and Czech developments after 1989 are also instructive in this respect, and can be seen as exemplary of similar processes across the new member states. Not unlike in Poland, in the Czech Republic too a divide emerged between the globalists and the nationalists. This Czech societal divide can be mapped onto two distinct aspects of shared national tradition. Assessing contemporary

Czech politics from the perspective of long-term developments, Radek Chlup identified 'two basic mythical perspectives that have been crucial for the Czechs since the 19th century: the "particularist" and the "universalist"' (2020: 179). It is the latter that became dominant in the 1990s, which was very much conducive to the key political agenda of that time—rebuilding democracy and the (re-) integration of the Czech Republic into Western political structures, including NATO and the European Union. The problem, which has exacerbated political polarisation since 1989, is the fact that this perspective was perceived by its proponents as the only one that was valid. Perhaps not entirely without justification, they saw their position 'as inherently rational and morally superior, denouncing illiberal sentiments as irrational and socially disruptive' (Chlup 2020: 180). On this view, people opposing this liberal, universalist position were not merely wrong, they were also morally inferior (compare Tamir 2019: 10). While Masaryk still managed to combine both the particularist and universalist tenets of Czech traditions, intellectuals and liberal political leaders post-1989 have been less successful in doing so.[6] Havel's adaptation of Masaryk's notion that 'the Czech question is either a world question or it is not a question at all', shifted its emphasis increasingly towards the *world*.

This was not much of a problem in the 1990s when many Czechs perceived nationalism as a predisposition that afflicted only less Western nations, and not their own. As the British anthropologist of Czech origin, Ladislav Holy, observed, the prevalent view of nationalism was as 'something that plagues others—Slovaks, Serbs, Croats, and the various nations of the former Soviet Union—but not the Czechs' (1996: 189). However, a decade or so later, as the long-anticipated 'return to the West' appeared to be proceeding far slower than many had expected (Chlup 2020: 193), the accumulated frustration gave rise to political leaders who tapped into a more particularist, ethno-nationalist conception of the Czech nation, which was critical of the European Union and at times even of the Western alliance.[7] This was reflected in the way in which the figurehead of the Velvet Revolution, Václav Havel, was eclipsed by his rival Václav Klaus. Initially working alongside Havel as an architect of economic transformation, Klaus quickly turned himself into a political leader in his own right, recognising the importance of political parties and of clearly defined agendas that would better resonate with voters. He thus both instigated and benefited from a changing popular mood that turned more sceptical of the West in general and of economic liberalism in particular (even though Klaus—a self-declared Thatcherite—was one of its most ardent proponents). With his particular libertarian brand of Euroscepticism, combined with wariness towards Western universalist agendas, Klaus decisively shaped Czech politics, first as Prime Minister (1993–8) and eventually as President, replacing Havel in 2003 and remaining in office for a decade, just like his predecessor. In fact, it was only in the 2000s that Klaus came to represent a more assertive, nationalist agenda, which helped him to obscure his own responsibility for the social dislocation caused by his economic reforms. Klaus successfully positioned himself as someone able and willing to defy any 'international dictate' (Chlup 2020: 192). As a result, 'the blame for the post-revolutionary frustrations was put on Havel rather than on Klaus' (ibid. 193).

The differences between Havel and Klaus, and the politics they represented, are encapsulated in the conflict over the US-led NATO intervention in Kosovo, which was embraced by the former and vehemently rejected by the latter. For Havel, then still President, the situation in Kosovo demanded that 'international law protecting the unique human being must be ranked higher than international law protecting the state' (Havel 1999: 5). While the idea that state sovereignty does not offer murderous regimes blanket immunity for crimes they commit against their own people is neither novel, nor controversial,[8] Havel's reasoning was more expansive and ambitious, and therefore also more problematic from both normative and pragmatic perspectives. For Havel, the wars in Yugoslavia represented a turning point in international relations that exposed the idea of the sovereign nation state as obsolete. Not only was this vision not realised, but the mixed legacy of the Kosovo intervention at least partially vindicated the concerns of realist critics, such as Klaus.

Far from becoming obsolete, as Havel intuited, the concept of national sovereignty was revived through the 1989 collapse of communism and the disintegration of the Soviet Union that followed, resulting in 'the second great wave of national liberation' (Tamir 2019: 18). Progressivist, liberal assumptions, according to which nationalism might have been important in moments of political birth, but would eventually be transcended, giving way to universalism, were proven premature. National sovereignty as a concept proved remarkably resilient, not merely in international relations, but within the European Union, which was meant to have become post-sovereign, serving as a vanguard for a better world to come. The superficial assimilation of the 1989 revolutions to the grand narrative of European unity, touched upon in the previous chapter, generated misunderstandings that continue to divide Europeans within and between EU member states. The lessons drawn from 1989 in Germany and France, for example, were strikingly different from those in Hungary, Poland, the Czech Republic and Slovakia. Notwithstanding the open-ended nature of liberal nationalist strands in the region, the aim of these revolutions was not to abolish borders and nation states. Rather, they were animated by a desire to end ideologically inspired projects that aimed at radical transformation. Nationalism and ethnic particularism should not be ascribed the sole responsibility for all of Europe's many problems, in contrast to supranational ideals that tend to be seen as progressive by definition.

As Gerard Delanty reminds us, creating 'a truly European supra-national civilisation' was also an explicit ambition 'of all fascists from Mosley via Mussolini to Hitler', whose post-historical order 'would both include and transcend the national traditions of the chosen nations' (1995: 112). Thus, not all attempts to assert national sovereignty should be dismissed as illegitimate and retrograde. The practice of democratic self-government has to be acquired locally, and the further it is removed from a particular place, the bigger the challenge is to keep the rule accountable to the people. This lies at the heart of Kant's warnings against the danger of 'a universal monarchy', which Palacký echoed in 1848 and which many people in Central Europe internalised further in the twentieth century. This is not to downplay the numerous threats to democratic governance that exist at local and national levels, including from extreme nationalist mobilisation. The question is how best to address them.

Democratic Backsliding

The continuing erosion of the quality of democracy and the rule of law in the new member states poses an enormous challenge for the EU as whole. This problem is commonly referred to as 'democratic backsliding', which frames the issue in a way that unwittingly contributes to the overall deterioration of democratic accountability at both European and national levels. Backsliding implies a unidirectional movement of history, which is precisely the proposition that ought to be questioned. This is not to deny the general sense of disillusionment that has occurred in the countries of Central and Eastern Europe since 1989. Rather it is to problematise the assumptions that underpin the dominant strand of transition literature—that is, the idea that the nations which had freed themselves from communism had no other choice but to adopt a particular version of free market capitalism and democracy. This is what Timothy Snyder called 'the *politics of inevitability*, a sense that the future is just more of the present, that the laws of progress are known, that there are no alternatives, and therefore nothing really to be done' (2018: 7). Presenting free markets and democracy as the only choice possible has backfired. Moreover, 'the return to Europe', which was a popular slogan of the 1989 revolutions, proved vastly more challenging than most people expected. This added to the sense of frustration caused by economic and political reforms, which led to a widespread sense of dislocation.

Another fallacy that the very notion of 'backsliding' entails is the idea that an accountable, Western-style liberal democratic system was already well established by the time the applicant member states became EU members. This fiction was reinforced by the process of EU enlargement. In the course of acceding to the *acquis communautaire*, the extensive body of pre-existing EU legislation, the applicant states also had to fulfil the 'Copenhagen Criteria'. Of particular importance was the expectation that—by the time of accession—they 'ha[d] achieved the stability of institutions guaranteeing democracy, the rule of law, human rights and the respect for and protection of minorities'. They had not.[9] The extent of corruption and state capture varied from country to country, but these problems predated the collapse of communism and have remained significant everywhere since 2004. Romania, which secured EU membership in 2007, stood out in this respect, with its elites being described as 'looters of the state by appointment of Brussels' (Gallagher 2005: 308) for their ability to raid EU funds for personal enrichment, while mimicking the 'social democratic vision' of their Western counterparts. The former communist elites embraced Europe not because of their commitment to the values it represented, but as a convenient vehicle that allowed them to transform their pre-1989 political privileges into economic ones (Tucker 2015).

The conservative Polish political philosopher Ryszard Legutko, currently an MEP for the Law and Justice Party, captured the mood in post-1989 post-communist societies in his polemical study *Demon in Democracy: Totalitarian Temptations in Free Societies* (2016). The process of gradual disenchantment with a particular version of Western-style democracy started with attempts at imitation:

> As if charmed by powerful but invisible political magicians, the East Europeans immediately succumbed to what they considered to be the imperative of the historical development of Western civilization. The required attitude of a newly liberated nation was not that of creativity, but conformity. ... The more we copied and imitated, the more we were glad of ourselves. Institutions, education, customs, law, media, language, almost everything became all of a sudden imperfect copies of the originals that were in the line of progress ahead of us. (Legutko 2016: 39, 41)

People's revolutions were driven by desires for 'humanity' (Krapfl 2013), 'human dignity' (Legutko 2016: 39) and solidarity. 'The key ideal of the revolution was humanism—no one was supposed to live in fear, be humiliated or be forced to act opportunistically' (Rychetský and Fiala 2014: 2). Yet, a few years later many people felt they had ended up with inferior copies of successful Western models. In fact, the models they followed were themselves not without problems, as Mair's 2013 diagnosis of 'the hollowing of Western democracy' suggested. The superficial adaptation of Western institutions and practices—the process aptly labelled 'Potemkin democratisation' (Ágh 2015)—enabled old elites to reinvent themselves as liberals and 'good Europeans'. This gave rise to a narrative that gained ever more credibility across the region, a narrative which claimed that the 1989 revolutions were stolen by elites. If such claims appear exaggerated, there are legitimate questions to be asked about the legacy of 1989, including whether these 'non-revolutionary revolutions' created pathologies that undermined the legitimacy of the new political orders.

Was there too much 'velvet' in the Velvet Revolutions of 1989? If yes, how is it possible to rectify this problem without betraying the very ideals in the name of which these corrective policies are advanced? EU power and credibility in this realm is rather limited. Having unwittingly assisted the old pre-1989 elites in their transition to become Western-style 'social democrats' and Europhiles—just think of Róbert Fico in Slovakia, Ferenc Gyurcsány in Hungary and Aleksander Kwaśniewski in Poland—the process of 'Europeanisation' has had a more mixed impact on democratic consolidation than is commonly acknowledged. The process has both reinforced certain pathologies and created new ones. The transposition of the EU rules (the *acquis*) privileged technocratic modes of government at the expense of open-ended democratic contestation. It has also resulted in the adoption of the EU's 'economic constitution' (Joerges 2014), which tended to elevate neoliberal principles of economic policy above other concerns. Far from being an impartial instrument to constrain power, law in post-communist societies became a major tool in the hands of political elites, 'safeguarding the vested interests of the political class and of the new capitalist entrepreneurs with political connections' (Czarnota 2019: 53). As they had learned from Marx before 1989, former apparatchiks-turned-capitalists utilised their political capital, transforming it into tangible economic benefits. This contributed to both the erosion of social democracy in Central Europe and the credibility of the European Union. It was particularly social democratic leaders who embraced 'a vision of Europe as a cosmopolitan, business-friendly technocracy' (Mudde 2016: 27), resulting in a strange reversal of roles. While many post-1989 leaders in the first couple of decades tended to be free market liberals who positioned themselves as being on the left, the 2010s witnessed the rise of conservative illiberalism accompanied by social policies that would normally be expected of social democrats. Populist revolts can thus be seen as 'an illiberal democratic response to decades of undemocratic liberal policies' (Mudde 2016: 30).

In this respect, there has been a strange convergence between Central and Eastern Europe and the West. The problem that the EU unwittingly reinforced is one that has characterised the West as a whole for some time: '*undemocratic liberalism*, a system of government in which individual rights are entrenched but too little of government is decided by the ballot box or heeds the welfare of the people' (Tucker 2018: 3). For example, the widespread perception in Poland between 1990 and 2015 was that 'in each election, no matter which party won, there was a continuation of the same economic policy' (Czarnota 2019: 57); and similar tendencies have been observed elsewhere, including in Germany, where the economic policies of both major parties have been converging to such an extent that Christian Democrats and Social Democrats are almost indistinguishable. By contrast, *illiberal democracies* are less concerned with minority rights and individual freedoms but promise—with various degrees of sincerity—to better reflect the will of the people. As a result of this new global constellation, Hungary has gained a preeminent role that defies its small size. The country of 10 million citizens is seen alternatingly as a deterrent—a preview of a possible descent to illiberalism that also threatens Western democracies—or as an example to follow, empowering 'the people' against their alienated, globalist elites.[10]

The global financial crisis (GFC) in 2008 further undermined the neoliberal consensus that had proved so influential in Central and Eastern Europe until then. In Hungary, the crisis benefited the Fidesz party, which comfortably won the April 2010 election. Amongst the first measures of the newly elected government were economic policies pursued in defiance of the International Monetary Fund (IMF) and the EU. As Adam Tooze noted, 'among Fidesz heresies was its refusal to separate the questions of political sovereignty and financial dependence' (2018: 491). Orbán's government, for example, forced foreign banks to share the losses that many ordinary Hungarians suffered as a result of the GFC. Against expectations, these and similar measures worked. Without much assistance from the EU, whose agenda was then dominated by the eurozone crisis, Hungary's economic position improved so much that by the summer of 2013 the government had 'paid off the IMF and asked the Fund to shut its office in Budapest' (Tooze 2018: 492). This has had further geopolitical consequences. Having succeeded in strengthening his country's economic position, Orbán was emboldened to pursue partnerships with Putin's Russia and Xi's China, openly expressing sympathy for their own illiberal regimes. The close links to Putin culminated in 2014 with 'a contract for a new nuclear power plant to be financed and built by Russia in Hungary' (Kovács and Trencsényi 2020: 411), followed by Orbán's government's ambiguous approach towards the Russian invasion of Ukraine. With respect to China, Hungary is one of the very few EU countries to join the 'Belt and Road Initiative', and in 2021 it effectively prevented the EU from taking a firm stance on China's crackdown on Hong Kong (Rohac 2021).

To be sure, the conservative, populist leaders of this new generation are no less corrupt than their predecessors, and their relationship with Europe is even more beset with contradictions. Unlike their predecessors though, they appear more successful in maintaining popular support. This is not to ignore the unsavoury methods employed by them. There is no denying, for example, that leaders like Jarosław Kaczyński and Viktor Orbán did not merely capitalise on grievances but instigated them too, partly by controlling significant segments of the media and resorting to propaganda tools that did not shy away from anti-Semitic tropes. Yet here too, the EU helps them as the target of people's discontent and a lucrative source of funds. While these leaders oppose EU technocracy, domestically they cultivate a form of *technocratic* populism. Exemplary of this trend was the then Czech Prime Minister Andrej Babiš—a Slovak billionaire businessman who presented himself as a passionate defender of Czech interests and a 'man of the people'. Formerly a member of the Czechoslovak Communist Party and a collaborator with its secret police (*Státní bezpečnost*), Babiš promised in the 2017 national elections 'to "make everything better for the ordinary people" by adopting an "expert and business-like" governance style—running "the state as a firm"' (Buštíková and Guasti 2019: 2). Even more than

Klaus, Babiš was Havel's nemesis. The release of a recording in which Babiš mused about the legacy of 1989, saying 'Truth and love … they can go f—k themselves' (ibid.) did nothing to diminish his popularity. While Orbán has benefited from EU grants by channelling them to businesses supportive of his government, amongst the main beneficiaries of EU largesse in the Czech Republic are the companies actually founded and owned by Babiš. This is clearly an area in which the EU could and should act. However, whether the EU Commission audit released in April 2021, which determined that 'Babiš was … in conflict of interest' (Murray 2021), will have the desired effect is questionable. When the European Parliament sought to assert its authority by adopting a resolution to halt EU funding to businesses controlled by Babiš and demanding more decisive steps from the EU Commission, including triggering procedures that would halt all EU finding to the Czech Republic, Babiš deflected the criticism by emphasising national sovereignty. Though this strategy did not pay off in the 9 October 2021 parliamentary elections, which resulted in a narrow defeat for Babiš' governing coalition, 'the Czech Republic's political turnaround isn't liberal victory' (Ditrych 2021).

While Babiš' electoral failure augurs well for the end of his particular brand of technocratic populism, it is worth noting that the new Prime Minister of the Czech Republic, Petr Fiala, has expressed sympathies for Orbán's policies in the past,[11] and his Civic Democratic Party, founded by Klaus, sits with Kaczyński's Law and Justice Party in the European Parliament. Like Klaus before him, Fiala is rather sceptical towards the European Union, especially with respect to its more progressivist, supranational ambitions. In particular, Fiala sees the role of the kind of conservative politics he advocates as being to 'reverse the current deleterious trend, which leads to weak states being dissolved in international structures' (Fiala and Mikš 2019: 133).[12] Prior to becoming Prime Minister, as a political scientist and prolific author Fiala argued against a further deepening of European integration, attributing to it the erosion of democracy (Fiala 2010: 114). Not unlike Orbán and Kaczyński, Fiala is also an unapologetic defender of the traditional family and opposed to LGBT agendas (Fiala and Mikš 2019)—a position that has far stronger popular resonance across Central and Eastern Europe than in the West.

If the EU struggles to exercise its power in a field where its authority should be self-evident—the integrity of the single market and the provision of EU funds—it finds it all the more difficult to do so in the realm of values (Furedi 2018).

European Cultural Wars and the Struggle for the Rule of Law

Conflict over values between the EU's new and old member states is fundamental because it concerns the very essence of the European project. No political project can survive without normative foundations. Yet, widespread rhetoric about the importance of European values notwithstanding, it is not clear who should have the final say on what constitutes such foundational values and how they ought to be policed and defended. As a supranational polity that relies on legal instruments and technocratic institutions, the EU does not have enough popular legitimacy to decide on what are fundamentally political questions, such as what its own ultimate purpose is and what the potential limits of European unity are.

This is not to deny that a firm commitment to democracy and the rule of law has become one of the key features of the European project. The question is how, and by whom, they will be defined. 'The nationalists are misguided when they claim to defend our identity by withdrawing from Europe, because it is the European civilisation that unites, frees and protects us', argued French President Macron, campaigning 'For European Renewal' in the 2019 elections to the European Parliament. It is not difficult to guess whom Macron was targeting: Matteo Salvini in Italy, Marine Le Pen in France and Orbán in Hungary are all possibilities. Yet none of them advocated a withdrawal from Europe, let alone from 'the European civilisation' (Macron 2019). Quite the opposite: in defending their nations they saw themselves as defending Europe. 'I am the most Christian, and thus the most European, of Europeans. Europe's DNA is me. I am its guardian', Orbán asserted in a lengthy interview with Bernard-Henri Lévy (Lévy 2019).

Though it was pursued by the means of economic integration, the European project has always had primarily political goals. The reconciliation of West European nations, including Germany, and their commitment to mutual cooperation and 'an ever-closer union' was to strengthen the Western alliance and its values. This might have been merely implicit in the 1950s, but there was no ambiguity about the EU's key political agenda by the time the nations of Central and Eastern Europe joined the Union in the 2000s. From this perspective, the posturing of politicians in the region who talk about their opposition to 'Brussels colonialism' is disingenuous—membership is voluntary, and the post-communist nations embraced Europe as they embraced democracy. Yet, certain EU strategies (and academic debates informing these strategies) make such claims about the EU's neocolonial mindset easier to sell to their electorates.

A recent commentary on a decision by the European Court of Justice (ECJ) offers a striking metaphor of what is at stake for both the EU and its new member states. In this article, the EU's power is likened to the time-limited magic that allows Cinderella's pumpkin to look like a diamond coach, but only until midnight. The analysis focuses on the ECJ's recent *Repubblika* judgment of April 2021, which dealt with the Maltese system for the appointment of judges and whether it was in line with the EU requirement of judicial independence. The particularities of the case are of less importance to us than its path-breaking character with respect to numerous EU efforts to uphold the rule of law. The judgment is said to have 'introduced the new principle of "non-regression" into the system of EU law' (Leloup, Kochenov and Dimitrovs 2021), which would prohibit member states from backsliding on whatever progress they had achieved in developing their legal and political systems. The *Repubblika* judgment is thus of obvious relevance for the post-communist countries of Central and Eastern Europe, which, having complied with EU conditionality, are now free to disown their promises about democracy and the rule of law. The Copenhagen Criteria were an ingenious device to protect both the EU as well as potential member states against democratic erosion. They were in place to ensure that the EU 'does not go to bed with bad guys', as the authors put it. The problem is that post-2004, 'the EU has now found itself precisely where it did not want to be: in bed with those very bad guys. Worse still, so far, the bad guys have absolutely no intention to leave' (Kochenov and Dimitrovs 2021). Just like the fairytale magic assisting Cinderella which ceased working at midnight, the EU's power appeared very limited once the countries became full members, which is the 'midnight terminus when crystal carriages tend to turn into pumpkins and pre-accession dreams of justice into Zbigniew Ziobro' (Leloup, Kochenov and Dimitrovs 2021: 18)—the Polish Minister for Justice who is widely considered responsible for the dismantlement of checks and balances.

What this analysis overlooks is the fact that there was no properly working rule of law state prior to 'backsliding'; or, to remain with the same metaphor, there was no 'diamond carriage' out there that suddenly transformed into a pumpkin. In fact, the metaphor could be extended. Granted, the nations of Central and Eastern Europe, like Cinderella, were poor. But their professional classes, including lawyers, were neither as poor nor as virtuous as Cinderella. Yet, the entire concept of an independent judiciary is predicated on the existence of professional lawyers who take pride in serving the ideal of justice, however imperfectly. Judges working within the Leninist legal system were unlikely to have these qualities.[13] The communist systems of power ruled *by* law, particularly in the final decades of their existence, but they were far removed from the principles of the rule *of* law. Post-communist legal culture combined elements of legal formalism, which can be traced to nineteenth-century German legal tradition, with sheer opportunism. As Adam Czarnota put it in his discussion of post-1989 Polish legal culture, its characteristic features entailed 'a kind of legalism understood as sticking closely to the legal text and at the same time a willingness to depart from the text if the political risk of a decision were too high' (2019: 60).

That is where one of the distinguishing features of the 1989 revolutions, which were seen positively shortly after the collapse of communism, proved to be a major liability. Andrew Arato spoke for many when he praised the reluctant revolutionaries of 1989, such as Adam Michnik, for their ability to demonstrate that 'the new can be built without total rupture with the past' (2000: xiv). These 'self-limiting revolutions', argued Arato, were 'highly innovative and worthy of imitation' because they managed 'to postulate the fiction of legal continuity with a past without legality' (ibid.; compare Auer 2004b: 376). As we now know, this continuity came at a price.

While it is difficult to imagine what the alternative would have been to simply keeping most judges in place, while expecting them to operate according to a set of radically different principles, this approach created its own problems. From the very beginning, the credibility and legitimacy of the newly emerging judicial system was tainted by its connection with the communist past. In stark contrast to the German Constitutional Court, for example, which has for decades enjoyed the highest level of trust amongst German citizens, the Constitutional Tribunal in Poland has been one of the least trusted institutions. This brings us to one of the main points of contention between Poland and the European Union, which is the legality and legitimacy of a series of judicial reforms which have been introduced in Poland since December 2015.

Rule of Lawyers or Rule of Law?[14]

At the heart of the dispute between the EU and the post-2015 Polish conservative governments is the extent to which the executive can interfere in the judiciary. A number of controversial steps taken by successive Polish governments to obtain control over the Constitutional Tribunal and undermine the independence of the Polish Supreme Court forced the EU Commission to take action. In January 2016, the Commission activated its rule of law framework, which was followed in December 2017 by its initiation of the Article 7 procedure of the Treaty on European Union. Article 7 is often referred to as the EU's 'nuclear option', as it forms the basis for the most severe sanction against a member state—the suspension of voting rights in the Council. For many critics of the Polish government, the EU has done too little, too late, to prevent 'Poland's Rule of Law Breakdown' (Pech, Wachowiec and Mazur 2021), while those who were more sympathetic towards the aims of the judicial reforms objected to what they viewed as a technocratic approach to a fundamentally political problem. 'The present constitutional crisis in Poland is not only a legal crisis; it is first and foremost a political crisis' (Czarnota 2019: 56).

This is not to deny the deficiencies of conservative Polish post-communist governments in implementing judicial reforms.[15] But neither can it be denied that the existing legal system was deficient, making judicial reforms necessary. 'The fiction of legal continuity with a past without legality' that was praised by Arato and many liberals as one of the key attributes of the 1989 transformation that ensured its non-violent character, resulted in the post-communist judiciary being largely unreformed. This significantly contributed to the low levels of public trust in both lawyers and judges. The name of Poland's ruling Law and Justice Party (PiS) sought to capitalise on the general public dissatisfaction with the legal profession. In 2013, for example, two years prior to the PiS victory in national elections, an opinion survey indicated that up to two thirds of Poles did not trust the independence of judges (Siedlecka 2013). This is not to suggest that the Law and Justice Party has always managed to live up to the principles it celebrates in its name.[16] But it has undoubtedly had a strong democratic mandate for judicial reforms, confirmed numerous times since 2015 in local, presidential, European and national elections.

At any rate, preserving the integrity of the rule of law is not the same as protecting the privileges of lawyers who helped to rule the country prior to 1989. Were the calls for the preservation of the rule of law rather attempts at the preservation of the rule of lawyers, as Czarnota suggested? 'Legalism as legal formalism', he argued, 'became the currency of the day and lawyers replaced citizens as the main actors on the scene' (2019: 57). To be sure, more than three decades later, there was little direct continuity left with the pre-1989 communist order. Not surprisingly, though, even the new generation of lawyers was socialised into practices and values that were at times at odds with the democratic ethos. While the political regime changed virtually overnight in 1989, legal education and established habits of mind acquired through the processes of socialisation were much harder to change.

As Paul Blokker has noted, Polish judicial reforms were driven by the desire to overcome what the PiS political leaders viewed as 'legal fundamentalism or an excessive juridification of society'. By contrast, they aimed at 'a significant reduction in the presence and status of public and constitutional law throughout society', prioritising instead 'informal local norms, traditions and conventions' (Blokker

2019a: 537). In Polish, this agenda is well captured by the term '*impossybilizm prawny*' (legal impossibilism), which refers to

> the constraints faced by the executive in bringing about extensive reform, and rejects excessive legal formalism. Legal impossibilism is a 'synonym of the embarrassing and irrational legal formalism, which allegedly prevents the adoption of certain and socially desirable regulations and constitutes a brake on progress'. (Blokker 2019a: 537)

Marek Cichocki cites Judith Shklar to make a similar point, bemoaning that the very essence of the rule of law is actually distorted by legalism, because it prioritises the status quo in contrast to

> the categories of freedom and justice, leading to the denial of fundamental European values. Shklar states that it is striking that supporters of the ideology of legalism use the category of the rule of law, to refer to the need to fight against arbitrary power, without seeing the threat of real tyranny in their own stance. (Cichocki 2020: 247)

It is in this context that one should read Frank Furedi's warning that 'illiberal anti-populism constitutes the principal threat to democracy in Europe' (2018: 129). Czarnota echoes this sentiment, interpreting 'the present constitutional crisis in Poland and some other countries in Central-Eastern Europe as an attempt to take the constitution seriously and return it to the citizens' (2019: 63). Whether numerous violations of the existing constitution in Poland will enhance its legitimacy may well be questioned, but the crisis has undoubtedly raised the general awareness of the issues at stake. Through ongoing discussions about both European and Polish constitutionalism, more Polish citizens learned to appreciate the importance of particular legal provisions and the extent to which they are open to interpretation.[17] By contrast, when the current Polish Constitution was conceived, the popular response was rather lukewarm. Adopted by a national referendum on 25 May 1997, the constitution was endorsed by only 53 per cent of voters, while the participation level in the referendum was at around 43 per cent. In other words, there was no strong popular support for this particular Constitution, and no 'constitutional moment' to speak of. Its adoption was widely seen as a victory for the then President Aleksander Kwaśniewski, a former communist, who was chairman of the Constitutional Convention and the text's co-author. The conservatives, on the other hand, were opposed both to Kwaśniewski and 'his' constitution. It is thus worth recalling that partisan struggles tainted the legitimacy of the Constitution and its framers from its inception.[18] In Czarnota's assessment, similar developments took place across Central and Eastern Europe, resulting in a situation in which 'liberal constitutionalism has been used as a smokescreen during transformation to arrange the social world according to the interest of those with political and economic capital' (2020: 47).

Challenging scholars sympathetic to the aims of the judicial reforms in his detailed and compelling study, *Poland's Constitutional Breakdown*, Wojciech Sadurski urges us to enquire into what the Polish government *does* rather than what it claims to do (2019: 253). There is no denying that the Law and Justice-led government has not lived up to its promises. As Sadurski documented, 'Kaczyńsky and his collaborators alternated between breaching certain express rules and working largely within the letter of the law while at the same time violating unwritten norms without which those rules lose meaning' (ibid.).

Drawing on these conflicting arguments, it is plausible to argue that democracy in Europe is endangered both by excessive reliance on formal legalism, deployed in support of 'authoritarian liberalism', as well as populist transgressions against judicial independence. At any rate, the rule of law crisis will not be solved simply by law. The crisis is essentially political, and calls for political solutions. As Martin Krygier has argued, 'populists' failure to honour what we might take to be fundamental principles of the rule of law is often not primarily a technical problem' (2020: 86). Therefore, the protection of the integrity of the legal system cannot be left simply to lawyers and courts, even if those lawyers are highly distinguished and courts powerful. There is a normative dimension to it too, as Krygier reminds us: 'For the values at stake are not ones that should be thought to matter only to lawyers; they matter to us all' (ibid. 91). The key question in our context is this: what level of polity is best suited to deal with these problems? In other words, who are the 'us all' who should be concerned? Is it primarily a challenge for the demos within individual member states, a European demos, or can the EU as a post-sovereign federation of sorts address these challenges too?

For proponents of a 'European superstate' the task at hand is clear, and so is the legitimacy of the European actors responding to populist rebellions. As noted above, Glyn Morgan is refreshingly honest in his advocacy of the EU practising 'imperialism in the fifth degree', in line with which,

> A more powerful state (or group of states) offers political membership to a weaker periphery, the members of which vote overwhelmingly in favor of membership. While all members of the periphery find that they enjoy free and equal membership in the sense that their civil and political rights are fully protected, the Center forces the abolition of all cultural and traditional practices incompatible with freedom and equality as the Center understands those terms. The Periphery finds that it can no longer ban gay marriage, discriminate against local minorities, or refuse to accept refugees. (Morgan 2020: 1428)

While few liberals would quarrel with the substantive points listed here, what is deeply problematic is the idea that cultural and traditional practices are to be banished if they are deemed to be in conflict with freedom and equality 'as the Center understands those terms'. The question that this prescription raises is not merely whether the EU, which itself is not sufficiently democratic, has the right to police the quality of democracy within its member states. It is more fundamental than this. The question is: who has the right to define what constitutes liberal democracy? The most obvious candidate for such a role would be *pouvoir constituant*, that is, constituent power, which is the only credible source of democratic legitimacy.

Jan-Werner Müller (2020) offers a solution that appears to be immune to some of the objections raised above. Unlike Morgan, Müller does not expect the EU to prescribe 'a uniform legislative stance on controversial questions such as same-sex marriage' (Müller 2020: 323). It is possible to 'have many legitimate *policy* disagreements in the EU'. The only thing that cannot be accepted is 'having one's preference for an undemocratic *polity* realized inside the Union' (ibid.). To ensure this, Müller proposes the creation of a new institution to strengthen democracy and the rule of law in the new member states. To extend the EU's power to enforce the Copenhagen Criteria, a Copenhagen Commission would be created, which 'could credibly act as a guardian of Europe's *acquis normatif*' (Müller 2015: 150). Yet as much as he tries, even Müller cannot escape the question of values and who is to define them.[19] The Copenhagen Commission—'composed of legal experts and statesmen and stateswomen'—would be tasked 'to effectively raise an alarm across a common European political space', which does not quite exist yet (Müller 2020: 319). Following the Copenhagen Commission's expert advice, Müller continues, the European Commission 'should be required to cut funds, for instance, or impose significant fines' (ibid. 320).

But wouldn't such a solution be undemocratic?—one commission advising another commission to impose a fine on one of the EU's member states? In Müller's view, no, because the people have already given their consent by supporting EU membership. Extrapolating from the specific German experience, and the idea of *wehrhafte Demokratie* I have discussed in Chapter 1, Müller argues that what the nations of Central and Eastern Europe *really* wanted was a 'constrained democracy'. This is the idea, going back to post-Second World War developments in West Germany and Italy, that political elites had good reason to be suspicious of the populace as they were rebuilding popular democracy. A similar approach was adopted after the collapse of authoritarian regimes in Spain, Portugal and Greece. In all these countries, a robust institutional framework was created— at the apex of which were usually constitutional courts—to protect the people against their worst instincts. European integration simply added another layer of protection. Müller's argument is thus a reminder that while the European project was pursued in the name of democracy and the defence of Western values, it was not democratic from the outset—its aim was to constrain democracy. In the German context, the idea that democracy needs to be protected *from* the people is entangled with the concept of *Rechtsstaat*, which 'had become the ultimate aim of politics', especially after the Second World War. On this reading, 'democracy itself served merely as a means to its realization' (Maier 2019: 1070).[20]

Proponents of European integration see a similar story unfolding after 1989. Many people in post-communist countries, so the argument goes, perceived EU accession as 'a guarantee that would solidify democracy and the rule of law against possible post-accession authoritarian and populist temptations', and thus their choice for Europe was a voluntary endorsement of 'a democratic straitjacket' (Sadurski 2019: 192, 199).[21] As we have seen, we are safe to assume that Cichocki, Czarnota and a significant number of Polish citizens who repeatedly voted for the Law and Justice Party and its coalition allies might disagree with this interpretation. The early post-1989 disillusionment documented by historians such as Krapfl (2013), was later exacerbated by the realisation that the more a country is embedded in a supranational governing structure, the less say its citizens appear to have in determining policies. While one of the guiding principles of the 1989 revolutions was 'nothing about us without us' (Rychetský and Fiala 2014: 1), people were soon to discover the iron logic of Dani Rodrik's trilemma: global economic integration, reinforced through European integration, comes at the expense of democracy and national sovereignty (Rodrik 2007). In practice, this meant, to cite Czarnota again, that 'in each election, no matter which party won, there was a continuation of the same economic policy' (2019: 57).

This is the background against which the popular appeal of claims about Brussels' colonialism has to be understood. When the Polish Justice Minister Ziobro rejected the idea that 'the EU is like a good uncle who offers us money and we simply need to follow all his demands and accept him at any price' (cited in Nizinkiewicz 2021), he is likely to speak for many in a nation proud of its rebellious history. While it is highly unlikely that there is ever going to be a majority of Poles following any of their politicians all the way to 'Polexit', it is equally doubtful that the threat of fines would have the desired effect. In fact, it might deliver quite the opposite result, as it would further undermine the democratic opposition in Poland, which is something that even commentators urging the EU to take a tougher stance acknowledge.[22] Would such a penalty be lawful? And even if it were, would it be *perceived* as legitimate and lawful?

Once again, Europe is damned if it does and damned if it doesn't take a more assertive role. And once again, the question arises as to who the final arbiter should be in such a conflict. If it is to be the European Court of Justice, the problem we have is that the rule of law crisis would be left to the lawyers. What is more, its authority is being contested not just by the Polish Constitutional Tribunal: even the German Bundesverfassungsgericht, for example, has never fully accepted the idea of the ECJ's supremacy. Further to this, open conflict between courts over their respective jurisdiction undermines the credibility of all courts, which has the potential to exacerbate the rule of law crisis across the Union (Nußberger 2021). Paradoxically, there is a very real possibility that such steps would neither advance the cause of democracy nor the rule of law. As Müller admits,

> sanctions would always go against the very EU ethos of consensus finding, mutual accommodation, and even mutual normative self-relativization which has worked so well, so often, and which is ultimately predicated on a shared willingness not to push things to the limit. They would also, prima facie, go against notions of constitutional tolerance, which valorizes particular national understandings of political values. (2020: 327)

'Mutual normative self-relativization' worked 'so well, so often', until it didn't. The very same Schmittian question—'which always asks for the identification of the final arbiter'—dismissed by the author as retrograde some twenty years ago (Müller 2000: 1779; see my Chapter 1 above)—comes back with a vengeance, and we still have no good response because of an emergency in which inaction is not an option either. As Müller continues:

> the actual choice might not be between upholding these ideals or serious sanctions. The choice is more likely to be between, on the one hand, accepting the (inevitable) risks of sanctions and, on the other, condoning a process where the core of the EU slowly rots. Ultimately, it is not in the Union's interest to have a periphery where everyone knows that things are not quite okay and yet no one dares to do anything. (2020: 327)

Clearly, 'legitimation through procedure' (Müller 2000: 1779) reaches its limits when fundamental questions of values and ideals arise. In fact, the question of sanctions on defiant member states and open conflicts between courts is no longer merely theoretical. In late 2021, a veritable lawfare of sorts started between key EU institutions on the one hand, and top courts and national governments in Poland and Hungary on the other. Frustrated with the lack of progress to reverse the erosion of the rule of law, in October 2021 the European Parliament decided to sue the European Commission for not taking adequate action against Poland and Hungary. This happened just a couple of weeks after the Polish Constitutional Tribunal declared the ECJ's interpretation of a number of articles of the Treaty on European Union unconstitutional. The decision represented a frontal attack on the well-established principle of EU legal supremacy, which underpins EU constitutionalism.

As discussed in Chapter 1, the decision was deeply problematic for three interrelated reasons. First, the Polish Tribunal's legitimacy was dubious, owing to the fact that the PiS-led government had stacked it with judges sympathetic to its aims. Second, the case was brought to the court by the Polish government, which was looking for a justification whereby it could disregard ECJ jurisprudence. Third, the reasoning of the ECJ appeared at odds even with the Polish Constitution, as many prominent critics in and outside Poland argued. However plausible these objections are, it is not clear what viable course of action the EU institutions can pursue to defuse this conflict. One of the purposes of the controversial judgment from the Polish perspective was to protect the government against EU demands to dismantle the Disciplinary Chamber of the Supreme Court through which it sought to control the judiciary (while claiming that it was an indispensable part of the judicial reforms). In response, the European Commission succeeded in imposing a record €1 million-per-day fine on Poland, through a decision of the ECJ. Even more far reaching might be the prospect of denying Poland the payment of its share of the coronavirus recovery package, worth in total almost €24 billion (the disbursement of which was being delayed at the time of writing).

Yet, the Polish government defended its position in the name of national sovereignty. However strong the European Union is,

Morawiecki argued in the European Parliament, it 'is not a state'. Member states 'are European sovereigns—they are the "masters of the treaties"', and it is for them to 'define the scope of the competences entrusted to the European Union'. Morawiecki was adamant that rather than betraying democratic principles, his government was defending them against the EU's illegitimate power grab:

> It is unacceptable to extend powers, to act by means of accomplished facts. It is unacceptable to impose one's decisions on others without a legal basis. It is all the more unacceptable to use the language of financial blackmail for this purpose, to talk about penalties, or to use even more far-reaching words against certain Member States. I reject the language of threats, hazing and coercion. I do not agree to politicians blackmailing and threatening Poland. I do not agree blackmail to become a method of conducting policy towards a Member State. That's not how democracies do things. (Morawiecki 2021a)

Needless to say, few Poles would think of themselves as living on Europe's periphery, to use Müller's term. They see themselves as being at the heart of the European continent and central to its political endeavour of unity. Thus, while up to 90 per cent of Poles remain in favour of EU membership (CBOS 2021), many of them expect Poland's national sovereignty to be respected. Morawiecki's arguments against the creation of a European superstate by stealth echo these sentiments and are thus likely to find a receptive audience. As a headline in the major national newspaper *Gazeta Wyborcza* put it,[23] 'We don't want Polexit, but PiS's anti-EU rhetoric works' (Kublik 2021). What's more, the appeal of such arguments is not limited just to Poland and other new member states. As noted in Chapter 3, it is revealing that Michel Barnier sought to rally public support for his presidential candidacy in late 2021 by promising to change the French Constitution to reaffirm 'French legal sovereignty over European courts'. Seeking to enhance his popularity with French voters by taking a firm stance towards migration—advocating a three- to five-year moratorium for non-EU immigrants—Barnier argued that France 'must not be permanently cowed by a ruling or a condemnation from the ECJ' (cited in Valentin and González-Gallarza

2021). Barnier's transformation from European Commissioner and Chief EU Brexit negotiator into a French politician seeking to outmanoeuvre Marine Le Pen by threatening an open confrontation with the EU reflects a general trend across Europe—which is the decline of support for mainstream political parties. Thus, Poland's problems are no longer confined to Europe's 'periphery'. Yet, the ideal of a 'militant democracy' which defends its values against the people it is meant to represent—labelled by Dyzenhaus' 'Schmittian liberalism with a vengeance' (see Chapter 1)—brings about its own challenges, which can be usefully illustrated by the EU attempts to rein in Hungary's illiberal turn, on which many Polish conservative policies have been modelled.

Böckenförde's Dilemma in Orbán's Hungary and Europe

'They don't like us [Hungarians] in Brussels', Viktor Orbán was cited as saying, after a heated European Council meeting in June 2021, in which he found himself on the defensive in response to discriminatory legislation against Hungarian LGBT communities, which implied a connection between homosexuality and paedophilia. The President of the European Commission, Ursula von der Leyen, did not hide her displeasure, stating, 'This bill clearly discriminates against people based on their sexual orientation. It goes against the fundamental values of the European Union: human dignity, equality and respect for human rights' (Erlanger 2021). The Hungarian government, by contrast, insisted that their intentions had been misconstrued and that the bill merely protected children from abuse, giving parents more control over their education in questions of sexuality. Fairly quickly, the conflict over that particular piece of legislation escalated into a veritable culture war between Budapest and a number of Western capitals and civil society activists, both in Hungary and across Europe. This was one of the low points in the East-West relationship, a synecdoche of sorts, in which mutual accusations exposed differing levels of mutual miscomprehension.

The West of which many Central Europeans had wanted to be a part turned out to be rather different from what they had imagined. Conversely though, West European expectations of Central and

East European nations also proved somewhat unrealistic. People there tended to be more sceptical about the advantages and virtues of multiculturalism (including LGBT rights) than their Western counterparts, and they grew to resent demands for change. This was also one of the rationales for the uncompromising positions that the governments in a number of new member states took during the 2015 migration crisis. Then, too, Hungary was at the centre of attention, owing to the images of tens of thousands of refugees stranded in Budapest and the very public opposition of Orbán's government. Yet his argument had a wide resonance across the region. The self-proclaimed Social Democrat Róbert Fico, then still the Slovak Prime Minister, defended his anti-immigration position by arguing that 'the idea of multicultural Europe failed and the natural integration of people who have another way of life, way of thinking, cultural background and most of all religion, is not possible' (cited in Zsolt 2020: 369).

Historically, this is a strange reversal of positions. Whereas high degrees of ethnic heterogeneity, which the nations of Central and Eastern Europe inherited from the collapse of the Austro-Hungarian Empire, had been seen as a major liability a century ago, today the West criticises its neighbours in the East for being too homogeneous (Krastev 2018). Yet, Western leaders are also not immune to charges of hypocrisy. It suffices to recall Angela Merkel's statement in 2010 about attempts to create a multicultural society in Germany, which she said had 'utterly failed' (see Chapter 2). And even with respect to LGBT rights, it seemed to have been forgotten that 'several of the 17 EU member states that called upon the EU to fight "anti-LGBT discrimination" do not legally recognize gay marriages (e.g., Cyprus, Italy) or some form of civil union (e.g., Latvia), which even Hungary accepts!' (Mudde 2021). Furthermore, those countries that have adopted more progressive legislation in this area have done so relatively recently, and only after decades of political contestation. For example, same-sex marriage was only legalised in 2000 in the Netherlands, 2013 in France and 2017 in Germany (Hefty 2021).

What these conflicts bring to light are different conceptions of the political community based on different prioritisations of values. This is what makes these disagreements so intractable. When societal changes are perceived as 'foreign' impositions, or as demands by judicial and technocratic bodies beyond democratic control, they are bound to lead to a backlash. The result is 'the European culture wars' (Furedi 2018), in which another version of TINA emerges: 'there is no alternative' to progressive liberal values on a number of issues, such as nationalism, religion or LGBT rights. This generates discontent that the conservative leaders in Hungary and Poland have exploited to their advantage. Many analysts of populism and 'democratic backsliding' overlook this challenge because they posit that populist leaders represent no values. This is a mistaken and unhelpful assumption. In a similar vein, while populists are usually seen as being opposed to constitutionalism, it is useful to think of populism 'as a constitutional project', even if not of a liberal kind (Blokker 2019b). It is prudent to take seriously the populists' claim that

> an emphasis on legal rationality, the neutrality of the state, and formal-legal proceduralism tends to weaken the polity, due to its lacking potentiality in terms of symbolic, sentimental, and collective engagement. Populist constitutionalism endorses, in this, a program that promises to reduce the distance between ordinary citizens and the institutions. Populists want to directly link the people to the institutions, and to re-enchant democracy, to make it meaningful to its citizens. (Blokker 2019b: 536)

In other words, what the populists respond to is the predicament recognised by Ernst-Wolfgang Böckenförde as a dilemma (discussed in Chapter 2), in which the liberal state draws on societal resources 'it cannot itself guarantee'. In particular, such a state 'can only survive if the freedom it grants to its citizens is regulated from within, out of the moral substance of the individual and the homogeneity of society' (Böckenförde 2017: 45). It is worth emphasising that the homogeneity Böckenförde refers to is not to be understood narrowly—a shared commitment to values, for example, may well be more important than ethnicity. Thus, however unappealing the populists' professed solutions might seem—unappealing particularly to their liberal, progressive critics—they respond to a very real dilemma which liberals have underestimated at their own peril. To be sure, 'a Europe of values' also attempts to 're-enchant democracy' and 'make it meaningful to its citizens', but it does so from a peculiar perspective, in which one's membership in the political community depends on 'whether one is a patriot of the principles of liberal democracy' (Dyzenhaus 2016: 504). This is both an impractical and normatively problematic position, particularly considering that the principles of liberal democracy themselves are open to legitimate contestation. Further to this, what are liberals to do with those who question liberal virtues? Expel them from their political community? This problem is intractable even within the confines of nation states; at the level of a transnational EU-wide polity it appears unmanageable.

Once again, it is instructive to turn to Schmitt to unpack the difficulties that liberals face when they confront the problem of how to tolerate those who are (in their view) intolerant. The ideal of neutrality with respect to the pursuit of a good life only takes us so far. The attempt to defuse potential conflicts by neutralisation has its limits when it comes to value judgments. In fact, presenting value judgments as objective, particularly in areas in which there is space for legitimate disagreements, can lead to the 'tyranny of values' (Schmitt 2011) which exacerbates conflicts:

> The subjective nature of ordering values is not overcome, and the objective values are not gained simply through a process, in which the subjects are concealed, in whose interests certain points of view and certain strategies for attack are offered by this same set of values. Nobody can value without devaluing, revaluing and exploiting. (Schmitt 2011: 46)

The question is no longer merely academic. He who values also devalues. In response to the recent anti-LGBT provocation by the Hungarian Prime Minister, which was followed by Orbán's call for a national referendum in support of the legislation, the Luxembourg Foreign Minister, Jean Asselborn, suggested an EU-wide referendum on whether Hungary should be expelled from the EU. There is no legal basis for such a radical step, as Asselborn, one of Europe's longest-serving politicians, is well aware. Thus, the suggestion only makes sense as an appeal to a European demos that needs to defend EU's democracy against its illiberal elements. Such a solution would not be merely undemocratic, it would be profoundly illiberal too, as it would strip all Hungarians (including those with liberal persuasion) of EU citizenship. However unrealistic such a step is, the mere fact that it was proposed reinforces divisions in Europe and challenges the very idea of parliamentary democracy. Ironically, such a referendum would replicate what is seen as the dysfunction of the Hungarian political system, which, under Orbán's leadership, has been moving towards a Schmittian 'acclamatory democracy', in which a powerful executive rules largely as he pleases, with an occasional endorsement—acclamation—of his policies in a referendum, or by other means.[24]

Even more radical is the suggestion to reconstitute the European Union in such a way that would exclude its illiberal member states. Responding to the growing realisation that the EU might prove unable to rein in Hungary's and Poland's anti-EU rebellions from within, Merijn Chamon and Tom Theuns warn against 'membership fatalism', advancing a plan that would make it possible to expel non-compliant countries. While they acknowledge that no state can be expelled against its will, they propose

> to explore the option of a collective withdrawal by the liberal democracies from the EU. A collective triggering of Article 50 TEU [Treaty on European Union] and a collective negotiation of a withdrawal agreement whereby all of the EU's assets are transferred (through the withdrawing Member States) to an EU 2.0 would leave autocratic Member States in the empty useless shell of the original EU. Rule of law compliant Member States could then pursue their cooperation in an EU 2.0. (Chamon and Theuns 2021)

While this solution could be advanced on the basis of existing treaty provisions, both its democratic credentials and political feasibility are highly questionable. The bold proposal ignores the fact that Polish and Hungarian citizens would be punished by such a measure regardless of their political affiliations and commitments. Once again, even passionate pro-Europeans would lose out, without having had a chance to contest the possibility of exit, as was done, for example, in the Brexit referendum, however imperfectly. Second, the proposal appears to assume that such rebellions would be limited to peripheral countries and thus that the damage of such a step to the European project as such could be contained. Could a similar scenario be applied to France, for example? In fact, is it even conceivable that it could ever be applied to Poland? Would any German government, whatever its ideological orientation, sign up to a radical step of reconstituting the EU in order to expel Poland? What would be left of the European project's greater historical rationale that served the purpose of post-Second World War reconciliation between Germany and France, and similarly, after 1989, between Germany and Poland?

Concluding Remarks

'We need to change the attitude in Europe that everyone thinks he is something better and the others are not so great', Wolfgang Schäuble, Germany's longest-serving politician said in an interview in June 2021, in which he reflected on the immense contribution of the nations of Central Europe to both German and European unity, and praised their 'courage and tenacity' (Karnitschnig 2021). While he spoke as a President of the German *Bundestag*, the role he has played since 2017, Schäuble is better known across Europe as Germany's Finance Minister during the eurozone crisis, in which he was feared and resented as the architect of austerity. His conciliatory attitude towards controversial political positions in Poland and Hungary are all the more remarkable. In the words of his interviewer, Schäuble believes that 'the growing East-West divide represents a greater danger to Europe's future than anything happening in an individual member state'. He is right. The East-West conflicts appear to make the series of crises discussed in previous chapters all the more intractable, revealing a fundamental dysfunction at the heart of a polity that is stuck between a nation state and a supranational polity in the making.

To return to the 'Habsburg myth', we are reminded of an obvious paradox. As Helen Thompson pointed out,

> Investing the EU with the Habsburg cosmopolitan promise runs into the hard fact that the Habsburg empire was replaced by

states legitimated by the very imaginative claims to nationhood once accommodated within its supranational polity. To think that the EU is like the Habsburg empire is to deny the teleological optimism in the idea that the EU is moving toward 'ever closer union'. (2020: 46)

An alternative approach would be to consider that historical experience as pointing towards the limits of the EU's teleology. The messianic promise of an 'ever-closer union' ought to be questioned against the possibilities of what such a multinational polity can deliver. If the EU's reluctant empire is to remain 'united in diversity'—a motto that it shares with its Habsburg predecessor—it might need more acceptance of its heterogeneity. It could do worse than to return to the initial meaning of that phrase, in which diversity stood primarily for the rich variety of national cultures rather than merely 'diverse minorities that inhabited a common geographical space'. In this latter and more recent interpretation, as Frank Furedi has noted, there is not much place left for national cultures, squeezed as they are 'between a transnational cosmopolitanism and diverse minority identities' (Furedi 2018: 69). To use Palacký's language, the EU should avoid the temptation to play the role of a 'universal state', notwithstanding the fact that many member states face very real internal challenges.

To be sure, conservative Polish and Hungarian visions for Europe are deeply unpalatable for those citizens and politicians across Europe who aspire to a post-national Europe—or even a sovereign Europe. These citizens and politicians envisage a far greater degree of political unity than the likes of Orbán would allow. Yet, there is no point denying that the populist appeal to nation and national sovereignty resonates with a significant part of the electorate, not only in the new member states. However objectionable their substantive responses might be to what we have discussed above as 'Böckenförde's dilemma', they offer solutions to problems, which some of their more liberal counterparts appear to wish away. What is the right balance, for example, between the emphasis on individual rights and concerns for societal cohesion? What person or institution is to have the final say in matters of great public concern, whether it is judicial reform, gender rights, or the extent to which borders are to be protected? Who, by extension, has the final responsibility for the well-being of citizens in times of emergency, and at what level is that responsibility to be acted upon—local, national or European? These questions take us to the final chapter of this book, which offers a short reflection on the phenomenon of 'emergency Europe'.

CONCLUSION

EMERGENCY EUROPE AND ITS LIMITS

*It is difficult to tell the truth, for though there is only one, it is lively
and thus has an ever changing, lively face.*

Franz Kafka cited by Hannah Arendt, in
The Difficulties of Understanding ([1952] 2018: 159)[1]

This book grapples with a few basic themes. What *is* the EU and
is it still fit for purpose? What is the appropriate size of a political
community? If a supranational state is undesirable, can Europeans
reclaim more democratic control at the level of nation states?[2]
Can Boris Johnson's Brexit deliver on the promise of 'taking back
control'? Can Emmanuel Macron's 'sovereign Europe' do the same
for French and European citizens? Can this experimental polity
prove itself an effective global actor, able to stand up for its interests
vis-à-vis China, Russia and the United States? These questions were
particularly pressing as European societies struggled to restore
normality after the veritable *annus horribilis* of 2020, which was
marked by the outbreak of the pandemic at its beginning and—in the
midst of a highly damaging second wave—acrimonious negotiations
of the modalities of Brexit towards its end. A lot was at stake, and
the EU's young polity was tested in the early 2020s as never before.
These exceptional challenges brought to the fore the question of

sovereignty which Europeans had sought to evade. Who was to decide for the EU and how? Who was truly in charge?

Further to this, in mid-2021 Europeans were reminded of the volatility of contemporary world politics, a volatility which accelerated as the US continued to relinquish its role as a global superpower. Though President Joe Biden's administration—in contrast to Trump's—spoke the language of multilateralism and globalisation, its policies continued to prioritise US interests. The hasty and chaotic retreat of the US military from Afghanistan in August 2021 proceeded without any meaningful consultation with America's European partners. The speedy collapse of the pro-Western government in Kabul that followed forced EU elites to think once again about European security, leading—rather predictably—to renewed calls for strategic autonomy. 'Europe only responds in a crisis', the EU's foreign policy chief Josep Borrell noted: 'Afghanistan could wake it up. The moment has come to give it a military force capable of fighting if necessary' (AFP, 22 August 2021). As the US struggled to maintain control over Kabul Airport, which was of crucial importance for evacuations, Armin Laschet, the then Christian Democratic candidate for German Chancellor, argued that more Europe was needed in the area of foreign policy. 'We [Europeans] have to be able to secure an airport like the one in Kabul even on our own' (Burger, Gerster and Schuller 2021). For Laschet (2021), Afghanistan represented 'the greatest fiasco for NATO since its very foundation'. What these early accounts had in common was that no individual nation state (or leader) wanted to be accountable for the outcome. That Germany, as the second largest financial contributor to NATO, had some responsibility for this 'fiasco' was underplayed in Laschet's call for 'more Europe'. And as Borell, Laschet and other European leaders should know, the chance of Europe developing military capabilities that would match those of the United States is small. Yet there seemed to be no harm in advocating them. The louder and more frequent the calls for more Europe were, the more vacuous they tended to get.

The new German governing coalition inaugurated in December 2021, comprising the Social Democrats, the Greens and Free Democrats, is unlikely to significantly alter Europe's direction of travel. Though the new Foreign Minister, Annalena Baerbock, has voiced robust criticisms of Germany's and Europe's major contenders, such as China and Russia, it is far from clear what impact such rhetoric will have on both Germany's and the EU's actual foreign policies. Remarkably, Macron's notion of a 'strategically sovereign European Union' is contained in the coalition agreement. Yet, the reluctance of the new German government to finance and deploy military force is unlikely to increase Europe's ability to project power. Revealing in this respect is the commitment to spend 3 per cent of the national budget on development, diplomacy and defence, but without any commitment to live up to the 2 per cent spending target on defence agreed at the 2014 NATO Wales Summit. In fact, on closer reading it appears that Germany's understanding of Europe's strategic sovereignty is more about reducing economic dependence on China and Russia than enabling Europe as a potential military actor. And even the aim of greater economic self-reliance might prove unrealisable, considering Germany's dependence on gas supplies from Russia, which is unlikely to decrease given the new government's stronger commitment to phase out German coal production and do without nuclear energy. The coalition government's promise to work towards an EU which 'decisively stands up to and protects its values and its rule of law within and without' sounds ambitious, but is also ambiguous, leaving many questions about implementation unanswered.

'Europe' as a term performs the function of a religious incantation. Far from empowering political communities and their leaders to take destiny into their own hands, as Merkel urged Europeans to do (see Chapter 2), calling for 'more Europe' obscures their responsibilities. It is fitting that the desired final destiny of the European project is seldom spelled out (Streeck 2021: 134). As a secularised religion, Europe can thus be embraced by mainstream politicians of vastly different persuasions, without any strong commitment on their part to any particular policy. Whatever problem you might have, 'Europe is the solution', as the book-length essay by Frank-Walter Steinmeier (2016), Germany's Social Democratic president since 2017, claims. The discussion about Europe's *finalité politique* is avoided because it would likely lead to more conflicts, as is obvious to anyone familiar with the many, radically different conceptions of Europe, including those discussed in the present book. It is revealing in this context that the 'Conference on the Future of Europe', launched in Strasbourg on 9 May 2021, steered away from big questions about the ultimate purpose of European unity. What is more, notwithstanding its promise to listen to 'European citizens, from all walks of life and corners of the Union', the Conference has been largely ignored by the people(s) of Europe. The idea that some of those Europeans would be willing to fight, and even die, for Europe, is hence rather outlandish. Whatever the likes of Emmanuel Macron, Bruno Le Maire and Guy Verhofstadt advocate when they talk about a 'sovereign Europe' (see Chapter 3), Europe is not and is unlikely to ever become a federal state.

We are thus brought back to the question of identity and to what extent individuals see themselves as part of a political community. Without such attachments it is not clear what would motivate people for action, particularly in times of crisis. As a prominent scholar of nationalism put it some time ago: 'Who will feel European in the depths of their being, and who will willingly sacrifice themselves for so abstract an ideal? In short, who will die for Europe?' (Smith 1995: 316). The very fact that this question sounds antiquated today is revealing. Over the last few decades, Europeans have grown accustomed to living in a post-political world where conflicts can and should be solved by conversation (Jones 2005). In such a world, instead of military might what is needed is global cooperation that can harness technical expertise to address the multifarious challenges that humanity faces, ranging from climate change, global pandemics and inequality, to threats of terrorism. Indeed, the realisation that so very few people in Europe (particularly in Germany) are willing to fight—or even just to support military expenditure—can be seen as a sign of moral progress. The violent conflagrations of the First and Second World Wars must not be repeated ever again. In this sense, one can safely surmise that Europe is *not* an empire, at least not of the kind that would be capable of standing up for its interests against those ready to resort to violence. As we have seen, Europe has the ability to inspire the people of Belarus to fight for their freedom, but it has no ability to effectively protect them against their tinpot dictator.

Similarly, with Europe's help Ukrainians might have succeeded in freeing themselves from their own corrupt government, but the EU has been less successful in helping Ukraine to protect its interests against Russia (see Chapter 4).

Yet, there is another sobering lesson to be drawn from the humiliating defeat of the US-led Western alliance in Afghanistan. No amount of money, multilateral cooperation, deployment of military force or effort of non-governmental organisations can create a political community where there is none. This is the meaning of Schmitt's famous dictum that the very existence of the state presupposes 'the concept of the political' ([1928] 2007: 19). Moreover, the societal stability provided by a well-functioning state is a precious good which ought not to be taken for granted. This basic insight no longer seems to apply to Europe's novel polity. In good times, it was indeed possible to legitimise the European Union by way of procedures and by delivering the goods that its citizens valued. The long decade of crises has upended this settlement. Can and should it be restored?

The European Union, of course, is not a state. Yet, having taken on an ever-increasing number of roles that a state is expected to fulfil, the Union has eroded the very democratic states that constitute it. The process that started as a pragmatic enterprise after the devastation of the Second World War, initially rescuing the nation state (Milward 2000), has ended up exacerbating the crisis of democratic legitimacy. Of course, the problem is neither new, nor is it unique to Europe: democracies everywhere have faced similar challenges. But the problem has been accelerated over the last couple of decades by the process of hyper-globalisation, of which Europeanisation became a part. The relentless move towards ever more governance disempowered governments, reducing their accountability to their electorates. Rather than providing a credible model of supranational governance for the world, Europe's missionary zeal to forge 'an ever-closer union' has reduced the attractiveness of contemporary Western liberalism. Europe's attempt to overcome a world of sovereign nation states has unwittingly weakened its ability to act. This was revealed by the number of crises that gave rise to an 'emergency Europe', in which exceptional challenges were to be met by the politics of the exception.

Eurozone Crisis and the Rule of Law

If the sovereign is the one who decides on the exception, emergency politics revealed the absence of sovereign power at the European level. Instead, we have seen action without agency and technocratic institutions taking on political roles. Exemplary of this was Draghi's bold promise that the European Central Bank (ECB) would 'do whatever it takes' to safeguard the currency union, downplaying the legal constraints. At the start of the pandemic, by contrast, a multitude of actors at all levels of the EU's system of governance largely failed to live up to the challenge of recognising and acting on the emergency. Both scenarios present a serious problem for the EU. Bold actions in the name of emergency, which violate the existing legal framework, undermine the EU's self-understanding as a community of law. Inaction exposes the EU to the charge of being a dysfunctional polity, unable to protect its citizens.

Though the intensity of concerns about the future of the eurozone have subsided, the conflict over the policies that eased the crisis continues. As discussed in Chapter 2, the disagreement over the legality of ECB measures led to an open confrontation between the constitutional courts of Germany and the EU. This conflict exposed two different understandings of the EU and the sources of its legitimacy. The Schmittian question of 'who is the guardian of the constitution?' thus becomes, in the European context, 'who is the guardian of *whose* constitution?' In other words, the hybrid nature of the EU, as a polity located somewhere between a fully-fledged federation (*Bundesstaat*) and a community of sovereign nation states (*Staatenverbund*), creates an irresoluble dilemma about who has the 'final say', which no number of legal proceedings is likely to settle. If one subscribes to the federalist position that a functioning EU requires the prioritisation of the European constitution over national constitutions, then the European Court must be the guardian of the European constitution, in which case the judgment of the German Federal Constitutional Court itself was an *ultra vires* act (Mayer 2020: 736). If, by contrast, the authority of EU law is ultimately derived from well-functioning national democracies, as the Bundesverfassungsgericht (BVerfG) understands it, then the 'final' authority of national constitutional courts over national constitutions is impossible to disentangle from their authority over European constitutional issues. Thus, as Everson and Joerges (2014: 198) have argued, the Union 'has both national and European masters: masters who may be in disagreement with one another', with disagreements becoming particularly heated in times of emergency.

The problem of ambiguity as to who is the final arbiter gained increased urgency because of the populist rebellions in Hungary and Poland; that is, in nations whose democratically elected governments were seen as dismantling democracy in their countries *and* in Europe. While the German Constitutional Court was targeted for its 'nationalist' judgments, there were no serious voices that questioned the quality of German democracy, let alone the independence of the German judiciary. In fact, one of the awkward consequences of the Commission's decision to launch infringement proceedings against Germany was that the very ideal of separation between politics and law was undermined by the implicit demand on the German government to somehow discipline its country's Constitutional Court—an impossible task. Not surprisingly then, when the Polish Constitutional Tribunal faced the prospect of an unfavourable judgment by the ECJ with respect to controversial judicial reforms in which the court played an important role, it declared that the EU's highest court was acting beyond its competence. This enabled the Polish government to dismiss the judgment as illegitimate, arguing that following the ECJ's decision would undermine the independence of the Polish judiciary. As discussed in Chapter 5, the rule of law crisis will not be solved simply by legal means, yet there are no obvious political solutions either.

Covid-19 Crisis

Invoking an emergency where there is none threatens the life of democracy. Yet not invoking one when the danger is real threatens the actual lives of citizens. And, indeed, many Italians perceived 'a Europe that protects' as a hollow promise in March 2020, when the virus outbreak was out of control in Lombardy, and again across Europe in late 2020 and early 2021, as EU citizens faced another wave of the pandemic accompanied by delays in vaccine rollouts.[3] As a post-sovereign polity, the EU's options for quick and decisive action are somewhat limited. This is a serious liability. As Machiavelli noted with respect to a 'wasting disease', in its early stages it 'is easy to cure but difficult to diagnose; after a time … it becomes easy to diagnose but difficult to cure' (2011: 12). It requires a prudent politician, Machiavelli argued, to live up to this challenge. In fact, deciding on what constitutes an emergency is a profoundly political act that should not be left to a technocratic body.

At the EU level, where we confront the phenomenon of 'emergency rule without a defined institutional sovereign' (White 2020: 34), the difficulty is even more pronounced. Decisions are still taken in the absence of a sovereign, but 'bureaucratic rule by nobody' (Arendt 2005: 78) tends to replace political rule. Instead of a political decision, Hannah Arendt warned, 'we find haphazard settlements of universal procedures, settlements which are without either malice or arbitrariness because there is no will behind them, but to which there is also no appeal' (ibid. 78). In other words: when power is dispersed, nobody rules and nobody is responsible.

Across the world, both politicians and experts failed to identify the seriousness of the danger that Covid-19 presented. Faced with an unprecedented pandemic, the devastating effects of which had been known for many weeks, owing to the experience in China, Europeans were paralysed. They acted just as Schmitt predicted liberals would in an emergency. When asked to decide between Jesus and Barabbas, they called a committee (Schmitt 1985a: 62).[4] The countries and territories that did well in suppressing the pandemic in its *early* stages (e.g., Taiwan, Hong Kong, Vietnam, Singapore, Australia and New Zealand) did so by taking the kind of drastic action that the EU with its multilevel system of governance could not. As late as the end of February 2020, more than a month after Wuhan was locked down and at a time when Italy had recorded 400 out of the 477 Europe-wide cases of Covid-19, the Commission advised national governments against border closures, dismissing the Italian government's concerns as unfounded (Gutschker 2020a). The assertion that 'Covid-19 does not respect borders' (Laffan 2020) became something of a platitude, obfuscating the fact that stricter border controls, when implemented early, could dramatically reduce the spread of the virus. Indeed, having failed to come up with a coordinated response on borders and other virus suppression measures, most European states ended up imposing much harsher and more haphazard restrictions on individual freedoms in the form of repeated 'lockdowns'.

Crisis as an Opportunity?

To suggest that the EU has *not* managed its many crises well is a heresy. It defies the insight of one of its founders, Jean Monnet, who in the 1970s professed his belief that 'Europe will be established through crises and that the outcome will be the sum of the outcomes of those crises' (1978: 518). It is thus an article of faith within EU studies that crises are conducive to European unity. Whenever Europe appears to be failing, it is 'failing forward' (Jones, Kelemen and Meunier 2021). In line with this, conventional narratives of European integration focus on how Europeans overcome initial difficulties only to emerge out of each crisis stronger. In this vein, one may observe that the eurozone crisis did *not* lead to the EU's disintegration, resulting instead in a far more intensive coordination of national economic policies. Similarly, after the initial upheavals caused by the Covid-19 crisis, a massive EU recovery fund was agreed on—a measure celebrated as Europe's 'Hamiltonian moment', implying that just like the United States towards the end of the eighteenth century, Europe was getting closer to becoming a true federation via debt mutualisation. Following the same logic, it may be argued that growing global instability will lead Europeans towards the realisation that they need a far greater degree of cooperation in the Common Foreign and Security Policy, including by developing shared military capabilities. And, finally, the transgressions of populist rebels in Hungary and Poland may merely serve as a reminder to progressive, liberal Europeans of the essential values that keep Europe together—making the EU stronger as a result. This book seeks to demonstrate that such optimism is unwarranted. Rather than failing forward, Europe is failing.

In order to endure, democracy requires a *demos*. If the EU is 'the future in the present, a laboratory for trying out new forms of government' (Kalmo and Skinner 2010: 19), then the value of its experiment with shared sovereignty should be questioned. This post-sovereign project has eroded democracy in Europe and its track record on delivering the goods for its people is mixed. Europe's political elites will need to stop chasing Arcadia—the promised land of a post-national, or supranational democracy—if they wish to regain popular support. 'Europeans must depart from utopian dreams', argued Donald Tusk (*Ekathimerini*, 2 June 2016). He was right. Less would be more.

AUTHOR'S NOTE

The war was predicted with remarkable precision, yet it took most people by surprise. It was observed from the air and on the ground, reported in major newspapers and broadcasts, and widely debated on social media. Authorised by President Vladimir Putin, about 150,000 Russian soldiers were amassed on the borders of Ukraine, including in Belarus, which supported Russian efforts. With the notable exception of the US and UK governments, which openly warned about an imminent attack on Ukraine,[1] most observers and major political leaders, including the French President Emmanuel Macron and the German Chancellor Olaf Scholz, appeared to believe that Putin's Russia was mainly posturing. Many observers assumed that Russia's intimidation was, at most, aimed merely at consolidation of its previous gains—the takeover of Crimea and some form of recognition for the self-proclaimed republics in eastern Ukraine. Such assumptions assigned a far greater degree of rationality to the autocratic and increasingly isolated Putin than was warranted. 'I got this totally wrong,' Andrew Moravcsik acknowledged, the day after the Russian invasion began on 24 February 2022 (Gilpin 2022). He was not alone. 'Almost everybody got it totally wrong,' Moravcsik added, 'because the tools we use to figure out what autocrats are going to do didn't work ... Putin had a 20-year record of being an aggressive but very risk-averse opportunist. This was a step change in his behavior.'

And yet, we should not have been surprised. The war that Russia has been waging against Ukraine started in 2014 with an illegal occupation of Crimea, followed by military support for the separatist forces in Donetsk and Luhansk (see Chapter 4). Instead of listening mostly to Putin, the 'risk-averse opportunist', we should have been more attentive to the voices of his opponents, who risked and lost their lives speaking truth to power. Think of Boris Nemtsov, who was assassinated in the vicinity of the Kremlin on 27 February 2015, just hours after denouncing Putin's war on Echo Moskvy radio station as 'insane, aggressive and deadly for our country'. Nemtsov was aware of the danger he was exposed to. In one of the last interviews he gave (Hille 2015), Nemtsov told the *Financial Times* that Putin was capable of murder: 'He is a totally amoral human being. Totally amoral. He is a Leviathan.'[2]

What was new was not Putin's willingness to wage a war, but the war's scale, mode and immediate proximity to the countries of the European Union. Unlike the initial invasion of Crimea, this was no longer a 'deniable intervention' that would give Western leaders enough pretext to shy away from far-reaching sanctions. It was an unprovoked war of territorial conquest pursued on the basis of grotesquely inaccurate claims. The purported aim of Russia's 'special military operation', as the war was described by Putin's propaganda machine, was to 'demilitarise and de-Nazify' Ukraine, a country whose democratically elected leader, Volodymyr Zelenskiy, was Jewish and a native Russian-speaker. Putin's reckless decision turned Russia into a pariah nation, while Zelenskiy did not merely manage to rally his own people to defend their nation, 'he also galvanised the world's democracies in ways that seemed unthinkable just a week before' (Shuster 2022). Led by the United States, European allies agreed to unprecedented economic penalties against Russia, excluding large parts of its economy from world markets. Germany and the European Union as a whole underwent a momentous transformation within days of the invasion. For EU enthusiasts, this was an impressive show of European unity, while critics continued to doubt the EU's resolve, pointing at past missed opportunities (Münchau 2022).

Against this background, the European transformation that occurred in the immediate aftermath of the invasion is all the more remarkable. As I am writing these remarks, Europeans are displaying an admirable degree of unity, in the face of a challenge that goes directly to the themes that animate this book: namely, democracy, sovereignty and the politics of emergency. Against an old-fashioned war of territorial conquest, the people of Ukraine defended their national sovereignty, with their fight widely seen as a battle between Putin's authoritarianism and liberal democracy. And clearly, the war has presented the most serious test of Europe's ability to act quickly and decisively, extending the need for the politics of emergency. In the first couple of weeks, the war overshadowed other challenges Europe had faced over its long decade of crises. Yet, not only did Russia's invasion of Ukraine do little to remove these challenges, it will likely make them even more intractable.

Firstly, the indiscriminate bombing of major Ukrainian cities produced a new refugee crisis, the scale of which has the potential to dwarf the crisis of 2015–16. Remarkably, the first wave of refugees—more than 2 million displaced Ukrainians less than two weeks after the start of the invasion[3]—were welcomed even by EU countries traditionally hostile to migration, including Hungary, Poland and the Slovak Republic, all of which share borders with Ukraine. Secondly, the severe economic sanctions imposed on Russia are bound to inflict significant costs on the EU economy too, making a revival of the eurozone crisis a distinct possibility. Thirdly, and arguably most importantly, the war in Ukraine presents a major challenge to the foundational values of the European project, whose very existence is meant to have defied the idea that 'might makes right' (see Chapter 1). This is also bound to reconfigure the EU's internal struggle for the rule of law. Can EU institutions afford ongoing confrontation with Poland over its judicial reforms at the same time as Poland is playing a leading role in assisting its neighbour's fight for survival?[4] Will the overwhelming feeling of European unity prove short-lived?

European Disunion

Indeed, it is worth recalling that Russia's military build-up prior to the invasion exposed Europe's divisions. Decisive actions came from within nation states rather than the EU. Attention was paid to what happened in Washington, London, Warsaw, Kyiv and Moscow, rather than Brussels, the seat of the major EU institutions. While the UK and Poland negotiated a security alliance with Ukraine, and alongside the United States urged their Western partners to adopt stringent economic sanctions, France and Germany remained hopeful about their ability to defuse the conflict via negotiations. Visiting Moscow on 7 February, for example, Macron once again advanced the idea of a 'new security architecture', which was to be negotiated with Russia.[5] This was, of course, yet another opportunity for the French President to muse about a 'sovereign Europe' that would reduce the EU's reliance on the United States and NATO (discussed in Chapter 3). How such a vision was to 'consolidate' Ukraine's sovereignty, as Macron promised to Zelenskiy (Robinet 2022), was far from clear, particularly considering Russia's intransigence. France's dogged determination to think of European security with Russia, rather than against it, was strongly supported by Germany. Not surprisingly, then, the German government was reticent about far-reaching economic sanctions and reluctant to debate the suspension of its controversial pipeline, Nord Stream 2.

In their opposition to a tough stance on Russia, France and Germany echoed an unlikely ally, Viktor Orbán, who called Russian demands 'reasonable' and dismissed calls for sanctions as 'pointless' (Hopkins 2022). Further to this, Germany also opposed deliveries of any military equipment to Ukraine, going so far as to block transfers of weapons and ammunition from Estonia and the Netherlands to Ukraine, because they originated from Germany. Foreign Minister Annalena Baerbock defended this non-confrontational stance, invoking Germany's historic legacies. Speaking at the Munich Security Conference on 18 February, just days before the invasion, Baerbock stressed,

> We have a different responsibility for securing international peace than others. If we are looking at Poland, if we are looking at France, they have been attacked by us like the Soviet Union countries, and therefore our responsibility after the Second World War was that never again from Germany [will there] be war, and never again [will there] be genocide (US Department of State 2022).

Reflecting this justification, Germany's legislation disallowed exports of weapons into areas of conflict—a position that had had strong cross-party support for many decades. Up to the last minute, the German government sought dialogue with Moscow, with Chancellor Scholz visiting Moscow on 15 February, as one of the last major Western leaders to negotiate with Putin before the invasion. Saskia Esken, the leader of Germany's senior governing party the Social Democrats, praised the Chancellor for the 'impressive crisis diplomacy' that led to Putin withdrawing some of his troops and indicating his willingness to pursue 'the path of negotiations'.[6] As we now know, such optimism proved premature. Peace was not to be. What Baerbock, Esken, Scholz and Macron underestimated was Putin's belligerent rhetoric, and the fact that he meant what he said when questioning Ukraine's very right to exist as an independent nation state (a basic misjudgment they shared with Angela Merkel, as discussed in Chapter 2). In fact, in her remarks at the Munich conference, Baerbock unwittingly followed some of the Kremlin's talking points. In a joint press briefing with Scholz, Putin took the opportunity to claim, 'What is happening in Donbass today is, in fact, genocide' (Kremlin 2022). This extraordinary statement remained unchallenged there and then, and later showed its true potential when Putin included it in his lengthy justification of war. Putin's ability to weaponise the 'memory of the World War II and the Holocaust' (Segal 2022) was facilitated by distorted views of European history, into which many sympathisers with Putin's Russia had been co-opted for decades.

Zeitenwende *and the Renewal of European Unity*

'We again have an enemy,' opined *Der Spiegel* in its account of the major epochal change, the *Zeitenwende*, which Germany underwent in the days following the Russian invasion (Gathmann et al. 2022). The 'return of the enemy' (Nassehi 2022) woke Germany from its post-political slumber. The stakes were high. As Chancellor Scholz put it (2022):

> The issue at the heart of this is whether power is allowed to prevail over the law. Whether we permit Putin to turn back the

clock to the nineteenth century and the age of the great powers. Or whether we have it in us to keep warmongers like Putin in check.

To keep Putin in check, the German government promised to massively expand funding for its military, reversed its opposition to sending lethal weapons to Ukraine, and embraced a series of unprecedented sanctions against Russia, including giving up on the Nord Stream 2 project. What had seemed impossible for many decades came to appear necessary in a matter of days. Germany's cherished reliance on the 'rule by rules' was no longer adequate. Supporting this sudden U-turn on its key positions, Germany's Foreign Minister Baerbock noted (2022), 'if our world is a different one, then our policy must also be different.'

The EU response too was as quick as it was bold. The challenge that European leaders faced was to break through the old pattern, in which they had done enough to strengthen the motivation of Ukrainians to fight for democracy and national independence, while denying them sufficient support to enable them to defy Russia. In other words, EU policies seemed to have given enough rhetorical ammunition to Putin in his outlandish claims about Russia's Western 'encirclement', while proving inadequate in containing his revisionist ambitions. At any rate, the time for Europe's 'bureaucratic answers' (Wolczuk 2016: 61) in response to its 'Eastern neighbourhood' was over; new and imaginative solutions were required. Would Europeans prove capable of delivering on their promise to stand with Ukraine? Would Europe, in dealing with Russia, show its ability to speak 'the language of power', as Josep Borrell, the EU's quasi-Foreign Minister, had demanded for some time?

The initial signs were somewhat mixed. To be sure, three days after the invasion, the EU seemed to be both determined and united in its support for Ukraine (Reuters 2022). Ursula von der Leyen, the European Commission President, proudly proclaimed: 'For the first time ever, the European Union will finance the purchase and delivery of weapons and other equipment to a country that is under attack'. Talking up the initiative, Borrell stressed that yet another taboo was being broken: 'The taboo that the European Union was not providing arms in a war.' And to reiterate just how significant the EU's transformation had been, Borrell added, 'we're going to provide even fighting jets' (Tambur 2022)—a promise which he had to disown just a day later, when it transpired that the tentative plan to transfer planes from Poland, Slovakia and Bulgaria did not have the support of these member states, NATO or the United States.

Borrell's attempt to demonstrate Europe's strength ended up as a very public display of its relative weakness. While the EU's financial support was considerable, major decisions about military equipment remained in the hands of national governments, rather than the EU Commission. In a similar way, von der Leyen's encouraging rhetoric about Ukraine's future membership in the European Union was not followed by any major step at the informal EU Council meeting held in Versailles on 10–11 March. Yet, it is the EU Council, not the EU Commission, that has the ultimate say on EU enlargement, and this can only occur with the unanimous support of member states.

What both episodes showed was that the powers of the EU Commission remained constrained. The backtracking on fighter jets was a reminder of the gap between the high expectations that EU rhetoric gives rise to time and again, and its somewhat limited ability to deliver. The blunder also showed the limited accountability of major EU officials. The call for Borrell to resign his position issued by an Estonian MEP, Riho Terras of the European People's Party Group, could safely be ignored. Such setbacks were also indicative of potential divisions within the EU in its approach to Russia. While Central European countries, particularly Poland, the Czech Republic and the Baltic states, were strong advocates of extensive support for Ukraine, including by accelerated accession procedures, the approach taken by Germany, France and the Netherlands was more guarded. 'There is no such thing as a fast track' to EU membership, Dutch Prime Minister Mark Rutte was cited as saying, dampening expectations that the EU could embrace Ukraine's ambition in a speedy manner, accepting it immediately as a candidate country. Timothy Garton Ash's call to reconcile the two Europes, 'the [Brussels] Europe of peacetime bureaucratic process and the [Kyiv] Europe of wartime existential struggle', went unheeded (Ash 2022).

However speedy and radical Europe's transformation was, it proved too little, too late for thousands of Ukrainians—mostly civilians—who perished in the first several weeks of the war, as well as for millions of refugees. At the time of writing in late March 2022, it seems clear that not only Europeans, but the West as a whole, 'will not abandon Ukraine, but nor will it intervene militarily', which awkwardly exposes 'the actual limits of Western commitment' (Tooze 2022). It remains to be seen whether Ukrainian resistance and Western economic sanctions will prove sufficient to stop Putin's expansion. Yet, whatever the outcome, one of the key assumptions that drove the entire project of European integration has been seriously undermined: the idea of the EU as 'the most ambitious and most successful example of peaceful international cooperation in world history' (Moravcsik 2001). While this liberal assumption proved beneficial within the EU, it disempowered Europe in relation to other major external actors. As Ivan Krastev astutely observed (2022), 'Europe's cherished conviction that economic interdependence is the best guarantee for peace has turned out to be wrong. Europeans made a mistake by universalizing their post–World War II experience to countries like Russia.'

The Return of Central Europe

The post–World War II experiences in Central and Eastern Europe were radically different from those of the Western European states that gave birth to the integration project. Thus, intellectuals, academics and political leaders in the Centre and East—whether they were liberal or conservative—were less likely to have any illusions about Russia.[7] Putin's sympathisers were more likely to be recruited from the extreme left or extreme right fringes of the political spectrum. Writing about 'Czech perspectives and British inspiration' for a 'conservative realism', Petr Fiala and František Mikš (2019), for example, warned against the idea that Putin's Russia could be seen as 'a saviour, an ally and a future partner in defence of conservative values'. Such an approach, they argued, ignores the historical experiences of countries that had suffered under Russian and Soviet domination. 'There could not be anything more naive,' Fiala and Mikš wrote, 'because Russia was, is and always will be ready to exploit any weakness of the West to pursue its own power ambitions'.

In a similar vein, Václav Havel, the first president of post-communist Czechoslovakia, warned against Putin's Russia as a 'new kind of dictatorship' with expansionist ambitions as early as 2008.[8] Not surprisingly, then, after becoming Czech Prime Minister, Petr Fiala was at the forefront of support for Ukraine, stressing that 'Ukrainians were fighting for us too' (Česká televize 2022). In a bold gesture, Fiala, alongside Poland's Prime Minister, Mateusz Morawiecki, and Slovenia's Prime Minister, Janez Janša, visited beleaguered Kyiv three weeks after the Russian invasion to express support for the Ukrainian people. After the meeting, Morawiecki noted, 'Europe must understand that if it loses Ukraine it will never be the same again. It will no longer be Europe. Rather it will be a defeated, humiliated and pathetic version of its former self. I want a strong and resolute Europe.'[9]

It remains to be seen whether that daring Prime Ministerial mission marks the return of Poland, the Czech Republic and Slovenia to the centre of EU politics. But there can be little doubt that most Central Europeans have felt vindicated in their choice of both NATO and Europe. The arguments of many West European sympathisers of Putin's Russia (dubbed *Russlandversteher* in German) about Moscow's 'legitimate security interests' in controlling its 'neighbourhood' had little resonance in the Czech Republic, Slovakia, Poland and the Baltic states. As happened with Ukraine, such arguments deny these countries agency by postulating that both EU and NATO enlargements were somewhat imposed on the nations of Central and Eastern Europe against their will. No less a figure than Havel advocated Czech membership of NATO, seeing this as a logical consequence of the country's troubled history. In fact, Czechs have been quick to recognise that Putin's arguments about Russia being threatened by Ukraine are reminiscent of Nazi Germany justifying its invasion of Czechoslovakia in 1938. Putin's real face, Erik Tabery opined, came to light when he expressed 'his deep hatred of [his] democratic neighbour' (2022). Tabery wrote,

In 1938 Adolf Hitler falsely claimed that the 'repression of three and half million of Germans had to stop'. This was the pretext for the occupation of Sudetenland and then the whole country. In 2022 Vladimir Putin untruthfully said that it is 'absolutely necessary to stop this horror, the genocide directed against millions of people, who live there, and rely solely on Russia'. This was the pretext to invade Ukraine.

In contrast to Central European approaches to Russia, Ukraine's vulnerability was exacerbated by Western reluctance to admit the country to both NATO and the European Union. Furthermore, Germany—in the name of interdependency—reduced Russia's dependence on Ukraine by building pipelines for natural gas to bypass Ukraine (Umland 2022), with the construction of Nord Stream 2 project starting just a year after the takeover of Crimea.[10] Merkel's comment about 'gas molecules not knowing what country they were from' has not aged well. In fact, her legacy will remain tarnished by her misjudgment of Russia, vindicating Wolfgang Münchau's earlier assessment of Merkel as 'the most over-rated politician of our time' (Münchau 2021). As shown in Chapter 2, she personified an apolitical approach to politics, which has badly backfired.

The return of war to Europe will further intensify the contest between technocratic 'rule of rules' and the 'politics of emergency', both of which have eroded democracy in Europe and reduced the ability of its sovereign nations to act. Whether Europe's post-heroical (Münkler 2022) and post-political societies will prove capable of overcoming their limitations will impact decisively not only on the future of Ukraine and Russia, but on the Western world as we know it. A rules-based international order can only be restored when democratic nations prove able and willing to fight for it. Is this asking too much? Western politicians who were still prevaricating about the severity of actions targeting Putin's Russia could do worse than find inspiration in Czesław Miłosz, the great Polish poet who was as 'tender toward innocence' as he was 'tough-minded when faced with brutality and injustice' (Heaney 2004). A discharged soldier in Miłosz's poem '1945', written forty years later in Berkeley (2004), 'grasped the futile pride of those lofty generations', who

> In their fine capitals ... still liked to talk
> Yet the twentieth century went on. It was not they
> Who would decide what words were going to mean.

NOTES

ACKNOWLEDGEMENTS

1. 'There are decades where nothing happens; and there are weeks where decades happen'; a Guardian commentator cited Lenin to describe just how turbulent February and March 2022 were because of the Russian invasion of Ukraine: https://www.theguardian.com/world/2022/mar/04/russia-ukraine-how-the-west-woke-up-to-vladimir-putin

2. https://www.iwm.at/event/the-challenge-of-technocracy

3. https://www.chathamhouse.org/2021/10/law-tool-eu-integration-could-be-ending

4. The 1–2 December 2014 Sino-European Dialogue was organised and hosted by the China Institutes of Contemporary International Relations (CICIR), one of the largest Chinese think-tanks on foreign and security policy, which is closely affiliated with the government. In response to my presentation, a senior official from the Chinese Ministry of Foreign Affairs referred to Mearsheimer to rebut my criticisms of Russian and Chinese fears of colour revolutions.

5. The 'Ten Years of the New Europe' conference was organised on the occasion of the tenth anniversary of the Eastern enlargement and took place at the European University Institute, Florence, on 29–30 May 2014. Individual presentations are available on YouTube, including Andrew Moravcsik: https://youtu.be/pAwJZQstS9w and my own: https://youtu.be/G6_NczGP3Uc

6. 'Carl Schmitt in the Kremlin: the Ukraine crisis and the return of geopolitics', *International Affairs*, 91(5), 2015: 953–68.

7. The 22nd Council for European Studies Conference, 'Contradictions: Envisioning European Futures', Sciences Po, Paris, 8–10 July 2015.

1. THE RETURN OF SOVEREIGNTY

1. *The Economist* 2015.
2. Orbán repaid the compliment, calling Juncker 'Grand Duke', in reference to his native Grand Duchy of Luxembourg, one of the world's smallest countries.
3. To make matters more confusing, the Council of Ministers, as opposed to the European Council, *does* have a legislative role. As the name suggests, the former consists of ministers with their different portfolios, while the latter brings together Heads of State and Government. An example of a particularly important Council of Ministers configuration is Ecofin (Economic and Financial Affairs), which has authority over economic policy, including taxation and financial services.
4. In a similar way, Kim Seongcheol (2020: 1) considers Merkel's 'market-conforming democracy', characterised by the 'denial of the need for democratic conflict … in the name of neoliberal economic rationality', as a mirror image of Orbán's 'illiberal democracy'.
5. I would like to thank the late György Schöpflin for this translation. Source: http://nol.hu/archivum/archiv-417593-228304 (accessed 19 November 2021).
6. Andrew Moravcsik is exemplary of this stance, praising the EU as 'the first postmodern institution in world politics and a possible harbinger of future global political structures' (Moravcsik 2001: 122).
7. Against this background, it can be safely surmised that Rousseau would not be impressed by the idea, advanced by a French diplomat, that 'the European Parliament expresses the position of the citizens, according to political trends, and therefore a form of majority European opinion, a European "general will"' (Lefebvre 2021: 6). For a more sophisticated account of Rousseau's conception of the general will and its applicability to the EU, see Bellamy 2019.
8. In a similar way, Bruce Ackerman's (2016) proposition to advance the cause of European integration by the creation of a European army, which would protect Europeans against revisionist Russia, would have to be rejected from such a Kantian perspective. More political unity would need to precede the centralisation of power required for an effective command of such a transnational army. The idea that the European Commission could be tasked with decisions on war and peace assumes a degree of European unity that is neither feasible, nor desirable.
9. For a rare Kelsenian perspective on EU constitutionalism, see Robert Schütze 2016. In his view, 'the ultimate normative base within

Europe—its originality hypothesis or *Grundnorm*—are the European Treaties as such' (58). For Schütze, 'the Union is not a State but constitutes a Federation of *States*' (46).

10. This term can also be traced back to Kelsen (see Busch and Ehs 2008: 195).

11. A possibility that Ernst B. Haas was fully aware of. The units of analysis for political scientists are different from those in natural sciences. 'Atoms, molecules and cells', Haas quipped, 'do not "talk back" to the scholar' (Haas and Haas 2002: 583).

12. Jonathan White's 2003 analysis of the 1965–6 period prefigures the intransigence of the European Commission regarding Brexit negotiations in 2017–20, which was informed by the assumption that the UK would not deal against its own interests (as understood mostly by those who opposed Brexit in the first place). See also Chapter 3 of this volume.

13. Revealingly, this aspect is rather underdeveloped in Weiler's account, other than the author noting that there are many signs indicating 'that the long period of the 70s and 80s has had the effect of introducing a measure of Community "loyalty" whereby the strict Exit-Voice paradigm no longer operates in the way it was established in the foundation period' (Weiler 1990: 25). With the privilege of hindsight, we are left wondering whether even this cautious statement was unduly optimistic.

14. More recently, he was also accused of collaborating with the Soviet KGB, allegations which remain somewhat inconclusive, as discussed in Nichols 2007: 133–7.

15. Yet even Beck (2012) came to the realisation that instead of Europe being exemplary of his 'cosmopolitan vision', it ended up being dominated by its largest member state, Germany.

16. 'A Europe of values' is no longer just a focus of scholarly debates. Before becoming President of the European Commission, on 16 July 2019 Ursula von der Leyen presented herself as a candidate to the European Parliament by thanking 'all the men and women who built a Europe of peace, a united Europe, a Europe of values', and promising to be a bitter opponent to 'anyone that wants to weaken or divide Europe or rob it of its values' (Von der Leyen 2019).

17. 'Only the "third way" remains for us … which is nothing other than the Hegelian synthesis between the thesis of the generally free world economy and the antithesis of autarky. I mean the integration of nations or national economies into larger living communities. In Germany we have coined the expression great space for this, and

this word has lost its meaning and significance abroad through the political conflict. But that should not obscure the fact that the actual content of this concept is an objective condition of our world.' Thus argued Ferdinand Fried in a lecture at the German Chamber of Commerce in Stockholm on 5 March 1943, which was a part of his concerted effort to convince neutral countries during the Second World War about the benefits of 'the Nazi New Order' (cited in Derman 2020: 18, 1).

18. Consider also the recent discussion by Perry Anderson (2020) on legal professionals who worked for and/or influenced the European Court of Justice immediately after the Second World War, with their democratic credentials tarnished by their involvement with Nazi Germany, Vichy France and fascist Italy.

19. This concept of 'militant democracy', that is, a democracy that's willing to stand up for its core principles, is traced back alternatively to Karl Loewenstein (1937) or Carl Schmitt. In his 1932 *Legality and Legitimacy*, Schmitt warned against an excessive commitment to value neutrality, which ultimately rendered the Weimar Republic defenceless against its illiberal enemies. If the legal system is committed to absolute neutrality, wrote Schmitt, it would offer a legal way to destroy itself, pushing value neutrality 'to the point of system suicide' ([1932] 2004: 48). For more recent debates on Schmitt as a theorist of 'militant democracy', see Hacke (2021: 163, 169).

2. A POST-SOVEREIGN EUROPE?

1. My translation.

2. However, strictly speaking, the EU has no single capital. The main seat of the European Parliament, for example, is meant to be Strasbourg, 'where 12 periods of monthly plenary sessions—including the budget session—shall be held' (Article 341, Protocol 6 of the Treaty on the Functioning of the European Union). In fact, most meetings of the Parliament and its many committees take place in Brussels. The result is a messy (and somewhat costly) compromise of the Parliament commuting between Brussels and Strasbourg—an arrangement that was temporarily suspended during the Covid-19 pandemic, much to the anger of French political leaders (Keiger 2020).

3. In contrast to Merkel, another self-declared music lover, the brilliant Hungarian Jewish philosopher Agnes Heller declared the Ninth Symphony dead *because* it became the European anthem (Buch 2003: 5).

4. Against this background, it is all the more astonishing that the musician commissioned with the adaptation was Herbert von Karajan, an Austrian Nazi sympathiser. As Esteban Buch observed, '"Ode to Joy" was chosen to represent Europe not only for its musical greatness, but also for the values proclaimed in Schiller's famous verse, which the instrumental melody evokes even in the absence of words: "All men become brothers." This is by definition less convincing coming from the mouth of a Nazi member, even if he is, according to some, the most brilliant of orchestra conductors' (Buch 2009: 17).

5. The powers of the European Parliament are limited and not comparable to its national counterparts, whether the UK's House of Commons, the German Bundestag, the Irish Dáil Éireann or the Polish Sejm. This did not stop Merkel from flattering MEPs by stressing the importance of the European Parliament as 'the heart of European democracy'.

6. Marking her tenth year as Chancellor, Merkel was *Time* magazine's Person of the Year in 2015, praised for her 'humanity, generosity, tolerance' and her ability 'to demonstrate how Germany's great strength could be used to save, rather than destroy' (Gibbs 2015). In a similar way, *The New York Times* celebrated Merkel as 'the Liberal West's Last Defender' (Smale and Erlanger 2016).

7. Revealing in this respect is the EU flag, which is not a flag, according to the relevant EU Treaties, including Maastricht, but rather 'a Community "logo"—or "emblem"—that was eligible to be reproduced on rectangular pieces of fabric, among other objects' (Theiler 2005: 1). This semantic obfuscation was the result of a compromise designed to allay the fears of those people, particularly in the UK, who were concerned about the EU becoming a federal state.

8. Jacques Delors is cited as saying that he had regrets about giving in too much to German demands, much to the detriment of broader European interests (Moravcsik 2012: 56).

9. Amongst influential policy-makers, only Pöhl, who was then the president of the German Bundesbank, opposed the project. Exceptionally astute was the judgment by Leszek Kołakowski, who was concerned about the loss of national sovereignty and predicted that 'a crisis of the common currency would … be a crisis for Europe as a whole, and in all respects. So if the common currency does not succeed, everyone will have to pretend otherwise' (2003: 20).

10. 'Sie war eine sehr schöne Währung' (She was a beautiful currency), read the headline in the major daily newspaper *Frankfurter Allgemeine Zeitung*, in an obituary of sorts, capturing the nostalgia felt for the German mark (Dieckmann 2001).

11. This was made even more explicitly pro-European in response to the Maastricht Treaty through the amended Article 23(1), which 'stipulates a positive obligation' for Germany's state institutions to 'participate in the development of the European Union', with the constitutional objective of 'establishing a united Europe' (*Staatszielbestimmung*) (cited in Grimm et al. 2019: 418).

12. Which is not to deny that Schmitt discussed the possibility of ethnic homogeneity even earlier, as Weiler highlighted in a recent blog, citing *Die geistesgeschichtliche Lage des heutigen Parlamentarismus* (*The Crisis of Parliamentary Democracy* [1923]), in which Schmitt states that democracy 'necessarily involves first homogeneity and secondly— if necessary—the elimination or annihilation of heterogeneity' (Weiler 2021). However appalling this statement is, even here, as Schmitt explains in numerous examples that follow, the ideal of homogeneity is not necessarily linked to ethnic purity; 'it can also be found in certain physical and moral qualities, for example, in civic virtue, in αρετή, the classic democracy of the *virtus* (*vertu*)' (Schmitt [1923], 1985b: 14). Consistent with this, Schmitt argues that 'the *volonté générale*—the way Rousseau constructs it—is in reality homogeneity' (Schmitt [1923], 1985b: 20). Anticipating the problem that is today known as Böckenförde's dilemma, discussed below, Schmitt concludes his preface by emphasising 'the inescapable contradiction of liberal individualism and democratic homogeneity'.

13. Judging Merkel's response to the pandemic outbreak, a biographer of Max Weber praised her for living up to the Weberian ideal of political leadership (Pergande 2020), an assessment echoed by an editorial in *Süddeutsche Zeitung* which contrasted her 'passion, a sense of responsibility and proportion' with the opportunistic and reckless behaviour of populist leaders like Viktor Orbán and Sebastian Kurz (Föderl-Schmid 2020). In a similar vein, an academic study analysed Merkel's remarkable transformation in 2015 'from committed pragmatist to "conviction leader"' (Helms et al. 2019).

14. Alexander echoes Habermas (2011), who chastised Merkel for 'demoscopic opportunism'.

15. Commission européenne@UEFrance, 9:45AM, 5 October 2020, https://twitter.com/UEFrance/status/1313037472427802625

16. This is an incomplete interpretation of the German Basic Law. Article 16a (§1), which ensures asylum to all 'those who are politically persecuted', is limited in (§2) to those who did not travel through 'other EU countries, or safe third countries'. As very few

refugees would comply with this requirement, almost none have a constitutional right to asylum (Palmer 2017: 37).

17. See Missing Migrants Project, https://missingmigrants.iom.int/region/mediterranean

18. Following the vote, the Czech Interior Minister Milan Chovanec tweeted that '[v]ery soon we will realise the emperor has no clothes. Today was a defeat for common sense.' @Milan_Chovanec, 4:39PM, 22 September 2015, cited in BBC News, Migrant crisis: Opponents Furious Over New EU Quotas, 22 September 2015, https://www.bbc.com/news/world-europe-34331126

3. A SOVEREIGN EUROPE?

1. From 'Extraits d'un inédit d'Alexandre Kojève: "Esquisse d'une doctrine de la politique française"', in *Hommage a Alexandre Kojève: Actes de la 'Journée A. Kojève' du 28 January* 2003 [online] (Éditions de la Bibliothèque nationale de France, 2007 [accessed 5 January 2022]); http://books.openedition.org/editionsbnf/389. With thanks to Alexandros Tsaloukidis for translation.

2. Translated by Alexandros Tsaloukidis.

3. As *The Guardian* reported enthusiastically, 'it was no coincidence that the music Emmanuel Macron chose to accompany him, as he walked in victory through the Louvre esplanade on Sunday night, was Beethoven's Ode to Joy, the official anthem of the European Union. This election was, first and foremost, the rebuttal of what could have been—for France, Europe and the west at large—a slide into a new dark age' (Nougayrède 2017).

4. On 5 December 2020, shortly before the conclusion of the deal, the EU's and the UK's chief negotiators, Michel Barnier and David Frost, released a shared statement in a tweet announcing a pause to the talks so that they could brief their respective 'Principals on the state of play of the negotiations', clarifying that the issues would be further discussed by 'President @vonderleyen and Prime Minister Johnson' (see @MichelBarnier 3:15 AM · Dec 5, 2020 https://twitter.com/michelbarnier/status/1334939381854040064). This was somewhat misleading, for the EU Commission President von der Leyen is *not* to the EU what Boris Johnson is to the United Kingdom.

5. This was an extraordinary claim, especially coming from the EU's chief Brexit negotiator, who, in that capacity, had insisted that the UK accept the jurisdiction of the ECJ over Northern Ireland—an aspect of the withdrawal agreement that Boris Johnson's government was

keen to remove. Furthermore, Barnier's objections to the EU's legal sovereignty coincided with the deteriorating situation in the 'rule of law' crisis, which was exacerbated by the 7 October 2021 decision of the Polish Constitutional Tribunal which openly challenged the supremacy of EU law.

6. In order to replace what Macron considered a discredited 'Washington Consensus'.

7. A few months after his spectacular electoral success, Macron imagined how 'Europe's transformation' might be celebrated seven years later: 'A few weeks after the European elections, Paris will host the Olympic Games. But it's not just Paris that is hosting. It's France and, with it, Europe that will keep alive the Olympic spirit born on this continent. It will be a unique time of coming together, a magnificent opportunity to celebrate European unity. In 2024, the Ode to Joy will ring out, and the European flag can proudly be flown alongside our national emblems.' See https://www.elysee.fr/en/emmanuel-macron/2017/09/26/president-macron-gives-speech-on-new-initiative-for-europe

8. The article by Farhad Khosrokhavar, director of studies at the Ecole des Hautes Etudes en Sciences Sociales, published in *Politico* on 31 October 2020, was later withdrawn as it was deemed too controversial for its suggestion that it was 'France's extreme form of secularism and its adherence to blasphemy, which fueled radicalism within a marginalized minority'. See https://www.politico.eu/article/france-attacks-religion-secularism-radicalism-blasphemy-islam/

9. The problem is bound to persist. As a recent study summarised, 'the EU's competencies in the field are significant, but they are largely centred on law enforcement cooperation, and exclude cooperation between (domestic) security services. These fall under the umbrella of "national security" and remain the sole responsibility of the Member States' (Bignami 2020: 25).

10. As foreshadowed in Schmitt's ([1942] 2008) short essay, *Land und Meer* ('Land and Sea'), a copy of which he sent to Kojève, according to their private correspondence.

11 'Our sea', which is what the Romans called the Mediterranean Sea—see Lepenies 2016.

12. Note that this is increasingly recognised by a number of economists who studied the eurozone crisis (also) as a 'cultural clash' (see, e.g., Guiso, Herrera and Morelli 2013).

13. This is arguably the most imminent challenge in countries like France, where President Macron seeks to end what he described as

'Islamist separatism'. The question of the appropriate response of a state committed to freedom—*der freiheitliche, säkularisierte Staat* (Böckenförde 2021: 228)—to those who detest a political order based on that commitment is one of the most intractable challenges linked to the European migration crisis, as Douglas Murray demonstrated in his 2017 study on immigration, identity and Islam.

14. One German economist criticised the facility as 'a powerful and disastrous precedent generating incentives for excessive debt financing', arguing that it was incompatible with 'the Treaties (notably Article 310 of the Treaty on the Functioning of the European Union) and the Budget Statute [according to which] the EU budget has to be balanced' (Vaubel 2020: 18).

15. Ulrich Beck and Edgar Grande (2007), for example, advocated a Europe based on cosmopolitan predispositions that would, in a Hegelian fashion, overcome (through *Aufhebung*, sublation [34]) the equally unappealing either/or options; that is, either national or European sovereignty by 'the both/and principle', which 'does not aim at a separate, completely independent European unit, but instead involves a doubling of the reference groups whose (mode of) existence is as a result transformed to its core' (35).

16. Thus, when Lord Astor argued that 'the EU referendum is merely advisory; it has no legal standing to force an exit' (Mance 2016), he was simply stating the obvious (though being David Cameron's father-in-law, he caused something of a stir). For a scholarly account of 'the defence of Parliamentary sovereignty through the invocation of popular sovereignty' as laying the foundation for contemporary English nationalism, see Wellings 2012. The arguments that Wellings advanced in relation to the 1975 referendum gained more relevance in 2016. By contrast, Martin Loughlin views 'the increased resort by [UK] governments to the use of referendums' as indicative of a major shift in the UK's constitutional order 'in favour of popular political sovereignty' (2018: 17–18).

17. What's more, parliamentary sovereignty is an English concept extended across the United Kingdom, with little resonance in Scotland (I am indebted to an anonymous reviewer for this point), further exacerbating the tensions between London and Edinburgh. In fact, Brexit has arguably strengthened the calls for another referendum on Scottish independence, which could overturn the result of the 2014 referendum, when Scots voted against independence by 55 per cent.

18. See https://www.times-series.co.uk/news/national/18206880.b-word-not-banned-insists-boris-johnson/

19. The irony, of course, is that 1688 was a parliamentary revolution, which was predicated on Britain 'receiving' a new king from the Netherlands—from continental Europe! I am indebted to Andrew Park for this observation.

20. If any reminder of the ambivalent British attitude towards Europe were needed, the UK's future king, Prince Charles, delivered it in a speech to the German Bundestag in November 2020, when he cited this very poem by Donne to stress the interconnectedness of both countries (Judah 2020).

21. Even more critical was Streeck's assessment, in which he viewed Brexit as a clear sign that 'supranational superstate-building has failed as a political programme', and argued that the result of the referendum was driven by 'the losers under neoliberal internationalism' who placed 'their hopes on their nation-state' (2016b).

22. Curiously, Offe actually misquoted Jandl's verse. The ingenious little poem plays ironically with the very idea of clearly defined categories in politics (and life). The full version in German is as funny as it is intriguing and untranslatable:

    lichtung

    manche meinen
    lechts und rinks
    kann man nicht
    velwechsern.
    werch ein illtum!

    The last verse that Offe cites to pass his verdict on Brexit is nonsensical in the original. By exchanging the letters r and l Jandl smashed 'the political code of left versus right' (Offe 2002: 84). A 'corrected' version in German could be translated as:

    direction

    some believe
    right and left
    cannot be confused
    what a mistake!

23. I have borrowed this title from an excellent survey article by Jill Rutter and Anand Menon (2020) presenting 'the mysterious story of how a split-down-the-middle nation killed off the chance to be half-in and half-out of Europe'.

24. This is not to underestimate other factors, including the mutual distrust exacerbated by the lack of clarity on the part of the UK government about the aims of Brexit.

25. On the completion of the negotiations on 14 November 2018, the front page of the *Irish Examiner* declared 'Victory in Dublin, Chaos in London'—a triumphalist headline that proved premature. It was clear from the outset that if 'chaos in London' was to persist, Ireland's victory would prove to be hollow.

4. THE RETURN OF GEOPOLITICS

1. Both epigraph quotes are my translations.

2. As the then Belgian Minister of Foreign Affairs, Mark Eyskens, quipped on the eve of the Gulf War in January 1991. Thirty years later, Europe is a somewhat diminished 'economic giant' too, as its economic preponderance is being eclipsed by the rise of China and the continuing expansion of the US economy. As *The Economist* reported on 5 June 2021, 'at the start of the 21st century 41 of the world's 100 most valuable companies were based in Europe (including Britain and Switzerland but excluding Russia and Turkey). Today only 15 are.'

3. There was nothing sinister about a British sociologist referring to 'the Ukraine' meaning 'borderland' a couple of decades ago (Delanty 1995: 147), but it would be reckless to do it now, considering the importance that Putin himself assigns to etymology. 'The Ukraine' is incorrect as it implies simply a territorial designation, rather than the name of the country, which is Ukraine (without the article). Putin claims that 'the name "Ukraine" was used more often in the meaning of the Old Russian word "okraina" (periphery), which is found in written sources from the 12th century, referring to various border territories', in order to argue that 'Russians and Ukrainians were one people—a single whole'—a statement that justifies Russia's revisionist claims towards its neighbour (Putin 2021).

4. This anxiety is captured in the opening line of the Ukrainian national anthem, which, like the Polish anthem, speaks of a nation that is not yet lost. The same anxiety and how it is perceived by other countries is cynically exploited by one of Putin's former propagandists, Vladislav Surkov, who is unrepentant about the role he played in the Russian 2014 invasion: 'Ukrainians are very well aware that for the time being, their country does not really exist' (Surkov 2021).

5. Grouped under Russia's leadership in the Collective Security Treaty Organization (CSTO), also referred to as the 'Tashkent Pact'.

6. In response to the allegations that Russia's security services targeted Navalny with a nerve agent, Putin did not deny that they would be able to do so, but instead claimed that they would have done so more effectively. 'Who needs to poison him', the Russian President said during a press conference. 'If they'd wanted to [poison him] then they probably would have finished the job' (cited in Roth 2020).

7. As Herpen points out, *gosudar* is an antiquated Russian term meaning '"ruler," "sovereign," but also "prince" or "monarch"' (2013: 83). Panarin cites Machiavelli's *Prince* for this unusual choice (cited in Herpen 2013: 83). Without overstating the point, it is worth noting that the etymology of 'the state' in Russian—*gosudarstvo*—differs from many Western languages. While in the West 'the state' ('der Staat' in German) is usually traced back to Machiavelli's discussion of 'lo stato', which amongst its multiple meanings indicated different forms of government and effective power, the Russian term *gosudarstvo* implies domination. For a detailed etymological study, see Kharkhordin (2001).

8. Sergey Lavrov, Russia's Foreign Minister, echoed these arguments in a programmatic article about 'The Law, the Rights and the Rules' (О праве, правах и правилах]), going so far as to suggest that Russia's deep-seated commitment to law- and rule-following is reflected in the Russian language. Because 'the words "law" and "rule" share a single root' ["право" and "правило"]', Lavrov suggested, 'to us [Russians], a rule that is genuine and just is inseparable from the law' (Lavrov 2021).

9. In May 2015, at the time that Greece was seeking to secure an extension to a massive €240 billion bailout, European leaders at an EU Eastern Partnership summit in Riga pledged merely €1.8 billion for Ukraine.

10. Even the EU Commission President José Manuel Barroso was able to see the manifold meanings of EU imagery in the Maidan. He observed in late 2013: 'When we see in the cold streets of Kiev, men and women with the European flag, fighting for that European flag, it is because they are also fighting for Ukraine and for their future' (cited in Byrne 2014).

11. It is following this logic that the Ukrainian government opposed the deal that Germany and the US finally reached in July 2021, overcoming their differences on Nord Stream 2. The Ukrainian Foreign Minister invoked the 2,135-page-long EU Association Agreement to remind Germany and the EU of the principle of solidarity under which such negotiations should have been conducted. Objecting to the fact that

Germany had made the decision about Ukraine without consulting Ukraine, the minister wrote an official note to Brussels, citing Article 274 of the Agreement, according to which the EU and its member states are obliged to 'consult and coordinate' with Ukraine on energy 'infrastructure developments' (Herszenhorn 2021).

5. A SOVEREIGNIST EUROPE?

1. 'Nationalism is an ideological poison', declared President Frank-Walter Steinmeier in a January 2019 speech to Germany's diplomatic corps, stressing that especially, 'we in Europe will never forget this' (*Die Welt*, 14 January 2019).

2. The more inclusive version of the Polish nation was represented by Józef Piłsudski—his authoritarian tendencies notwithstanding—while his opponent, Roman Dmowski, stood for a more ethnocentric conception of nationhood.

3. Though far from being non-violent, the Hungarian freedom fighters of 1956 were praised by Hannah Arendt in terms better applicable to the peaceful revolutions of 1989 (Arendt 1958: 487).

4. Born to a Slovak father and Czech/Moravian mother who received German education, Tomáš Masaryk married a fellow student in Leipzig, an American woman, Charlotte Garrigue, whose name he adopted as his own middle name. Before becoming President, he was a truly worldly philosopher at the University of Vienna.

5. As regional centres of the revolution opposed the attempts at consolidation of power in Prague and Bratislava, 'a pattern of 1848 in the Habsburg Empire was repeated at a smaller scale—with mid-level powers protesting the domination of higher-level powers, only to have lower-level powers appeal to the higher entities in protest of mid-level domination' (Krapfl 2013: 131). Thus, my hometown Košice in eastern Slovakia, for example, appealed to Prague as its citizens were fearful of domination by Bratislava.

6. For Masaryk, for example, the Czech national programme served humanity at large, but was based on its unique tradition. 'Humanity can be seen as our national task prepared and bequeathed to us by the Brethren: the humanitarian ideal is the entire meaning of our national life' (Masaryk, cited in Chlup 2020: 187).

7. Ironically, a recent Pew Research Center survey suggests that Czechs are on average *more* 'likely than Slovaks to agree with nationalist statements'. For example, 'more Czechs than Slovaks say being born in their country is important (78% vs. 56%). And more Czechs than

Slovaks agree with the statement "Our people are not perfect, but our culture is superior to others" (55% vs. 44%)' (cited in Starr 2019). I would like to thank Dasha Auer for alerting me to this point.

8. In making 'the legal case for violating Yugoslavia's national sovereignty in the absence of Security Council Approval', Klinton W. Alexander (2000: 403) cites Hugo Grotius in support of NATO's intervention in Kosovo: 'If a tyrant practices atrocities towards his subjects, which no just man can approve, the right of human social connection is not cut off in such a case …. [I]t would follow that others may take up arms for them.'

9. As Martin Krygier wryly observed, 'notwithstanding the implausible optimism of the tense chosen, everyone knew there was work still to be done' (Krygier 2021: 358).

10. Budapest has thus become a veritable place of pilgrimage for conservative pundits, with Tucker Carlson of Fox News fame hosting his show from the city for a week in August 2021.

11. Having said that, it is important to note that Orbán openly supported Babiš in the 2021 Czech parliamentary elections.

12. My translation from the Czech.

13. Consider the situation in Ukraine, where a liberal, pro-Western government led by President Volodymyr Zelenskiy was hindered in its anti-corruption drive by the Ukrainian Constitutional Court—a step described as a veritable 'counter-revolution' (see Veser 2020), which attempted to undo the achievements of the 2014 'Revolution of Dignity'. In its October 2020 decision, the court declared a crucial piece of legislation to be unconstitutional, invoking the independence of the judicial branch. Zelenskiy thus faced an impossible dilemma— he could either respect the independence of the court, jeopardising his anti-corruption reforms, or he could defy the court in order to fight the corruption (including amongst judges), jeopardising the political independence of the judiciary. It is worth remembering that 'the independence of constitutional justice is not an end in itself but a means of ensuring the constitutional limitations of state power and guaranteeing freedom and human rights' (Boryslavska and Granat 2021: 10). It follows, then, that 'if the independence of the constitutional court is used to the detriment of these ideas, the body of constitutional justice loses its legitimacy' (ibid. 24).

14. The subheading is borrowed from Czarnota (2019).

15. Even observers sympathetic to the Law and Justice Party-led government acknowledge that numerous mistakes were made. According to Cichocki and Grosse, for example, 'Poland has failed

to present convincing arguments that would defend the country and alleviate the fears of other Member States' (2019: 261).

16. An opinion poll in 2018, for example, saw a further significant decline in levels of trust for judges, from 54 per cent to 46 per cent from the previous year—a timeframe that may reflect the impact of the July 2017 reform which 'allowed the Polish Minister of Justice, among other things, to dismiss judges without citing any reasons and to appoint others instead' (GfK Verein 2018, 49).

17. I would like to thank Adam Czarnota for alerting me to this point (private email correspondence, 27 November 2021).

18. As Wiktor Osiatynski noted, 'because the drafting process took place in the lion's den of daily politics, the very legitimacy of the framers was repeatedly called into question' (1997: 66).

19. Assessing the compliance with the EU's *normative acquis* is not the same as 'ascertaining belief in values', stresses Müller, adding in jest: 'whatever the latter might mean concretely: a Committee on "Un-European" Beliefs and Activities in the European Parliament' (Müller 2020, 318).

20. Clara Maier offers a useful corrective to the received wisdom on the origins of this model, by arguing that 'West Germany's specific model of judicialized constitutionalism was developed not simply as a reaction and certainly not as a solution to the political and legal problems that Nazism brought to the fore. Rather … the West German *Rechtsstaat* with its "eternal" basic rights and the strong role of the constitutional court was developed already in the Weimar years' (2019: 1071).

21. It should be mentioned, however, that 'a quasi-mythical trust in Brussels' (Sadurski 2019: 200), which overwhelming majorities of citizens had in accession countries, was not based on adequate knowledge of the way the EU worked.

22. Supporting such sanctions would create 'a very delicate and uncomfortable situation', writes Sadurski, predicting that 'a financial stick will be used against Poland if the carrot does not turn out to be an effective incentive for respecting the rule of law' (2019: 232).

23. With Adam Michnik as its editor-in-chief, *Gazeta Wyborcza* is known and respected for its opposition to the conservative government.

24. There is a lively scholarly debate about how to classify Hungarian democracy, with labels ranging from 'managed democracy', 'illiberal democracy', 'populist democracy', 'defective democracy' to 'hybrid regime', 'authoritarian regime', 'operetta dictatorship', 'semi-dictatorship', 'electoral democracy' or even 'mafia state'. See an

excellent survey in Körösényi, Illés and Gyulai (2020), who describe the Orbán regime as a 'plebiscitary leader democracy'.

CONCLUSION

1. My translation.
2. While it is no longer taboo in EU scholarship to discuss the possibility that the EU might disintegrate (Webber 2014: 2019), there are far fewer voices contemplating the possibility of (partial) disintegration as something desirable (Streeck 2021).
3. This is corroborated by a recent survey conducted by the European Council on Foreign Relations, which found that 'many European citizens [had] less confidence in EU institutions' (Dennison and Puglierin 2021) more than a year after the outbreak of the pandemic (April 2021). High levels of dissatisfaction reached even Europe's core, including Germany, where the number of people believing that 'the EU system is broken' increased significantly (55 per cent in April 2021, from 44 per cent in November 2020), alongside a number of Germans expressing the view that 'EU integration has gone too far'.
4. An obvious objection could be made here that the United States, which had the advantage of a powerful executive, did not perform well either. There, the problem was thus not the lack of executive powers, but rather that these powers were in the hands of an erratic, narcissistic leader, President Donald Trump.

AUTHOR'S NOTE

1. Relying on US intelligence reports, which were widely shared to an incredulous press, the US administration led by President Joe Biden successfully foiled Russia's attempt to create a false pretext for the invasion.
2. Apart from referencing the classic image of an all-powerful leader associated with Thomas Hobbes—Leviathan—Nemtsov invoked the eponymous movie by Andrey Zvyagintsev (discussed in Chapter 4). In fact, shortly before he was killed, Nemtsov argued that Zvyagintsev's movie would serve as a monument to 'Putinism' (Wengle et al. 2018: 1012).
3. See AFP via *Frankfurter Allgemeine Zeitung*, https://www.faz.net/aktuell/ukraine-konflikt/mehr-als-zwei-millionen-menschen-sind-bislang-aus-der-ukraine-geflohen-17861322.html

4. Poland and Ukraine share a history of conflict, not just cooperation, but the war brought the two nations arguably closer than ever. The threat that a belligerent Russia represents to their statehood is reflected in their respective national anthems, which both start with the line that their nation 'has not perished yet'.
5. An idea that the French President had pursued for years. 'Macron: Europe needs to team up with Russia to build new security architecture', read the headline of the Russian news agency TASS on 30 August 2018: https://tass.com/world/1019244
6. @EskenSaskia, 4:37 PM, 15 February 2022, https://twitter.com/ EskenSaskia/status/1493625593841299459
7. With the notable exception of Orbán's Hungary, which prevaricated in the immediate aftermath of the invasion. Yet, even Orbán recognised that his past closeness to Putin was an electoral liability; he changed a number of key positions, including by supporting Ukraine's expedited membership in the EU and even allowing 'NATO arms shipments to pass through Hungary—a NATO member—on their way to Ukraine after previous refusals to do so'. See Coakley 2022.
8. Early on, Havel also warned against excessive dependency on Russian gas and oil, stressing the importance of dealing with Russia as an equal partner 'even if the result was to be less gas and oil'. See https://www.tyden.cz/rubriky/domaci/havel-rusko-je-novy-druh-diktatury_76846.html
9. @MorawieckiM, 10:27 PM, 15 March 2022, https://twitter.com/ MorawieckiM/status/1503860434918846464/retweets/with_ comments
10. Sigmar Gabriel, who as Germany's Economic Affairs Minister authorised Nord Stream 2 in 2015, acknowledged his mistake, all the while arguing that the German government's responsibility was limited because the EU had previously liberalised the market with gas. Apart from misconstruing the history—the EU attempted on numerous occasions to stop the project—this stance exemplifies how Germany sought to hide its power behind 'Europe'. See Steppat 2022.

BIBLIOGRAPHY

Ackerman, B. (2016). *Reorganizing NATO: Europe's Last Chance to Preserve Fundamental Rights*. Global Constitutional Discourse and Transnational Constitutional Activity, Venice. https://www.venice.coe.int/webforms/documents/default.aspx?pdffile=CDL-PI(2016)014-e

Adelman, J. (2013). *Worldly Philosopher: The Odyssey of Albert O. Hirschman*. Princeton University Press.

AFP (23 August 2021). Borrell: EU Should Prepare for the New Crises. *Euractiv*. https://www.euractiv.com/section/global-europe/news/borrell-eu-should-prepare-for-the-next-crises-iraq-sahel/

Agamben, G. (2013). The 'Latin Empire' Should Strike Back. *Voxeurop*. https://voxeurop.eu/en/the-latin-empire-should-strike-back/

Ágh, A. (2015). De-Europeanization and De-Democratization Trends in ECE: From the Potemkin Democracy to the Elected Autocracy in Hungary. *Journal of Comparative Politics*, 8(2): 4–26.

— (2019). *Declining Democracy in East-Central Europe: The Divide in the EU and Emerging Hard Populism*. Edward Elgar.

Alexander, K. W. (2000). NATO's Intervention in Kosovo: The Legal Case for Violating Yugoslavia's National Sovereignty in the Absence of Security Council Approval. *Houston Journal of International Law*, 22: 403–44.

Alexander, R. (2017). *Die Getriebenen: Merkel und die Flüchtlingspolitik*. 4th edition. Siedler.

Ali, T. (9 April 2015). The New World Disorder. *London Review of Books*, 37(7): 19–22.

———— (6 July 2021), US Hates Russia for Regaining its Sovereignty! *Russia Today*. https://www.youtube.com/watch?v=DvVOMf_AE3M&ab_channel=GoingUndergroundonRT

Anderson, P. (17 December 2020). The European Coup. *London Review of Books*, 42(24).

Arato, A. (2000). *Civil Society, Constitution, and Legitimacy*. Rowman & Littlefield.

Arendt, H. (1958). *The Origins of Totalitarianism*. Meridian Books.

——— (1968). *Men in Dark Times*. Harcourt, Brace & World, Inc.

——— (1982). *Lectures on Kant's Political Philosophy*. University of Chicago Press.

——— (2005). *The Promise of Politics*. Schocken Books.

Ash, T.G. (4 March 2022). In this moment of crisis, opening the door to Ukraine is one thing the EU can do. *The Guardian*. https://www.theguardian.com/commentisfree/2022/mar/04/ukraine-eu-membership-zelenskiy-european-values-war

Auer, S. (2004a). *Liberal Nationalism in Central Europe*. Routledge.

——— (2004b). The Paradoxes of the Revolutions of 1989 in Central Europe. In J. Rundell (ed.), *Contemporary Perspectives in Critical and Social Philosophy* (pp. 361–90). Brill.

——— (2010). 'New Europe': Between Cosmopolitan Dreams and Nationalist Nightmares. *JCMS: Journal of Common Market Studies*, 48(5): 1163–84.

Auer, S., and Scicluna, N (2021). The Impossibility of Constitutionalizing Emergency Europe. *JCMS: Journal of Common Market Studies*, 59: 20–31.

Avbelj, M. (2020). A Sovereign Europe as a Future of Sovereignty. *European Papers*, 5(1): 299–302.

Bach, J. (2007). Keep Sovereignty Sovereign! *International Studies Review*, 9(4): 714–17.

Baerbock, A. (27 February 2022). Statement by Foreign Minister Annalena Baerbock at the special parliamentary session on the Russian war. Federal Foreign Office of Germany. https://www.auswaertiges-amt.de/en/newsroom/news/-/2513998

Bajon, P. (2018). 'The Human Factor': French–West German Bilateralism and the 'Logic of Appropriateness' in the European Crisis of the Mid-1960s. *Diplomacy & Statecraft*, 29(3): 455–76.

Beck, U. (2006). *The Cosmopolitan Vision*. Polity Press.

——— (2012). *Das deutsche Europa*. Suhrkamp.

Beck, U., and Grande, E. (2007). *Cosmopolitan Europe*. Trans. C. Cronin. English paperback edition. Polity Press.

Behnke, A. (2008). 'Eternal Peace' as the Graveyard of the Political: A Critique of Kant's *Zum Ewigen Frieden*. *Millennium: Journal of International Studies*, 36(3): 513–31.

———— (2012). The Theme that Dare Not Speak its Name: Geopolitik, Geopolitics and German Foreign Policy Since Unification. In *The Return of Geopolitics in Europe?* Ed. S Guzzini (pp. 101–26). Cambridge University Press.

Belavusau, U., and Gliszczyńska-Grabias, A. (2020). *Constitutionalism under Stress: Essays in Honour of Wojciech Sadurski*. Oxford University Press.

Bellamy, R. (2019). *A Republican Europe of States: Cosmopolitanism, Intergovernmentalism and Democracy in the EU*. Cambridge University Press.

Berman, R. A., and Marder, M. (2009). Carl Schmitt and the Event: Introduction. *Telos* (147): 3–13.

Betts, A., and Collier, P. (2017). *Refuge: Transforming a Broken Refugee System*. Allen Lane.

Bickerton, C. J. (2012). *European Integration: From Nation-States to Member States*. Oxford University Press.

Bignami, F. (2020). *EU Law in Populist Times: Crises and Prospects*. Cambridge University Press.

Blinken, A. J. (1987). *Ally versus Ally: America, Europe, and the Siberian Pipeline Crisis*. Praeger.

Blokker, P. (2019a). Populist Counter-Constitutionalism, Conservatism, and Legal Fundamentalism. *European Constitutional Law Review*, 15(3): 519–43.

———— (2019b). Populism as a Constitutional Project. *International Journal of Constitutional Law*, 17(2): 535–53.

Böckenförde, E.-W. (21 June 2010). Kennt die europäische Not kein Gebot? *Neue Zürcher Zeitung*.

———— (2017). *Constitutional and Political Theory*. Ed. M. Künkler and T. Stein. Oxford University Press.

———— (2021). *Religion, Law, and Democracy: Selected Writings*. Ed. M. Künkler and T. Stein. Oxford University Press.

Bogdandy, A. von. (2017). Von der technokratischen Rechtsgemeinschaft zum politisierten Rechtsraum. *MPIL Research Paper Series* (12).

Bogdanor, V. (2019). *Beyond Brexit: Towards a British Constitution*. I.B. Taurus.

Boryslavska, O., and Granat, M. (2021). Independence of Constitutional Justices: Stumbling Blocks in Ukraine and Poland. *Access to Justice in Eastern Europe*, 2(10): 8–24.

Braun, E. (31 January 2020). Macron: Brexit Campaign Based on 'Lies' but EU Must Reform. *Politico*. https://www.politico.eu/article/macron-brexit-campaign-based-on-lies-but-eu-must-reform/

Brinkbäumer, K., Heyer, J. A., and Sandberg, B. (13 October 2017). Interview with Emmanuel Macron: We Need to Develop Political

Heroism. https://www.spiegel.de/international/europe/interview-with-french-president-emmanuel-macron-a-1172745.html?utm_medium=twitter&utm_source=dlvr.it#ref=rss

Browning, C. S. (2018). Geostrategies, Geopolitics and Ontological Security in the Eastern Neighbourhood: The European Union and the 'New Cold War'. *Political Geography*, 62: 106–15.

Bruckner, P. (4 November 2020). Frankreich ist nicht verhasst, weil es die Muslime unterdrückt. Sondern weil es sie befreit. *Neue Zürcher Zeitung*. https://www.nzz.ch/feuilleton/terror-in-frankreich-die-laizitaet-unterdrueckt-nicht-sie-befreit-ld.1585011?reduced=true

Brunnermeier, M., James, H., and Landau, J.-P. (2016). *The Euro and the Battle of Ideas*. Princeton University Press.

Buch, E. (2003). *Beethoven's Ninth: A Political History*. University of Chicago Press.

——— (2009). Beethoven in the Shadows of Berlin: Karajan's European Anthem. *Dissent*, 56(4): 14–17.

Burger, V. R., Gerster, L., and Schuller, K. (21 August 2021). Bidens Anküdigung hat mich enttäuscht. *Frankfurter Allgemeine Sonntagszeitung*. https://www.faz.net/aktuell/politik/inland/laschet-zu-afghanistan-biden-hat-mich-enttaeuscht-17494200.html

Burgess, J. P. (2007). The Evolution of European Union Law and Carl Schmitt's Theory of the Nomos of Europe. In *The International Political Thought of Carl Schmitt: Terror, Liberal War and the Crisis of Global Order*. Ed. L. Odysseos and F. Petito (pp. 185–201). Routledge.

Busch, J., and Ehs, T. (2008). The EU as Rechtsgemeinschaft: A Kelsenian Approach to European Legal Philosophy. *Rivista Internazionale di Filosofia del diritto*: 195–224.

Buštíková, L., and Guasti, P. (2019). The State as a Firm: Understanding the Autocratic Roots of Technocratic Populism. *East European Politics and Societies and Cultures*, 33(2): 302–30.

Byrne, A. (8 May 2014). EU's Response to Ukraine Crisis Highlights Limits to Power. *Financial Times*.

Canovan, M. (1999). Lasting Institutions: Arendtian Thoughts on Nations and Republics. *Graduate Faculty Philosophy Journal*, 21(2): 133–51.

Carens, J. H. (2015). *The Ethics of Immigration*. Oxford University Press.

CBOS (2021). Stosunek do członkostwa Polski w Unii Europejskiej. *Centrum Badania Opinii Społecznej*. https://cbos.pl/PL/trendy/trendy.php?trend_parametr=stosunek_do_integracji_UE

Česká televize. (1 March 2022). Ukrajinci bojují i za nás, zásah NATO by vedl ke světové válce, myslí si premiér Fiala. https://ct24.ceskatelevize.

cz/domaci/3449396-zive-premier-fiala-mluvi-ve-specialu-udalosti-komentaru-o-invazi-na-ukrajinu

Chamon, M., and Theuns, T. (11 October 2021). Resisting Membership Fatalism: Dissociation through Enhanced Cooperation or Collective Withdrawal. *VerfBlog*. https://verfassungsblog.de/resisting-membership-fatalism/

Chimni, B. S. (2015). Peace Through Law: Lessons from 1914. *London Review of International Law*, 3(2): 245–65.

Chlup, R. (2020). Competing Myths of Czech Identity. *New Perspectives*, 28(2): 179–204.

Chuanjia, Z., Xu, Y., and Peiyu, C. (25 May 2012). See through the Nature of Western Push for Human Rights and Democracy 认清西方"民主人权输出"的实质. *People's Daily* 人民网. http://politics.people.com.cn/GB/30178/17981157.html

Cichocki, M. A. (2020). *Contemporary States and the Crisis of the Western Order*. Peter Lang.

Cichocki, M. A., and Grosse, T. G. (eds.) (2019). *The Many Faces of Crisis: An Analysis of Crisis Management from an Economic and Political Perspective*. Peter Lang.

Clark, C. (1997). Forging Identity: Beethoven's 'Ode' as European Anthem. *Critical Inquiry*, 23(4): 789–807.

——— (2013). *The Sleepwalkers: How Europe Went to War in 1914*. Harper.

Coakley, A. (14 March 2022). Hungary's Orbán Pivots Away From Putin as Elections Loom. *Foreign Policy*. https://foreignpolicy.com/2022/03/14/hungary-orban-russia-war-election/

Collier, P. (2013). *Exodus: How Migration is Changing Our World*. Oxford University Press.

Connelly, J. (2020). *From Peoples into Nations: A History of Eastern Europe*. Princeton University Press.

Connolly, K. (16 July 2015). Angela Merkel Comforts Sobbing Refugee but says Germany Can't Help Everyone. *The Guardian*. https://www.theguardian.com/world/2015/jul/16/angela-merkel-comforts-teenage-palestinian-asylum-seeker-germany

Cooper, R. (1996). *The Post-Modern State and the World Order*. Demos.

Copsey, N. (2015). *Rethinking the European Union*. Palgrave Macmillan.

Curtin, D. (1993). The Constitutional Structure of the Union: A Europe of Bits and Pieces. *Common Market Law Review*, 30: 17–69.

Czarnota, A. (2019). Rule of Lawyers or Rule of Law? On Constitutional Crisis and Rule of Law in Poland. In *Governance and Constitutionalism: Law, Politics and Institutional Neutrality*. Ed. B. Iancu and S. E. Tănăsescu (pp. 51–63). Routledge.

————— (2020). Constitutional Breakdown, Backsliding, or New Post-Conventional Constitutionalism? In *Constitutionalism under Stress: Essays in Honour of Wojciech Sadurski*. Ed. U. Belavusau and A. Gliszczyńska-Grabias (pp. 39–50). Oxford University Press.

Dausend, P., and Schieritz, M. (20 May 2020). Jemand muss vorangehen [An Interview with Olaf Scholz]. *Die Zeit*. https://www.zeit.de/2020/22/olaf-scholz-europaeische-union-reform-vereinigte-staaten

Dawson, M. (2019). Juncker's Political Commission: Did it Work? *SIEPS: Swedish Institute for European Policy Studies*. https://www.sieps.se/globalassets/publikationer/2019/2019_8epa_.pdf

Deák, I. (1976). Lajos Kossuth's Nationalism and Internationalism. *Austrian History Yearbook*, 12(1): 48–51.

de Gaulle, C. (9 September 1965). Twelfth Press Conference held by General de Gaulle as President of the Fifth Republic in Paris at the Elysee Palace. Speeches & Press Conferences No. 228 [EU Speech]. Archive of European Integration. http://aei.pitt.edu/5356/

Delanty, G. (1995). *Inventing Europe: Idea, Identity, Reality*. Macmillan.

Delcker, J. (2016). Angela Merkel: Brexit is 'Watershed for Europe'. *Politico*.

Delors, J. (17 October 1989). Speech by President Delors at the Opening Session of the 40th Academic Year of the College of Europe – Bruges. https://ec.europa.eu/commission/presscorner/detail/en/SPEECH_89_73

Dennison, S., and Puglierin, J. (9 June 2021). Crisis of Confidence: How Europeans See their Place in the World. *European Council on Foreign Relations*. https://ecfr.eu/publication/crisis-of-confidence-how-europeans-see-their-place-in-the-world/

Derman, J. (2011). Carl Schmitt on Land and Sea. *History of European Ideas*, 37(2): 181–9.

————— (2020). Prophet of a Partitioned World: Ferdinand Fried, 'Great Spaces,' and the Dialectics of Deglobalization, 1929–1950. *Modern Intellectual History*, 18(3): 1–25.

Dieckmann, F. (1 December 2001). Sie war eine sehr schöne Währung. *Frankfurter Allgemeine Zeitung*, VI.

Dinan, D. (2005). *Ever Closer Union: An Introduction to European Integration*. 3rd edition. Lynne Rienner.

Ditrych, O. (2 November 2021). The Czech Republic's Political Turnaround isn't a Liberal Victory. *Foreign Policy*. https://foreignpolicy.com/2021/11/02/czech-republic-election-liberal-democracy-babis-zeman/

Dixon, D. (2018). Article 50 and Member State Sovereignty. *German Law Journal*, 19(4): 901–40.

Dunn, E. C., and Bobick, M. S. (2014). The Empire Strikes Back: War without War and Occupation without Occupation in the Russian Sphere of Influence. *American Ethnologist*, 41(3): 405–13.

Dyson, K., and Maes, I. (2016). *Architects of the Euro: Intellectuals in the Making of European Monetary Union*. Oxford University Press.

Dyzenhaus, D. (2016). The Concept of the Rule-of-Law State in Carl Schmitt's *Verfassungslehre*. In *The Oxford Handbook of Carl Schmitt*. Ed. J. Meierhenrich and O. Simons (pp. 490–509). Oxford University Press.

The Economist (27 May 2015). Hungary and the EU: Love Tap. https://www.economist.com/europe/2015/05/27/love-tap

————(5 June 2021). Europe is Now a Corporate Also-Ran. Can it Recover its Footing? https://www.economist.com/briefing/2021/06/05/once-a-corporate-heavyweight-europe-is-now-an-also-ran-can-it-recover-its-footing

Ekathimerini [Greece] (2 June 2016). EU's Tusk Urges End to 'Utopian Dreams' of Europe. https://www.ekathimerini.com/news/209245/eus-tusk-urges-end-to-utopian-dreams-of-europe/

Ellison, H. (May 2019). For a New Capitalism and a New European Union. *Paris Update*, 1. https://www.parisupdate.com/le-nouvel-elmpire-leurope-du-vingt-et-unieme-siecle/ [sic]

Enyedi, Z. (2020). Right-Wing Authoritarian Innovations in Central and Eastern Europe. *East European Politics*, 36(3): 363–77.

Enzensberger, H. M. (2011). *Sanftes Monster Brüssel oder Die Entmündigung Europas*. Suhrkamp.

Erlanger, S. (23 June 2021). A Culture War Between Hungary and Europe Escalates Over L.G.B.T. Bill. *The New York Times*. https://www.nytimes.com/2021/06/23/world/europe/hungary-europe-lgbt-culture-war.html

Euractiv (4 November 2020). Austria's Kurz Urges EU to do More to Fight 'Political Islam'. https://www.euractiv.com/section/global-europe/news/austrias-kurz-urges-eu-to-do-more-to-fight-political-islam/

European Council (17 December 2020). Belarus: EU Imposes Third Round of Sanctions over ongoing Repression. Council of Europe Press Release. https://www.consilium.europa.eu/en/press/press-releases/2020/12/17/belarus-eu-imposes-third-round-of-sanctions-over-ongoing-repression/

Evans, R. J. W. (2020). Remembering the Fall of the Habsburg Monarchy One Hundred Years On: Three Master Interpretations. *Austrian History Yearbook*, 51: 269–91.

Everson, M., and Joerges, C. (2014). Who is the Guardian of Constitutionalism in Europe after the Financial Crisis? In *Political Representation in the European Union*. Ed. Sandra Kröger (pp. 197–211). Routledge.

Fabbrini, F., and Kelemen, R. D. (7 May 2020). With One Court Decision, Germany may be Plunging Europe into a Constitutional Crisis. *Washington Post*. https://www.washingtonpost.com/politics/2020/05/07/germany-may-be-plunging-europe-into-constitutional-crisis/

Faiola, A. (13 November 2014). Juncker Scandal Prompts Sniping at European Commission Election System. *Washington Post*. https://www.washingtonpost.com/world/europe/juncker-scandal-prompts-sniping-at-european-commission-election-system/2014/11/13/cf8804e8-69c0-11e4-bafd-6598192a448d_story.html

Ferguson, N. (1 January 2005). Look Back at Weimar – and Start to Worry About Russia. *The Telegraph*. https://www.telegraph.co.uk/comment/personal-view/3613907/Look-back-at-Weimar-and-start-to-worry-about-Russia.html

Fiala, P. (2010). *Politika, jaká nemá být*. Centrum pro studium demokracie a kultury.

Fiala, P., and Mikš, F. (2019). *Konzervatismus dnes: Politika, společnost a zdravý rozum v době nerozumu*. B&P Publishing.

Filippov, A. (May 2008). Ожиревший Левиафан. Читают ли в Кремле Карла Шмитта? *Русский Журнал [Russian Journal]*, 1: 50–7.

Föderl-Schmid, A. (13 September 2020). Der Typus Merkel. *Süddeutsche Zeitung*. https://www.sueddeutsche.de/politik/krisenpolitik-der-typus-merkel-1.5029987

Fontaine, P. (2000). *A New Idea for Europe: The Schuman Declaration – 1950–2000*. Office for Official Publications of the European Communities. http://aei.pitt.edu/13909/1/EURDOC_newidea.PDF

Foy, H., and Buckley, N. (7 September 2016,). Orban and Kaczynski Vow 'Cultural Counter-Revolution' to Reform EU. *Financial Times*.

Fried, F. (7 June 1955). Krise der Europäer. *Die Welt*, 2. https://www.cvce.eu/content/publication/1999/1/1/3b63acf4-efdc-45eb-8ef5-7d0f1e9f6591/publishable_en.pdf [English translation]

Friedman, M. (28 August 1997). The Euro: Monetary Unity to Political Disunity? *Project Syndicate*.

Fukuyama, F. (1989). The End of History? *The National Interest* (16): 3–18.

Furedi, F. (2018). *Populism and the European Culture Wars: The Conflict of Values between Hungary and the EU*. Routledge.

Gallagher, T. (2005). *Theft of a Nation: Romania Since Communism*. Hurst & Co.

Gathmann, F. et al. (9 March 2022). Inside Germany's Foreign and Security Policy Revolution. *Der Spiegel.* https://www.spiegel.de/international/germany/standing-up-to-putin-inside-germany-s-foreign-and-security-policy-revolution-a-31fd2aba-bc08-4711-bb98-bd9fab99d908

German Federal Ministry of Defence (3 May 2021). The Strategic Compass: Developing Strategic Principles. https://www.bmvg.de/en/news/the-strategic-compass-5058518

GfK Verein (March 2018). Trust in Professions 2018 – A GfK Verein Study. https://www.nim.org/sites/default/files/medien/135/dokumente/2018_-_trust_in_professions_-_englisch.pdf

Gibbs, N. (2015). Person of the Year: Angela Merkel. *Time.* https://time.com/time-person-of-the-year-2015-angela-merkel-choice/

Gillingham, J. (2003). *European Integration, 1950–2003: Superstate or New Market Economy?* Cambridge University Press.

———— (2016). *The EU: An Obituary.* 1st edition. Verso.

Gilpin, D. (2 March 2022). Princeton Responds in Shock, Distress To War in Ukraine. *Town Topics.* https://www.towntopics.com/wordpress/2022/03/02/princeton-responds-in-shock-distress-to-war-in-ukraine/

Glendinning, S. (20 November 2014). Europe's Goal Should Not be a United States of Europe, but a Better United Europe of States. *LSE EUROPP Blog.* http://bit.ly/1ucUcyq

Goodhart, D. (2017). *The Road to Somewhere: The New Tribes Shaping British Politics.* Hurst & Co.

———— (6 March 2020). Farewell Free Trade, and Good Riddance. *UnHerd.* https://unherd.com/2020/03/its-time-liberals-embraced-economic-nationalism/

Gore, L. L. P. (2014). The Political Limits to Judicial Reform in China. *Chinese Journal of Comparative Law*, 2(2): 213–32.

Grimm, D. (2015). *Sovereignty: The Origin and Future of a Political and Legal Concept.* Columbia University Press.

———— (2016). *Europa ja – aber welches?* C. H. Beck.

———— (2017). *The Constitution of European Democracy.* Trans. Justin Collings. Oxford University Press.

———— (2020). A Long Time Coming. *German Law Journal*, 21(5): 944–9.

Grimm, D., Wendel, M., and Reinbacher, T. (2019). European Constitutionalism and the German Basic Law. In *National Constitutions in European and Global Governance: Democracy, Rights, the Rule of Law.* Ed. A. Albi and S. Bardutsky (pp. 407–92). T. M. C. Asser Press.

Gruyter, C. de (24 March 2021). What Europe can Learn from the Habsburgs. *The New European*. https://www.theneweuropean.co.uk/brexit-news-europe-news-lessons-for-the-eu-from-the-habsburgs-7813024/

The Guardian (23 September 2016). France and Germany Brush Off Johnson's EU 'Baloney' Jibe. https://www.theguardian.com/politics/2016/sep/23/france-germany-brush-off-johnsons-eu-baloney-jibe

Guérot, U. (2016). *Warum Europa eine Republik werden muss! Eine politische Utopie*. J. H. W. Dietz.

— (2020). *Nichts wird so bleiben, wie es war? Europa nach der Krise – eine Zeitreise*. Molden.

Guiso, L., Herrera, H., and Morelli, M. (2013). A Cultural Clash View of the EU Crisis. *CEPR Discussion Paper* (2–48). https://www.ecb.europa.eu/events/pdf/conferences/131128/06-Paper-Guiso-with_Herrera_Morelli.pdf?ac6788da50ae692206b5108713d2c45a

Gutschker, T. (28 February 2020a). EU-Kommission lehnt neue Grenzkontrollen ab. Risiko von Infektionshäufungen wie in Italien 'mäßig bis hoch'. *Frankfurter Allgemeine Zeitung*, 2.

——— (18 November 2020b). Wer blockiert, trägt schwere Verantwortung. *Frankfurter Allgemeine Zeitung*, 6.

Guzzini, S. (2012). The Framework of Analysis: Geopolitics Meets Foreign Policy Identity Crisis. In *The Return of Geopolitics in Europe?* Ed. S. Guzzini (pp. 45–74). Cambridge University Press.

Haas, E. B. (1958). *The Uniting of Europe: Political, Social, and Economic Forces, 1950–1957*. Stevens.

——— (1976). Turbulent Fields and the Theory of Regional Integration. *International Organization*, 30(2): 173–212.

Haas, P. M., and Haas, E. B. (2002). Pragmatic Constructivism and the Study of International Institutions. *Millennium: Journal of International Studies*, 31: 573–601. https//doi:10.1177/03058298020310031001

Habermas, J. (1990). *Die nachholende Revolution*. Suhrkamp.

——— (2001a). Why Europe Needs a Constitution. *New Left Review*, 11 (September/October): 5–26.

——— (2001b). *The Postnational Constellation: Political Essays*. MIT Press.

——— (7 April 2011). Merkels von Demoskopie geleiteter Opportunismus. *Süddeutsche Zeitung*. http://www.sueddeutsche.de/politik/europapolitik-merkels-von-demoskopie-geleiteter-opportunismus-1.1082536

——— (2015). *The Lure of Technocracy*. Polity Press.

——— (3 October 2020). Year 30: Germany's Second Chance. *Eurozine*. https://www.eurozine.com/year-30-germanys-second-chance/

Hacke, J. (2021). Carl Schmitt als Klassiker? Über das Anregungspotential denkerischer Provokation. *Rechtsphilosophie: Zeitschrift für die Grundlagen des Rechts*, 7(2): 158–73.

Haddad, B. (2020). France's War on Islamism Isn't Populism. It's Reality. *Foreign Policy*. https://foreignpolicy.com/2020/11/03/frances-war-on-islamism-isnt-populism-its-reality/

Hall, B. (9 November 2021). France's Centre-Right Dances to Eric Zemmour's Immigration Tune. *Financial Times*.

Hallstein, W. (1973). *Europe in the Making*. W. W. Norton.

Hallstein, W., Götz, H. H., and Narjes, K.-H. (1969). *Der unvollendete Bundesstaat: Europäische Erfahrungen und Erkenntnisse*. Econ Verlag.

Hansen, P., and Jonsson, S. (2014). *Eurafrica: The Untold History of European Integration and Colonialism*. Bloomsbury.

Hanson, S. E., and Kopstein, J. S. (1997). The Weimar/Russia Comparison. *Post-Soviet Affairs*, 13(3): 252–83.

Havel, V. (10 June 1999). Kosovo and the End of the Nation-State. *The New York Review of Books*, 4–5.

Hazony, Y. (2018). *The Virtue of Nationalism*. Basic Books.

Heaney, S. (13 September 2004). The Door Stands Open. *The New Republic*.

Hefty, G. P. (29 July 2021). Die westeuropäische Gedankenlosigkeit hilft Viktor Orbán. *Frankfurter Allgemeine Zeitung*.

Hegel, G. W. F. ([1821] 1989). *Grundlinien der Philosophie des Rechts*. Suhrkamp.

Heine, S. (2019). *For a Sovereign Europe*. Peter Lang.

Helms, L., Van Esch, F., and Crawford, B. (2019). Merkel III: From Committed Pragmatist to 'Conviction Leader'? *German Politics*, 28(3): 350–70.

Herpen, M. H. Van (2013). *Putinism: The Slow Rise of a Radical Right Regime in Russia*. Palgrave Macmillan.

Herszenhorn, D. M. (26 July 2021). In Nord Stream 2 Fight, Ukraine Gives EU Taste of its Own Bureaucracy. *Politico*. https://www.politico.eu/article/in-gas-fight-ukraine-gives-eu-taste-of-its-own-bureaucracy/

Heuser, B. (2019). *Brexit in History: Sovereignty or a European Union?* Hurst & Co.

Hewitt, G. (15 July 2014). The Real Jean-Claude Juncker. *BBC News*. https://www.bbc.co.uk/news/world-europe-28317790

Hill, C. (1993). The Capability-Expectations Gap, or Conceptualizing Europe's International Role. *JCMS: Journal of Common Market Studies*, 31(3): 305–28.

Hille, K. (1 March 2015). Boris Nemtsov: FT interview days before he was murdered. *Financial Times*. https://www.ft.com/content/e288978c-c024-11e4-a71e-00144feab7de?siteedition=intl

Hirschman, A. O. (1970). *Exit, Voice, and Loyalty: Responses to Decline in Firms, Organizations, and States*. Harvard University Press.

Holbrook, M. B., and Hirschman, E. C. (1993). *The Semiotics of Consumption: Interpreting Symbolic Consumer Behavior in Popular Culture and Works of Art*. Mouton de Gruyter.

Holy, L. (1996). *The Little Czech and the Great Czech Nation*. Cambridge University Press.

Hopkins, V. (15 July 2019). Hungary's Viktor Orban and the Rewriting of History. *Financial Times*. https://www.ft.com/content/c7032cb2-aca5-11e9-8030-530adfa879c2

——— (1 February 2022). Hungary's leader, visiting Moscow, calls Russian demands reasonable and says sanctions are pointless. *The New York Times*.

Horvath, R. (2013). *Putin's Preventive Counter-Revolution: Post-Soviet Authoritarianism and the Spectre of Velvet Revolution*. Routledge.

Howse, R., and Frost, B.-P. (2000). Introductory Essay: The Plausibility of the Universal Homogeneous State. In Alexandre Kojève, *Outline of a Phenomenology of Right*. Ed. B.-P. Frost, Tran. R. Howse (pp. 1–27). Rowman & Littlefield.

Isiksel, T. (2016). *Europe's Functional Constitution: A Theory of Constitutionalism Beyond the State*. Oxford University Press.

Jestaedt, M., and Lepsius, O. (2006). Der Rechts- und der Demokratietheoretiker Hans Kelsen – Eine Einführung. In Hans Kelsen, *Verteidigung der Demokratie*. Ed. M. Jestaedt and O. Lepsius (pp. vii–xxix). Mohr Siebeck.

Joerges, C. (2014). Europe's Economic Constitution in Crisis and the Emergence of a New Constitutional Constellation. *German Law Journal*, 15(5): 985–1027.

Joerges, C., and Ghaleigh, N. S. (eds.) (2003). *Darker Legacies of Law in Europe: The Shadow of National Socialism and Fascism over Europe and its Legal Traditions*. Hart Publishing.

Jones, D. M. (2005). Peace through Conversation. *The National Interest*, 79: 93–100.

Jones, E., Kelemen, R. D., and Meunier, S. (2021). Failing Forward? Crises and Patterns of European Integration. *Journal of European Public Policy*, 28(10): 1519–36.

Jörke, D. (2019). *Die Größe der Demokratie*. Suhrkamp.

Judah, B. (2 December 2020). 'The Crown' Casts Prince Charles as a Villain. Here's Why it's Wrong. *Washington Post*. https://www.

washingtonpost.com/opinions/2020/12/02/crown-casts-prince-charles-villain-heres-why-its-wrong/

Kahl, B. (1994). Europäische Union: Bundesstaat—Staatenbund—Staatenverbund? Zum Urteil des BVerfG vom 12. Oktober 1993. *Der Staat*, 33(2): 241–58.

Kalmo, H., and Skinner, Q. (2010). Introduction: A Concept in Fragments. In *Sovereignty in Fragments: The Past, Present and Future of a Contested Concept*. Ed. H. Kalmo and Q. Skinner (pp. 1–25). Cambridge University Press.

Kant, I. (1992). *Über den Gemeinspruch: Das mag in der Theorie richtig sein, taugt aber nicht für die Praxis; Zum ewigen Frieden*. Felix Meiner Verlag.

Karnitschnig, M. (24 June 2021). The World According to Wolfgang Schäuble. *Politico*. https://www.politico.eu/article/wolfgang-schauble-germany-bundestag/

Katzenstein, P. J. (ed.) (1997). *Tamed Power: Germany in Europe*. Cornell University Press.

Keiger, J. (17 September 2020). How the EU is Breaking its own Lisbon Treaty. *Spectator*. https://www.spectator.co.uk/article/how-the-eu-is-breaking-its-own-lisbon-treaty

Kelemen, R. D. (2020). The European Union's Authoritarian Equilibrium. *Journal of European Public Policy*, 27(3): 481–99.

Kelsen, H. (1928). *Das Problem der Souveränität und die Theorie des Völkerrechts: Beitrag zu einer reinen Rechtslehre*. Mohr Siebeck.

———— ([1929] 2019). *Vom Wesen und Wert der Demokratie*. Reclam.

———— (1944). *Peace Through Law*. University of North Carolina Press.

Kenney, P. (2002). *A Carnival of Revolution: Central Europe, 1989*. Princeton University Press.

Kharkhordin, O. (2001). What is the State? The Russian Concept of Gosudarstvo in the European Context. *History and Theory*, 40(2): 206–40.

Khosrokhavar, F. (31 October 2020). France's Dangerous Religion of Secularism. *Politico*.

Kochenov, V. D., and Dimitrovs, A. (28 April 2021). Solving the Copenhagen Dilemma: The *Reppublika* Decision of the European Court of Justice. *Verfassungsblog*. https://verfassungsblog.de/solving-the-copenhagen-dilemma/

Kirkegaard, J. F. (8 May 2017). Macron's Victory Signals Reform in France and a Stronger Europe. *Peterson Institute for International Economics*. https://www.piie.com/blogs/realtime-economic-issues-watch/macrons-victory-signals-reform-france-and-stronger-europe

Kojève, A. ([1957] 2001). Colonialism from a European Point of View. Trans. E. de Vries. *Interpretation*, 29(1): 115–30.

———— ([1945] 2004). Outline of a Doctrine of French Policy. *Policy Review*, 28(3). https://www.hoover.org/research/outline-doctrine-french-policy

———— (2000). *Outline of a Phenomenology of Right*. Ed. and trans. B.-P. Frost. Rowman & Littlefield.

Kołakowski, L. (2003). Can Europe Happen? *New Criterion*, 21(9): 19–27.

Körösényi, A., Illés, G., and Gyulai, A. (2020). *The Orbán Regime: Plebiscitary Leader Democracy in the Making*. Routledge.

Korosteleva, E. (2017). Eastern Partnership: Bringing 'the Political' Back In. *East European Politics*, 33(3): 321–37.

Koselleck, R. (1988). *Critique and Crisis: Enlightenment and the Pathogenesis of Modern Society*. MIT Press.

Kovács, J. M., and Trencsényi, B. (eds.) (2020). *Brave New Hungary: Mapping the 'System of National Cooperation'*. Lexington Books.

Kramer, M. (2009). The Myth of a No-NATO-Enlargement Pledge to Russia. *The Washington Quarterly*, 32(2): 39–61.

Krapfl, J. (2013). *Revolution with a Human Face: Politics, Culture, and Community in Czechoslovakia, 1989–1992*. Cornell University Press.

Krastev, I. (2017). *After Europe*. University of Pennsylvania Press.

———— (27 July 2018). Eine Geschichte zweier Europas. *Wiener Zeitung*. https://austria-forum.org/af/Wissenssammlungen/Essays/Internationale_Politik/Geschichte_zweier_Europas

———— (27 February 2022). We Are All Living in Vladimir Putin's World Now. *The New York Times*. https://www.nytimes.com/2022/02/27/opinion/putin-russia-ukraine-europe.html

Krastev, I., and Holmes, S. (2019). *The Light that Failed: A Reckoning*. Allen Lane.

Kreuder-Sonnen, C. (2018). An Authoritarian Turn in Europe and European Studies? *Journal of European Public Policy*, 25(3): 452–64.

Kremlin. (15 February 2022). News conference following Russian–German talks. http://en.kremlin.ru/events/president/news/67774

Król, M. (1999). *Liberalizmus strachu a liberalizmus odvahy*. Kalligram.

———— (2015a). *Byliśmy głupi*. CzerwIne I Czarne.

———— (2015b). Kończy się świat demokracji. In *Kultura Liberalna*. Ed. Ł. Pawłowski and T. Sawczuk. https://www.tttdebates.org/the-end-of-the-democratic-world

Krygier, M. (2020). Polish Lessons: Backsliding, Sabotage, and the Rule of Law. In *Constitutionalism Under Stress: Essays in Honour of Wojciech Sadurski*. Ed. U. Belavusau and A. Gliszczyńska-Grabias (pp. 79–94). Oxford University Press.

———— (2021). The Spirit of Constitutionalism. In *Law in a Time of Constitutional Crisis: Studies Offered to Mirosław Wyrzykowski*. Ed. J. Urbanik and A. Bodnar (pp. 357–72). C. H. Beck.

Kublik, A. (25 November 2021). Polexitu nie chcemy, ale antyunijna retoryka PiS-u działa. *Gazeta Wyborcza*. https://wyborcza.pl/7,75398, 27842910,polexitu-nie-chcemy-ale-antyunijna-retoryka-pis-u-dziala. html?fbclid=IwAR2GFVQAgQxfAPjNUI1kmaP54kIN8Fgw4Col4 QTG4srDamvdFsEZS2QaoBk

Kumar, K. (2017). *Visions of Empire: How Five Imperial Regimes Shaped the World*. Princeton University Press.

Kundera, M. (1984). The Tragedy of Central Europe. *The New York Review of Books*, 33–36.

Kundnani, H. (2014). *The Paradox of German Power*. Hurst & Co.

———— (2018). Discipline and Punish. *Berlin Policy Journal* (May/June). https://berlinpolicyjournal.com/discipline-and-punish/

Kuzio, T. (2017). Ukraine Between a Constrained EU and Assertive Russia. *JCMS: Journal of Common Market Studies*, 55(1): 103–20.

Kwaśniewski, A. (2004). Udział Prezydenta RP z Małżonką w uroczystości na Placu Piłsudskiego z okazji przystąpienia Polski do Unii Europejskiej. *The Official Website of the Polish President*. https://www.prezydent. pl/archiwalne-aktualnosci/rok-2004/art,225,udzial-prezydenta-rp-z-malzonka-w-uroczystosci-na-placu-pilsudskiego-z-okazji-przystapienia-polski-do-unii-europejskiej.html

Laffan, B. (2019). How the EU27 Came to Be. *JCMS: Journal of Common Market Studies*, 57 (Annual Review): 13–27.

———— (2 April 2020). Europe in the Time of Covid-19. *Bridge Blog*. https://bridgenetwork.eu/2020/04/02/europe-in-the-time-of-covid-19/

———— (12 January 2021). Brexit has Enabled the EU to Reveal its Essential Essence. *The Irish Times*. https://www.irishtimes.com/opinion/brexit-has-enabled-the-eu-to-reveal-its-essential-essence-1.4455620

Lapavitsas, C. (2019). *The Left Case Against the EU*. Polity Press.

Laruelle, M. (25 March 2015). Scared of Putin's Shadow. *Foreign Affairs*. https://www.foreignaffairs.com/articles/russian-federation/2015-03-25/scared-putins-shadow

Laschet, A. (16 August 2021). Afghanistan ist 'größtes Debakel für die Nato'. Video recording provided by the *Frankfurter Allgemeine Zeitung*. https://www.faz.net/aktuell/politik/laschet-afghanistan-ist-groesstes-debakel-fuer-die-nato-17487592.html

Lau, J., and Topçu, Ö. (24 June 2021). 'Das ist die Schuld des Westens' Der Sicherheitsexperte Carlo Masala über außenpolitische Fehler. *Die Zeit*.

Lavrov, S. (28 June 2021). О праве, правах и правилах. *Коммерсантъ*, 109: 1. https://www.kommersant.ru/doc/4877702 (English summary available at https://tass.com/politics/1307755)

Lefebvre, M. (2021). Europe as a Power, European Sovereignty and Strategic Autonomy: A Debate that is Moving Towards an Assertive Europe. *Fondation Robert Schuman Policy Paper* (582): 1–10. https://www.robert-schuman.eu/en/doc/questions-d-europe/qe-582-en.pdf

Legutko, R. (2016). *The Demon in Democracy: Totalitarian Temptations in Free Societies*. Encounter Books.

Leloup, M., Kochenov, D. V., and Dimitrovs, A. (2021). Non-Regression: Opening the Door to Solving the 'Copenhagen Dilemma'? All the Eyes on Case C-896/19 *Repubblika v Il-Prim Ministru*. *RECONNECT Working Paper (Leuven)* (15).

Leonard, M. (2005). *Why Europe will Run the 21st Century*. Fourth Estate.

Lepenies, W. (2016). *Die Macht am Mittelmeer: Französische Träume von einem anderen Europa*. Carl Hanser Verlag.

Lev, A. (2017). *The Federal Idea: Public Law Between Governance and Political Life*. Hart Publishing.

Lévy, B.-H. (13 May 2019). How an Anti-totalitarian Militant Discovered Ultranationalism. *The Atlantic*.

Lewis, D. G. (2020). *Russia's New Authoritarianism: Putin and the Politics of Order*. Edinburgh University Press.

Loewenstein, K. (1937). Militant Democracy and Fundamental Rights, I. *American Political Science Review*, 31(3): 417–32.

Lokdam, H. (2020). 'We Serve the People of Europe': Reimagining the ECB's Political Master in the Wake of its Emergency Politics. *JCMS: Journal of Common Market Studies*, 58(4): 978–98.

Loughlin, M. (2018). The British Constitution: Thoughts on the Cause of the Present Discontents. *New Zealand Journal of Public and International Law*, 16(1): 1–20.

McCormick, J. P. (2003). Carl Schmitt's Europe: Cultural, Imperial and Spatial Proposals for European Integration, 1923–1955. In *Darker Legacies of Law in Europe*. Ed. C. Joerges and N. S. Ghaleigh (pp. 133–42). Hart.

MacCormick, N. (1995). The Maastricht-Urteil: Sovereignty Now. *European Law Journal*, 1(3): 259–66.

———— (2010). Sovereignty and After. In *Sovereignty in Fragments: The Past, Present and Future of a Contested Concept*. Ed. H. Kalmo and Q. Skinner (pp. 151–68). Cambridge University Press.

McEwan, I. (1 February 2020). Brexit, the Most Pointless, Masochistic Ambition in our Country's History, Is Done. *The Guardian*. https://

www.theguardian.com/politics/2020/feb/01/brexit-pointless-masochistic-ambition-history-done

Macfarlane, N., and Menon, A. (2014). The EU and Ukraine. *Survival*, 56(3): 95–101.

Machiavelli, N. (2011). *The Prince*. Trans. George Bull. Penguin Books.

MacMillan, M. (2002). *Paris 1919: Six Months that Changed the World*. Random House.

Macron, E. (24 January 2017a). Europe Holds its Destiny in its Own Hands. https://www.ft.com/content/3d0cc856-e187-11e6-9645-c9357a75844a

———— (2017b). *Revolution*. Scribe.

———— (4 March 2019). Europe is a Historic Success – We Should Never Forget That. *The Irish Times*. https://www.irishtimes.com/opinion/emmanuel-macron-europe-is-a-historic-success-we-should-never-forget-that-1.3813926

———— (12 November 2020). The Macron Doctrine: A Conversation with the French President. *Le Grand Continent*. https://geopolitique.eu/en/macron-grand-continent/

Maier, C. (2019). The Weimar Origins of the West German Rechtsstaat, 1919–1969. *The Historical Journal*, 62(4): 1069–91.

Maier, C. S. (2002). Does Europe Need a Frontier? From Territorial to Redistributive Community. In *Europe Unbound: Enlarging and Reshaping the Boundaries of the European Union*. Ed. J. Zielonka (pp. 17–37). Routledge.

Mair, P. (2013). *Ruling the Void: The Hollowing of Western Democracy*. Verso.

Majone, G. (2005). *Dilemmas of European Integration: The Ambiguities and Pitfalls of Integration by Stealth*. Oxford University Press.

Mallet, V. (20 October 2020a). Islamist Killing Prompts French Crackdown on Militants. *Financial Times*. https://www.ft.com/content/acb1b83a-ea73-45a6-b6c8-8f2635acddbc

———— (6 November 2020b). France to Double Border Security Forces to Combat Terrorism. *Financial Times*. https://www.ft.com/content/57cc134b-b3b7-4fef-b047-b956129af2ef

Mance, H. (8 June 2016). Brexit Countdown: 15 Days to Go. *Financial Times*. https://www.ft.com/content/f7f065d0-2cc7-11e6-a18d-a96ab29e3c95

Manners, I. (2010). Global Europa: Mythology of the European Union in World Politics. *JCMS: Journal of Common Market Studies*, 48(1): 67–87.

Manow, P. (2018). *Die politische Ökonomie des Populismus*. Suhrkamp.

———— (2020). *(Ent-)Demokratisierung der Demokratie*. Suhrkamp.

Markell, P. (2000). Making Affect Safe for Democracy? On 'Constitutional Patriotism'. *Political Theory*, 28(1): 38–63.

Marks, G., Attewell, D., Rovny, J., and Hooghe, L. (2021). Cleavage Theory. In *The Palgrave Handbook of EU Crises*. Ed. M. Riddervold, J. Trondal and A. Newsome (pp. 173–93). Springer International Publishing.

Marsh, D. (2009). *The Euro: The Politics of the New Global Currency*. Yale University Press.

Maull, H. W. (2018). Reflective, Hegemonic, Geo-economic, Civilian…? The Puzzle of German Power. *German Politics*, 27(4): 460–78.

Mayer, F. C. (2020). The Ultra Vires Ruling: Deconstructing the German Federal Constitutional Court's PSPP Decision of 5 May 2020. *European Constitutional Law Review*, 16(4): 733–69.

Mearsheimer, J. J. (2014). Why the Ukraine Crisis is the West's Fault: The Liberal Delusions That Provoked Putin. *Foreign Affairs*, 93(5): 77–89.

Merkel, A. (16 February 2019). Speech by Federal Chancellor Dr Angela Merkel … at the 55th Munich Security Conference. https://www.bundesregierung.de/breg-en/news/speech-by-federal-chancellor-dr-angela-merkel-on-16-february-2019-at-the-55th-munich-security-conference-1582318

——— (8 July 2020). Speech by Federal Chancellor Angela Merkel on the German Presidency of the Council of the EU 2020 to the European Parliament in Brussels. https://www.eu2020.de/eu2020-en/news/reden/speech-chancellor-merkel-european-parliament/2366782

Middelaar, L. van (2013). *The Passage to Europe: How a Continent Became a Union*. Yale University Press.

——— (2016). The Return of Politics – The European Union after the Crises in the Eurozone and Ukraine. *JCMS: Journal of Common Market Studies*, 54(3): 495–507.

——— (2019). *Alarums and Excursions: Improvising Politics on the European Stage*. Columbia University Press.

Miller, D. (1995). *On Nationality*. Clarendon Press.

——— (2016). *Strangers in Our Midst: The Political Philosophy of Migration*. Oxford University Press.

Miller-Melamed, P., and Morelon, C. (10 September 2019). What the Hapsburg Empire Got Right. *The New York Times*.

Miłosz, C. (2004). *Selected Poems 1931–2004*. Selected by Robert Hass with a foreword by Seamus Heaney. HarperCollins.

Milward, A. S. (2000). *The European Rescue of the Nation-State*. 2nd edition. Routledge.

Mishra, P. (28 October 2020). Macron's Clash of Civilizations is Misguided. *Bloomberg Opinion*. https://www.bloomberg.com/opinion/articles/2020-10-28/macron-s-clash-of-civilizations-with-islam-is-misguided

Monnet, J. (1978). *Memoirs*. Collins.

Moravcsik, A. (1998). *The Choice for Europe: Social Purpose and State Power from Messina to Maastricht*. Cornell University Press.

———— (2001). Despotism in Brussels? Misreading the European Union. *Foreign Affairs*, 80(3): 114–22.

———— (17 June 2002). The Quiet Superpower. *Newsweek*.

———— (2010). Europe, the Second Superpower. *Current History*, 109 (725): 91–8.

———— (2012). Europe After the Crisis: How to Sustain a Common Currency. *Foreign Affairs*, 91(3): 54–68.

———— (24 September 2020). Why Europe Wins. *Foreign Policy*: 46–52. https://www.princeton.edu/~amoravcs/library/Moravcsik%20 WHY%20EUROPE%20WINS.pdf

Morawiecki, M. (19 October 2021a). Statement by Prime Minister Mateusz Morawiecki in the European Parliament. https://www. gov.pl/web/primeminister/statement-by-prime-minister-mateusz-morawiecki-in-the-european-parliament

———— (30 October 2021b). Primacy of Constitution, Primacy of Democracy. *Cyprus Mail*. https://cyprus-mail.com/2021/10/30/ primacy-of-constitution-primacy-of-democracy/

Morgan, G. (2009). *The Idea of a European Superstate: Public Justification and European Integration*. Princeton University Press.

———— (2020). Is the European Union Imperialist? *Journal of European Public Policy*, 27(9): 1424–40.

———— (2021). Europe's Commercial Order and the Crisis of Nationalism. In *Imagining Europe: Essays on the Past, Present, and Future of the European Union*. Ed. H. T. Edmondson III and P. Metnzel (pp. 19–38). Rowman & Littlefield.

Mudde, C. (2016). Europe's Populist Surge: A Long Time in the Making. *Foreign Affairs*, 95(6): 25–30.

———— (30 June 2021). Homoliberalism is Not the Answer to Homophobic Nationalism. *Voxeurop*. https://voxeurop.eu/en/homoliberalism-is-not-the-answer-to-homophobic-nationalism/

Mulder, N. (2019). Homo Europus. *New Left Review* (120). https:// newleftreview.org/issues/ii120/articles/homo-europus

Müller, J.-W. (31 October 2018). Angela Merkel Failed. *Foreign Policy*. https://foreignpolicy.com/2018/10/31/angela-merkel-failed/

———— (2000). Carl Schmitt and the Constitution of Europe. *Cardozo Law Review*, 21(5–6): 1777–95.

———— (2015). Should the EU Protect Democracy and the Rule of Law Inside Member States? *European Law Journal*, 21(2): 141–60.

———— (2020). What, If Anything, Can the EU Do? In *Brave New Hungary: Mapping the 'System of National Cooperation'*. Ed. J. M. Kovács and B. Trencsényi (pp. 311–30). Lexington Books.

Münchau, W. (26 June 2021). Overrated – Now Fading: Angela Merkel is the Most Over-Rated Politician of OurTime. *Euro Intelligence*. https://www.eurointelligence.com/column/merkel

———— (4 March 2022). How Putin wins the war. *The Spectator*. https://www.spectator.co.uk/article/how-putin-wins-the-war

Münkler, H. (2015). *Macht in der Mitte: Die neuen Aufgaben Deutschlands in Europa*. Körber-Stiftung.

———— (16 March 2022). Mit politischer Romantik ist niemandem geholfen. *Frankfurter Allgemeine Zeitung*. https://www.faz.net/aktuell/feuilleton/debatten/ukraine-wie-falsches-heldentum-alle-in-einen-krieg-hineinzieht-17879373.html

Murray, D. (2017). *The Strange Death of Europe: Immigration, Identity, Islam*. Bloomsbury Continuum.

Murray, S. (10 June 2021). MEPs Want Brussels to Act over Czech PM's Alleged Conflict of Interest. *Euronews*. https://www.euronews.com/2021/06/10/meps-want-brussels-to-act-over-czech-pm-s-alleged-conflict-of-interest

Musil, R. (1930). *Der Mann ohne Eigenschaften* [The Man Without Qualities]. Erstes Buch. Rowohlt Taschenbuch. http://musilonline.at/archiv/erstausgabe-1930

Mussler, W. (27 January 2021). Europäischer Impfnationalismus. *Frankfurter Allgemeine Zeitung*.

Nassehi, A. (25 February 2022). Die Rückkehr des Feindes. *Die Zeit*. https://www.zeit.de/kultur/2022-02/demokratie-bedrohung-russland-ukraine-krieg-wladimir-putin/komplettansicht

Nichols, J. H. (2007). *Alexandre Kojève: Wisdom at the End of History*. Rowman & Littlefield.

Nicolaidis, K. (2019). *Exodus, Reckoning, Sacrifice: Three Meanings of Brexit*. Unbound Publishing.

———— (2020). In Praise of Ambivalence – Another Brexit Story. *Journal of European Integration*, 42(4): 465–88.

Niemann, A., Lefkofridi, Z., and Schmitter, P. C. (2019). Neofunctionalism. In *European Integration Theory*. Ed. A. Wiener, T. Börsel and T. Risse (pp. 43–63). Oxford University Press.

Nizinkiewicz, J. (5 August 2021). Zbigniew Ziobro: Obecność Polski w Unii Europejskiej nie za wszelką cenę. *Rzeczpospolita*. https://www.rp.pl/polityka/art18464921-zbigniew-ziobro-obecnosc-polski-w-unii-europejskiej-nie-za-wszelka-cene

Nougayrède, N. (8 May 2017). Macron's Victory March to Europe's Anthem Said More than Words. *The Guardian.* https://www.theguardian.com/commentisfree/2017/may/08/macron-europe-president-nationalism

Nußberger, A. (12 August 2021). Der europäische Rechtsstaat in der Sackgasse. *Frankfurter Allgemeine Zeitung.*

Offe, C. (1998). Demokratie und Wohlfahrtsstaat: Eine europäische Regimeform unter dem Streß der europäischen Integration. In *Internationale Wirtschaft, nationale Demokratie: Herausforderungen für die Demokratietheorie.* Ed. W. Streeck (pp. 99–136). Campus Verlag. Reprinted in Claus Offe (2019). *Staatskapazität und Europäische Integration* (pp. 245–278). Springer Verlag.

———— (2002). 1968 Thirty Years After. *Thesis Eleven* (68): 82–8.

———— (2017). Referendum vs. Institutionalized Deliberation. *Daedalus*, 146(3): 14–27.

Olsen, J. (2020). *The European Union: Politics and Policies.* Routledge.

Onfray, M. (8 October 2018). L'Empire Maastrichtien (Populistes contre Populicides). https://michelonfray.com/interventions-hebdomadaires/l-empire-maastrichtien-populistes-contre-populici?mode=video

Orbán, V. ([1989] 2013). Fill in the Blanks [Speech at the reburial of 1956 revolutionary Prime Minister Imre Nagy]. Trans. S. Lambert. In *The Orange Files: Notes on Illiberal Democracy in Hungary.* https://theorangefiles.hu/2013.06/20/fill-in-the-blanks/

Osiatynski, W. (1997). A Brief History of the Constitution. *East European Constitutional Review*, 6(2/3): 66–76.

Outhwaite, W. (2021). The Postnational Constellation Revisited: Critical Thoughts on Sovereignty. *Berlin Journal of Critical Theory*, 5(1): 31–57.

Palmer, B. (2017). *Wir können nicht allen helfen.* Siedler.

Pech, L., Wachowiec, P., and Mazur, D. (2021). Poland's Rule of Law Breakdown: A Five-Year Assessment of EU's (In)Action. *Hague Journal of the Rule of Law*, 13(1): 1–43.

Pergande, F. (18 June 2020). Merkel verkörpert das Ideal Max Webers. *Frankfurter Allgemeine Zeitung.*

Pernice, I. (September 2001). Der Beitrag Walter Hallstein zur Zukunft Europas – Begründung und Konsolidierung der Europäischen Gemeinschaft als Rechtsgemeinschaft. *WHI-Paper 9/2001.* https://www.rewi.hu-berlin.de/de/lf/oe/whi/publikationen/whi-papers/2001/whi-paper0901.pdf

Peyrefitte, A. (2002). *C'était de Gaulle,* Vol. 1. Gallimard.

Pfaff, W. (2007). Happy Birthday! *The New York Review of Books*, 54(7): 20.

Pinkoski, N. (13 August 2019). Hannah Arendt: Thinking Pariah. *Public Discourse, The Journal of the Witherspoon Institute*. https://www.thepublicdiscourse.com/2019/08/55405/

Plickert, P. (7 February 2017). Wovor die Euro-Kritiker schon früh warnten. *Frankfurter Allgemeine Zeitung*.

Preuss, U. K. (2011). The Implications of 'Eternity Clauses': The German Experience. *Israel Law Review*, 44(3): 429–48.

——— (2017). Die Krise der Europäischen Union als Ausnahmezustand? *Kritische Justiz*, 50(1): 51–67.

Putin, V. (18 March 2014). Address by President of the Russia Federation. http://en.kremlin.ru/events/president/news/20603

——— (12 July 2021). On the Historical Unity of Russians and Ukrainians. http://en.kremlin.ru/events/president/news/66181

Qvortrup, M. (2016). *Angela Merkel: Europe's Most Influential Leader*. Abrams Press.

Rankin, J. (11 December 2017). EU Could 'Scrap Refugee Quota Scheme'. *The Guardian*. https://www.theguardian.com/world/2017/dec/11/eu-may-scrap-refugee-quota-scheme-donald-tusk

Rasmussen, M. (2021). Towards a Legal History of European Law. *European Papers: A Journal on Law and Integration*, 6(2): 923–32.

Rasmussen, M., and Martinsen, D. S. (2019). EU Constitutionalisation Revisited: Redressing a Central Assumption in European Studies. *European Law Journal*, 25(3): 251–72. https://doi:10.1111/eulj.12317

Rau, Z. (30 June 2021). Putin Wants to Lure Germany into a Trap. *Frankfurter Allgemeine Zeitung*. https://www.gov.pl/web/diplomacy/article-by-minister-zbigniew-rau-in-the-frankfurter-allgemeine-zeitung

Ray, J., and Esipova, N. (2014). Russian approval of Putin soars to highest level in years. Gallup. http://www.gallup.com/poll/173597/russian-approval-putin-soars-highest-level-years.aspx

Reuters (20 November 2020). UK, EU Need to Avoid Blame Game as 'Truth of Brexit' Emerges, Coveney Says. https://www.reuters.com/article/uk-britain-eu-coveney-idUKKBN28A0W7

——— (27 February 2022). EU tightens Russian sanctions and buys weapons for Ukraine. https://www.reuters.com/world/europe/eu-close-airspace-russia-curb-media-target-belarus-2022-02-27/

Robinet, F. (11 February 2022). Emmanuel Macron's Overtures to Vladimir Putin, and the Race to Prevent War in Ukraine. *The New Yorker*. https://www.newyorker.com/news/daily-comment/emmanuel-macrons-overtures-to-vladimir-putin-and-the-race-to-prevent-war-in-ukraine

Rodrik, D. (27 June 2007). The Inescapable Trilemma of the World Economy. *Dani Rodrik's Weblog*. https://rodrik.typepad.com/dani_rodriks_weblog/2007/06/the-inescapable.html

Rohac, D. (1 July 2021). How Viktor Orbán Became China's Most Reliable European Ally. *AEI Dispatch*. https://www.aei.org/op-eds/how-viktor-orban-became-chinas-most-reliable-european-ally/

Rone, J. (2021). Backsliding of the Left: Or How Viktor Orbán's Right-Wing Conservative Illiberalism Emerged as a Normative Ideal in Bulgarian Political Discourse. *European Politics and Society*: 1–18.

Rose, R. (2020). *How Referendums Challenge European Democracy: Brexit and Beyond*. Palgrave Macmillan.

Roshwald, A. (2006). *The Endurance of Nationalism: Ancient Roots and Modern Dilemmas*. Cambridge University Press.

Roth, A. (17 December 2020). Putin Rejects Navalny Poisoning Allegations as 'Falsification'. *The Guardian*.

Rousseau, J.-J. (1968). *Discourse on Political Economy and The Social Contract*. Trans. and intro. C. Betts. Oxford University Press.

——— ([1756] 1991). Abstract and Judgement of Saint-Pierre's Project for Perpetual Peace. In *Rousseau on International Relations*. Ed. S. Hoffmann and D. P. Fidler (pp. 53–100). Clarendon Press.

Roussinos, A. (11 December 2020). Je ne Bregret rien. *Unherd*. https://unherd.com/thepost/je-ne-bregret-rien/

Ruggie, J. G. (1993). Territoriality and Beyond: Problematizing Modernity in International Relations. *International Organization*, 47(1): 139–74.

Rutter, J., and Menon, A. (2020). Who Killed Soft Brexit? *Prospect Magazine*. https://www.prospectmagazine.co.uk/magazine/who-killed-soft-brexit-eu-european-union-no-deal

Rychetský, L., and Fiala, J. (2014). Czechs Look Back on 1989, a Revolution Betrayed: A Reflection on the Mythology of the Velvet Revolution. *Class, Race and Corporate Power*, 2(3). https://digitalcommons.fiu.edu/cgi/viewcontent.cgi?article=1043&context=classracecorporatepower

Sadurski, W. (2019). *Poland's Constitutional Breakdown*. Oxford University Press.

Sakwa, R. (2015). *Frontline Ukraine: Crisis in the Borderlands*. I. B. Tauris.

Sarmiento, D., and Utrilla, D. (22 May 2020). Germany's Constitutional Court has gone Nuclear. What Happens Next Will Shape the EU's Future. *Euronews*. https://www.euronews.com/2020/05/15/germany-constitutional-court-gone-nuclear-what-happens-next-will-shape-the-eu-future-view

Scharpf, F. W. (2017). De-Constitutionalisation and Majority Rule: A Democratic Vision for Europe. *European Law Journal*, 23(5): 315–34.

Schlögel, K. (2018). *Ukraine: A Nation on the Borderland*. Trans. G. Jackson. Reaktion Books.

Schmidt, V. A. (2020). *Europe's Crisis of Legitimacy: Governing by Rules and Ruling by Numbers in the Eurozone*. Oxford University Press.

Schmit, L., Stoldt, J., and Thomas, B. (2012). Der Mann ohne Eigenschaften. *Forum für Politik, Gesellschaft und Kultur*, (324): 4–11.

Schmitt, C. (1985a). *Political Theology: Four Chapters on the Concept of Sovereignty*. Trans. G. Schwab. University of Chicago Press.

———— ([1923] 1985b). *The Crisis of Parliamentary Democracy*. Trans. E. Kennedy. MIT Press.

———— (1991). *Glossarium: Aufzeichnungen der Jahre 1947–1951*. Duncker & Humblot.

———— (1996). *Roman Catholicism and Political Form*. Trans. G. L. Ulmen. Greenwood Press.

———— ([1950] 1997). *Der Nomos der Erde im Völkerrecht des Jus Publicum Europaeum*. 5th edition. Duncker & Humblot.

———— ([1932] 2004). *Legality and Legitimacy*. Trans. J. Seitzer. Duke University Press.

———— ([1928] 2007). *The Concept of the Political*. Trans. G. Schwab. University of Chicago Press.

———— ([1928] 2008a). *Constitutional Theory*. Trans. J. Seitzer. Duke University Press.

———— ([1942] 2008b). *Land und Meer: Eine weltgeschichtliche Betrachtung*. Klett-Cotta.

———— (2011). *Die Tyrannei der Werte*. Duncker & Humblot.

Scholz, O. (27 February 2022). Policy statement by Olaf Scholz, Chancellor of the Federal Republic of Germany and Member of the German Bundestag, Berlin. https://www.bundesregierung.de/breg-en/news/policy-statement-by-olaf-scholz-chancellor-of-the-federal-republic-of-germany-and-member-of-the-german-bundestag-27-february-2022-in-berlin-2008378

Schütze, R. (2016). *European Constitutional Law*. 2nd edition. Cambridge University Press.

Scicluna, N. (2015). *European Union Constitutionalism in Crisis*. Routledge.

———— (2018). Integration through the Disintegration of Law? The ECB and EU Constitutionalism in the Crisis. *Journal of European Public Policy*, 25(12): 1874–91.

———— (17 April 2019). Integration-through-Crisis: The Triumph of Expediency over Democratic Legitimacy? *EuVisions*. http://www.euvisions.eu/integration-through-crisis-expediency-or-democratic-legitimacy/

Scruton, R. (2006). *A Political Philosophy*. Continuum.

Segal, R. (7 March 2022). Putin and the Weaponization of the Memory of World War II and the Holocaust. *The New Fascism Syllabus*. http://newfascismsyllabus.com/contributions/putin-and-the-weaponization-of-the-memory-of-world-war-ii-and-the-holocaust/

Seongcheol, K. (24–28 August 2020). *From Berlin to Budapest and Back: 'Illiberal Democracy' and the Mirror of Neo-Liberal Post-Democracy*. European Consortium for Political Research, Virtual Event. https://ecpr.eu/Events/Event/PaperDetails/55539

Shagina, M. (2021). East–West Divides and Nord Stream 2. *Russian Analytical Digest* (267): 2–5. https://www.css.ethz.ch/content/dam/ethz/special-interest/gess/cis/center-for-securities-studies/pdfs/RAD267.pdf

Sheng, Y., and Qingqing, C. (15 April 2021). West-Backed Color Revolution a 'Top Threat' to China's National, Political Security. *Global Times*. https://www.globaltimes.cn/page/202104/1221182.shtml

Shevtsova, L. (2015). Russia's Political System: Imperialism and Decay. *Journal of Democracy*, 26(1): 171–83.

Shuster, S. (2 March 2022). How Volodymyr Zelensky Defended Ukraine and United the World. *Time*. https://time.com/6154139/volodymyr-zelensky-ukraine-profile-russia/

Siddi, M. (2018). The Role of Power in EU–Russia Energy Relations: The Interplay between Markets and Geopolitics. *Europe-Asia Studies*, 70(10): 1552–71.

Siedlecka, E. (21 January 2013). Sądy niegodne zaufania, ale przyjazne. *Gazeta Wyborcza*. https://www.wyborcza.pl/7,75398,13266735,sady-niegodne-zaufania-ale-przyjazne.html

Sikorski, R. (28 November 2011). I Fear Germany's Power Less than her Inactivity. *Financial Times*. https://www.ft.com/content/b753cb42-19b3-11e1-ba5d-00144feabdc0

Sinn, H.-W. (2014). *The Euro Trap: On Bursting Bubbles, Budgets, and Beliefs*. Oxford University Press.

———— (22 May 2020). Der Hamilton-Moment. *Frankfurter Allgemeine Zeitung*.

Skinner, Q. (2010). The Sovereign State: A Genealogy. In *Sovereignty in Fragments: The Past, Present and Future of a Contested Concept*. Ed. H. Kalmo and Q. Skinner (pp. 26–46). Cambridge University Press.

Smale, A. and Erlanger, S. (12 November 2016). As Obama Exits World Stage, Angela Merkel May Be the Liberal West's Last Defender. *The New York Times*. https://www.nytimes.com/2016/11/13/world/europe/germany-merkel-trump-election.html

Smith, A. D. (1995). *Nations and Nationalism in a Global Era*. Polity Press.

Smith, L. V. (2018). *Sovereignty at the Paris Peace Conference of 1919*. Oxford University Press.

Snyder, T. (2018). *The Road to Unfreedom: Russian, Europe, America*. Penguin.

South China Morning Post (11 October 2014). Occupy Central – Day 14: Full Coverage of the Day's Events. https://www.scmp.com/news/hong-kong/article/1614307/live-occupy-continues-push-democracy-hong-kongs-leaders-head-mainland

Speck, U. (2006). Vom Aufstieg und Niedergang des Europäismus. *Merkur*, 60(683): 243–8.

Starr, K. J. (2 January 2019). Once the Same Nation, the Czech Republic and Slovakia Look Very Different Religiously. Pew Research Center. https://www.pewresearch.org/fact-tank/2019/01/02/once-the-same-nation-the-czech-republic-and-slovakia-look-very-different-religiously/

Stein, E. (1981). Lawyers, Judges, and the Making of a Transnational Constitution. *American Journal of International Law*, 75(1): 1–27.

Steinmeier, F.-W. (2016). *Europa ist die Lösung*. Ecowin.

Stephens, P. (16 December 2020). The UK will Now Count the Cost of Brexit Sovereignty. *Financial Times*.

Steppat, T. (15 March 2022). Sigmar Gabriel im Interview über Russlandpolitik: 'Wir haben Fehler gemacht'. *Frankfurter Allgemeine Zeitung*. https://www.faz.net/aktuell/ukraine-konflikt/ukraine-krieg-sigmar-gabriel-gibt-fehler-in-der-russlandpolitik-zu-17879603.html

Stilz, A. (2019). *Territorial Sovereignty: A Philosophical Exploration*. Oxford University Press.

Strauss, L., and Kojève, A. (2013). *On Tyranny: Including the Strauss-Kojève Correspondence*. Ed. M. S. Roth and V. Gourevitch. Corrected and expanded edition. University of Chicago Press.

Streeck, W. (2014). Small-State Nostalgia? The Currency Union, Germany, and Europe: A Reply to Jürgen Habermas. *Constellations*, 21(2): 213–21.

———— (2016a). Scenario for a Wonderful Tomorrow. *London Review of Books*, 38(7): 7–10.

———— (2016b). After the British Referendum. *London Review of Books*, 38(14): 15.

———— (2018). Europe under Merkel IV: Balance of Impotence. *American Affairs*, 2(2): 162–92. https://americanaffairsjournal.org/2018/05/europe-under-merkel-iv-balance-of-impotence/

———— (2019). Reflections on Political Scale. *Jurisprudence*, 10(1): 1–14.

———— (2021). *Zwischen Globalismus und Demokratie: politische Ökonomie im ausgehenden Neoliberalismus*. Suhrkamp.

Surkov, V. (2 November 2019). Долгое государство Путина. *Nezavisimaya Gazeta*.

———— (18 June 2021). An Overdose of Freedom is Lethal to a State. *Financial Times*.

Tabery, E. (28 February 2022). Pravá tvář Adolfa Putina. *Respekt*. https://www.respekt.cz/tydenik/2022/9/prava-tvar-adolfa-putina

Tambur, S. (3 March 2022). Updated: Estonian MEP Terras asks Borrell to resign over the 'EU fighter jets for Ukraine' blunder. *Estonian World*. https://estonianworld.com/security/estonian-mep-terras-asks-borrell-to-resign-over-the-eu-fighter-jets-for-ukraine-blunder/

Tamir, Y. (1993). *Liberal Nationalism*. Princeton University Press.

———— (2019). *Why Nationalism*. Princeton University Press.

Thatcher, M. (30 October 1990). House of Commons Statement. Hansard HC [178/869-92]. Margaret Thatcher Foundation. https://www.margaretthatcher.org/document/108234

Theiler, T. (2005). *Political Symbolism and European Integration*. Manchester University Press.

Ther, P. (2017). *Europe Since 1989: A History*. Trans. C. Hughes-Kreutzmüller. Princeton University Press.

Thompson, H. (2020). The Habsburg Myth and the European Union. In *Europe's Malaise*, Vol. 27. Ed. F. Duina and F. Merand (pp. 45–66). Emerald Publishing Limited.

———— (2021). Pandemic Borrowing. *Internationale Politik Special, Covid 19: Global Impacts*, (2): 20–4. https://internationalepolitik.de/system/files/pdf_issues/IPS-02-2021_Cov19_Gesamt.pdf

Tombs, R. (2021). *This Sovereign Isle: Britain In and Out of Europe*. Allen Lane.

Tooze, A. (2018). *Crashed: How a Decade of Financial Crises Changed the World*. Viking.

————(8 March 2022). John Mearsheimer and the dark origins of realism. *The New Statesman*. https://www.newstatesman.com/ideas/2022/03/john-mearsheimer-and-the-dark-origins-of-realism

Trachtenberg, M. (2021). The United States and the NATO Non-extension Assurances of 1990: New Light on an Old Problem? *International Security*, 45(3): 162–203.

Traub, J. (2016). The Death of the Most Generous Nation on Earth. *Foreign Policy*. https://foreignpolicy.com/2016/02/10/the-death-of-the-most-generous-nation-on-earth-sweden-syria-refugee-europe/

Tucker, A. (2015). *The Legacies of Totalitarianism: A Theoretical Framework*. Cambridge University Press.

Tucker, P. (2018). *Unelected Power: The Quest for Legitimacy in Central Banking and the Regulatory State*. Princeton University Press.

Tusk, D. (13 September 2016). Letter from President Donald Tusk before the Bratislava Summit. European Council Press Release. https://www.consilium.europa.eu/en/press/press-releases/2016/09/13/tusk-invitation-letter-bratislava/

Umland, A. (2 April 2021). Russia's Annexation of Crimea Seven Years After: Why it Happened and What it Means for Europe. Centre for Democratic Integrity [Online Seminar]. https://democratic-integrity.eu/russias-annexation-of-crimea-seven-years-after/

——— (2022). Germany's Russia Policy in Light of the Ukraine Conflict: Interdependence Theory and Ostpolitik. *Orbis*, 66(1): 78–94.

US Department of State. (18 February 2022). Secretary Antony J. Blinken and German Foreign Minister Annalena Baerbock at the Munich Security Conference. https://www.state.gov/secretary-antony-j-blinken-and-german-foreign-minister-annalena-baerbock-at-the-munich-security-conference/

Vachudova, M. A. (2014). EU Leverage and National Interests in the Balkans: The Puzzles of Enlargement Ten Years On. *JCMS: Journal of Common Market Studies*, 52(1): 122–38.

Valentin, F., and González-Gallarza, J. (25 November 2021). Losing Precedence: The ECJ is Losing Out in Poland and Beyond: Is the Primacy of EU Law Ebbing Away? *The Mace*. https://macemagazine.com/losing-precedence/

Vaubel, R. (2020). Chancellor Merkel's Christian Democrats are Insisting that this Analogy is Misplaced. *The International Economy* (Summer): 18–19. http://www.international-economy.com/TIE_Su20_EUHamiltonSymp.pdf

Veser, R. (31 October 2020). Konterrevolution. *Frankfurter Allgemeine Zeitung*, 8.

von der Leyen, U. (16 July 2019). Opening Statement in the European Parliament Plenary Session by Ursula von der Leyen, candidate for President of the European Commission. https://ec.europa.eu/commission/presscorner/detail/pt/speech_19_4230

——— (24 December 2020). Remarks by President Ursula von der Leyen at the Press Conference on the Outcome of the EU-UK Negotiations. https://ec.europa.eu/commission/presscorner/detail/ov/SPEECH_20_2534

De Vries, C. E. (2018). *Euroscepticism and the Future of European Integration*. Oxford University Press.

De Vries, E. (2001). Alexandre Kojève and Carl Schmitt Correspondence. *Interpretation: A Journal of Political Philosophy*, 29(1): 91–115.

Weaver, M. (17 October 2010). Angela Merkel: German Multiculturalism has 'Utterly Failed'. *The Guardian*. https://www.theguardian.com/world/2010/oct/17/angela-merkel-german-multiculturalism-failed

Webber, D. (2014). How Likely is it that the European Union will Disintegrate? A Critical Analysis of Competing Theoretical Perspectives. *European Journal of International Relations*, 20(2): 341–65.

———— (2019). Trends in European Political (Dis)Integration: An Analysis of Postfunctionalist and Other Explanations. *Journal of European Public Policy*, 26(8): 1134–52.

Weber, M. (2004). *The Vocation Lectures*. Trans. R. Livingstone. Hackett.

Weiler, J. (1990). The European Community in Change: Exit, Voice and Loyalty. *Irish Studies in International Affairs*, 3(2): 15–25.

———— (1991). The Transformation of Europe. *Yale Law Journal*, 100(8): 2403–83.

———— (1994). A Quiet Revolution: The European Court of Justice and its Interlocutors. *Comparative Political Studies*, 26(4): 510–34.

———— (1995). Does Europe Need a Constitution? Demos, Telos and the German Maastricht Decision. *European Law Journal*, 1(3): 219–58.

———— (2012). Europe in Crisis: On 'Political Messianism', 'Legitimacy' and the 'Rule of Law'. *Singapore Journal of Legal Studies*, 2: 248–68.

———— (2020). Europe Must Learn Quickly to Speak the Language of Power: Part I. EJIL: Talk! Blog of the *European Journal of International Law*. https://www.ejiltalk.org/europe-must-learn-quickly-to-speak-the-language-of-power-part-i/

———— (2021). Cancelling Carl Schmitt? EJIL: Talk! Blog of the *European Journal of International Law*. https://www.ejiltalk.org/cancelling-carl-schmitt/

Wellings, B. (2012). *English Nationalism and Euroscepticism: Losing the Peace*. Peter Lang.

Die Welt (14 January 2019). Nationalismus ist ideologisches Gift. https://www.welt.de/politik/deutschland/article187018420/Bundespraesident-Steinmeier-Nationalismus-ist-ideologisches-Gift.html

Wendt, A. (2003). Why a World State is Inevitable. *European Journal of International Relations*, 9(4): 491–542.

Wengle, S., Monet, C., and Olimpieva, E. (2018). Russia's Post-Soviet Ideological Terrain: Zvyagintsev's *Leviathan* and Debates on Authority, Agency, and Authenticity. *Slavic Review*, 77(4): 998–1024.

White, J. (2003). Theory Guiding Practice: The Neofunctionalists and the Hallstein EEC Commission. *Journal of European Integration History*, 9(1): 111–31.

———— (2015). Emergency Europe. *Political Studies*, 63(2): 300–18.

———— (2020). *Politics of Last Resort: Governing by Emergency in the European Union*. Oxford University Press.

———— (2021). The De-institutionalisation of Power Beyond the State. *European Journal of International Relations*. Early view.

Wolczuk, K. (2016). Ukraine and Europe: Reshuffling the Boundaries of Order. *Thesis Eleven*, 136(1): 54–73.

Wolf, M. (13 May 2020). German Court Decides to Take Back Control with ECB Ruling. *Financial Times*.

Yack, B. (2003). Nationalism, Popular Sovereignty, and the Liberal Democratic State. In *The Nation-State in Question*. Ed. T. V. Paul, G. J. Ikenberry and J. A. Hall (pp. 29–50). Princeton University Press.

Yiwen, H. (11 October 2014). Why is the US so Keen on 'Color Revolutions'? *People's Daily*.

Youngs, R. (2017). *Europe's Eastern Crisis: The Geopolitics of Asymmetry*. Cambridge University Press.

Zielonka, J. (2006). *Europe as Empire: The Nature of the Enlarged European Union*. Oxford University Press.

———— (2018). *Counter-Revolution: Liberal Europe in Retreat*. Oxford University Press.

Zolo, D. (1998). Hans Kelsen: International Peace through International Law. *European Journal of International Law*, 9(2): 306–24.

Zsolt, E. (2020). Right-wing Authoritarian Innovations in Central and Eastern Europe. *East European Politics*, 36(3): 363–77.

INDEX